RESEARCH
METHODS
MADE SIMPLE

RESEARCH METHODS MADE SIMPLE

Stories, Games & Puzzles to Help You Understand

CATHERINE DAWSON

1 Oliver's Yard
55 City Road
London EC1Y 1SP

2455 Teller Road
Thousand Oaks
California 91320

Unit No 323-333, Third Floor, F-Block
International Trade Tower
Nehru Place, New Delhi – 110 019

8 Marina View Suite 43-053
Asia Square Tower 1
Singapore 018960

Editor: Jai Seaman
Editorial assistant: Becky Oliver
Assistant editor, digital: Ben Hegarty
Production editor: Nicola Marshall
Copyeditor: William Baginsky
Proofreader: Leigh Smithson
Indexer: Author
Marketing manager: Ben Sherwood
Cover design: Sheila Tong
Typeset by: C&M Digitals (P) Ltd, Chennai, India
Printed by CPI Group (UK) Ltd, Croydon CR0 4YY

Library of Congress Control Number: 2024936656

British Library Cataloguing in Publication data

A catalogue record for this book is available from the British Library

ISBN 978-1-5296-2320-8
ISBN 978-1-5296-2319-2 (pbk)

CONTENTS

Contents

LIST OF FIGURES AND ACTIVITIES

CHAPTER 1

Figures

Activities

CHAPTER 2

Figures

Activities

CHAPTER 3

Figures

Activities

CHAPTER 4

Figures

Activities

CHAPTER 5

Figures

Activities

CHAPTER 6

Figures

Activities

CHAPTER 7

Figures

Activities

CHAPTER 8

Figures

Activities

CHAPTER 9

Figures

Activities

CHAPTER 10

Figures

Activities

CHAPTER 11

Figures

Activities

CHAPTER 12

Figures

Activities

CHAPTER 13

Figures

Activities

ABOUT THE AUTHOR

Dr Catherine Dawson studied at university in the UK for an undergraduate degree in Combined Humanities, a Master's degree in Social Research and a PhD researching the learning choices of adults returning to education. She has worked as a research assistant, research associate and educator at various UK universities and as a research and training officer in both the public and private sectors. Over the years she has developed and taught research methods courses for undergraduate and postgraduate students and has designed and delivered bespoke research methods courses to employees in the private sector. At this present time, Catherine is writing online courses in research methods for postgraduate students and continuing to write research methods books for students and educators.

INTRODUCTION

Welcome to *Research Methods Made Simple: Stories, Games & Puzzles to Help You Understand*. This book is different from the norm. It introduces you to research methods in a creative and entertaining way by using activities, stories, games and visualization. It is a unique type of book that makes learning enjoyable and memorable. Complex text, terms, tables and equations, which can be daunting and overwhelming, have no place in this book. Instead, core principles and practicalities are introduced through activities, images and visualization. You are encouraged to get involved and learn through action rather than read and digest chapters of complicated text. This enables you to gain deeper insight, develop your understanding, overcome blocks, build motivation and enjoy your learning.

The content is guided by questions that have been asked by students on my research methods courses over the years. You can adopt a pick and mix approach, choosing areas that are of most interest, or those that answer specific questions you might have. You can do this simply and quickly as clear signposting is provided and chapters are divided by relevant and coherent topics. Or you can choose to work through the book from beginning to end: it flows in a logical order, taking you through the various steps required in research and testing your understanding of each step before moving to the next one.

Activities, stories and games cover a variety of subject areas and disciplines, which means that the book has relevance if you are studying in the arts, social sciences or sciences. They include undergraduate and postgraduate study, with practical examples and scenarios from students and research communities around the globe. Important ethics and integrity issues are introduced in concise, informative and relevant thought boxes, and interesting student and tutor tips appear throughout. 'Go further' boxes provide useful information and guidance about videos, podcasts and further reading to help you find out more about a particular topic.

The book enables you to build your understanding so that you feel comfortable moving forward with your research. It will also help you to understand the relevance of research methods to your course, your research and your personal and professional life. Research can be exciting and fun: don't be deterred by complex terms and off-putting statistics. Instead, work your way through the activities, read the stories and embark with enthusiasm on your research journey. Good luck with your research: I wish you every success and hope that you enjoy your research as much as I have done.

1

REFLECTION – LET'S THINK ABOUT THIS THING CALLED RESEARCH ...

CHAPTER CONTENTS

CHAPTER ACTIVITIES

CHAPTER OBJECTIVES

By the end of this chapter, you will be able to:

- Explain what research is
- Discuss the purpose of research
- Describe how research starts and ends
- Explain how research builds on research
- Illustrate how research can be used and abused, and explain how to avoid this
- Summarize the reasons why students undertake research
- List the benefits to be gained from undertaking research
- Provide practical examples of different types of student research project

A really good place to start your research journey is at the beginning. This might seem a very odd thing to say, but it needs to be said. This is because some research methods education does not start at the beginning. It expects a certain amount of knowledge and understanding, and moves straight into the complex worlds of methodology and method. You are not given the basics:

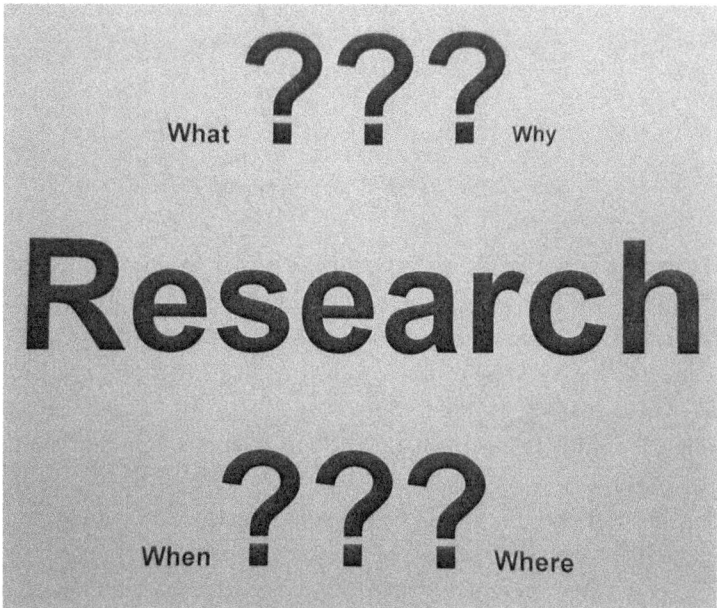

Figure 1.1   Research image

a grounding in the foundational questions and concepts, the 'why' and 'what' of research. Omitting this can be confusing, off-putting and demotivating. Also, as your course moves forward, it is easy to get left behind if you do not have a sturdy foundation.

Sometimes, you are expected to undertake research for your course without knowing why. Why should you do research? What is its purpose? Why is it important? These questions are often taken for granted and it can be confusing for those of you who need to know more about this before you start to think about how you actually do your research. If we start at the beginning (a very logical place to start) it will help you to gain a deeper understanding of this thing called research.

This chapter takes you through some of the foundational questions you might have about research (see Figure 1.1). They are all questions that have been asked by my research methods students in the past. It will help you to understand more about what research is and why it is done; who does research; how it can be misused and abused; and how it starts and ends.

WHAT IS RESEARCH?

I am always very pleased with my students when they ask, 'What is research?'. Some of the group might look surprised at the question, whereas others nod in agreement. It's a great way to start a course and a perfect way to start a research methods book. The question is perhaps best answered through a real-world example. Let me tell you a story …

Activity 1.1: Story

Liyana had to go into hospital for surgery on her stomach. As part of her recovery, she started walking. On the first walk, people were very friendly, wishing her good morning and smiling. On the second day, the same. And on the third. She really began to notice and she was happy. People were being very nice. Why? Not that people in her home town weren't friendly, but they were being more friendly than usual.

Perhaps it was Liyana herself? She'd had quite a serious operation and come out of it alive and well. Maybe she was being overly friendly with her new lease of life and people were responding to that? The next day she looked out for clues. But no, she wasn't the first to smile or say good morning, they were.

What else could be different? Perhaps the weather? Liyana thought back to the weather on these walks. No, she had experienced all types of weather and people were still being friendly, even when it was pouring with rain. It must be something else. But what?

Liyana spent a few days taking notice of how friendly people were on the walk and she was baffled. Perhaps it was time to forget about it and just be pleased that people were being so pleasant?

Then, for no apparent reason, it all changed. People weren't being so friendly. The odd one or two would smile and say good morning, but many wouldn't. What had changed? Why were they behaving so differently over such a short space of time?

Liyana thought long and hard. Something must be different. Then she had a brainwave. Surely that wasn't it? But it was worth a try. The next day she tested out her idea. And yes, all of a sudden people were being friendly again. The following day she changed that one thing again and yes, people were being less friendly.

Clothes. Surgery on her stomach meant that Liyana couldn't wear anything around her waist for a few weeks, so she'd bought three dresses. She'd been walking in them from the start but, once she'd recovered, she reverted back to T-shirts and jeans. And then people were less friendly. When she changed back into a dress, people were more friendly.

Liyana was surprised. This observation raised many questions:

- What was happening?
- Was she holding herself differently, or acting differently, because she was wearing a dress?
- Were people perceiving her to be more approachable or friendly because she was wearing a dress?
- Do people feel more comfortable with women who wear dresses?
- Do people think a woman deserves more respect if she wears a dress?
- Would the same happen if a man or a trans or non-binary person wore a dress?
- How do people react to the different clothes worn by women, men, trans and non-binary people?
- Does this occur only in the society, culture or country in which Liyana lives?
- Would reactions be different within other societies, cultures or countries?
- Are people conscious of their reactions to what others wear?
- Do different styles, colours or fabrics of dress get different responses?
- Can we predict what type of outfit would get what type of response?

Liyana was starting to do research by making this observation, testing her ideas and asking questions. Perhaps, after having read this story, you might have some other questions about what she observed. Or perhaps you might want to question the way she developed and tested her idea (see Figure 1.2). This is important. It will help you to think about the research process and illustrates that research builds on research: we will return to this later in the chapter.

If we want to do research, we might observe, question, explore, test, hypothesize, model or predict, and we do this in a disciplined and scientific way. This might sound

Figure 1.2 Questions image

daunting, but it's not. There are plenty of practices, procedures, instructions and advice that we can follow to help us carry out good, effective, valid and ethical research that other people value and trust. This book guides you through these issues.

THINK ETHICS 1.1

Research ethics refers to the moral and ethical principles that govern and guide all types of research. You must think about ethics throughout your project, from planning and design to implementation and reporting. 'Think ethics' boxes appear throughout this book, helping you to consider important ethical issues that will enable you to respect human dignity, privacy and rights; consider the ethics of consent and purpose; evaluate bias with reference to equality, diversity and inclusion; and address issues of confidentiality and anonymity when collecting and analysing data.

Think about the words we use. Research can be described in many different ways. It is both a noun and a verb: a thing and an activity. Activity 1.2 will help you to think about this in more detail.

Activity 1.2: Word search

Below are 20 words that can be used to describe research (or the activity of con-ducting research). They are nouns and/or verbs. Find them in the puzzle before checking the answers, which can be found at the end of the chapter.

analysis

discover

examine

experiment

explain

explore

find

inquire

inspect

investigate

probe

question

review

scrutinize

search

solve

study

synthesis

test

theorize

WHY DO WE DO RESEARCH?

We do research for many different reasons. Activity 1.3 will help you to think about what these reasons might be.

```
D S V Q U E S T I O N Y C Q J
R T D E X P E R I M E N T W N
L U N R H I E K E N B D I A Y
S D Q X E V N X T X A X N P V
Q Y X S O V P S P K A B Q Z M
R A N C C I I T P L T M U U W
W Y S T E R S E L E O D I A T
S I R T H E U S W P C R R N H
D M I N V E S T I G A T E A E
Y V N L Z X S K I V B B D L O
M V O S T N L I M N O N M Y R
A S E A R C H P S R I J F S I
I J E B R S B O P F T Z X I Z
E W I D M G M M T Q M R E S E
I B D F Q E X P L A I N G Z R
```

Activity 1.3: Missing-word puzzle

Complete this missing-word puzzle by filling in the blanks from the list of words provided. It will help you to think about why we do research. Answers can be found at the end of the chapter.

Research is an intellectually stimulating process that helps us to answer [_____], solve [_____], improve decision-making and tackle many of the issues faced in the world today. It is an innovative and creative process that enables us to generate, build and advance [_____] and ideas.

Research inspires us to work together on a national and [_____] basis. It facilitates the cross-fertilization and generation of ideas and encourages us to transfer and [_____] skills, techniques, equipment and knowledge.

Research benefits [_____], communities, society, industry, the economy and the environment. It enables us to combat disease, increase life expectancy, become more energy efficient and understand how to stop wasting precious resources. Through research we can improve our mental health, understand how people interact and work out what makes us tick. It is a way to combat lies and provide evidence for the [_____].

individuals

international

knowledge

problems

questions

share

truth

HOW IS RESEARCH USED AND ABUSED?

Research that is carried out with integrity and high levels of professionalism benefits people, communities, industry and the environment. It is trusted and respected and leads to the advancement of knowledge and humanity. Poor research, or pseudo-science, can be used to manipulate, mislead or perpetuate falsehoods. It can give researchers a bad name and lead to lack of trust in experts. Therefore, it is impera-tive that you act with integrity and high levels of professionalism when undertaking research. Activity 1.4 will help you to think about these issues in more detail and the 'Think integrity 1.1' box explains more about what is meant by integrity.

Activity 1.4: Checklist (right and wrong answers)

Work through the following list, putting 'yes' next to the statements you think are correct and 'no' next to those you think are wrong. This will help you to think about how research can be used and abused, by researchers and by others. Answers and explanations can be found at the end of the chapter.

Statement (yes or no)

Researchers must identify and declare conflicts of interest.

It is not necessary to declare who has funded a research project.

Researchers should not criticize other science without justification and evidence.

Researchers should allow their political opinion to influence their research.

Media and social media can sometimes misrepresent good research.

It is important to know the original source of research.

Researchers must back up statements with evidence.

All research methods must be well documented and clear to see.

Researchers should use conjecture when reporting their results.

Politicians sometimes quote research that goes against their political beliefs.

Tabloid newspapers prefer research that has a sensationalist or newsworthy headline.

Research findings should be placed in context.

Researchers should stretch findings to make them a little more publishable.

THINK INTEGRITY 1.1

The term 'research integrity' covers the professional standards, codes and practice along with the moral principles required to conduct research to the highest standards. This enables researchers to build trust and confidence in their research methods and outputs. 'Think integrity' boxes appear throughout this book, helping you to consider important integrity issues that will enable you to: view integrity as an individual and collective responsibility; foster research integrity through practice; cultivate transparency and openness; and avoid research misconduct (see Figure 1.3).

Figure 1.3 Responsible research image

GO FURTHER 1.1

Sanne Blauw, on TEDxMaastricht, has produced an interesting video on the misuse of statistics in the media: 'How to defend yourself against misleading statistics in the news': www.youtube.com/watch?v=mJ63-bQc9Xg [accessed 17 June 2022].

You can find out more about the misuse of science and statistics in the news, by politicians and others, by visiting Bad Science (www.badscience.net). This is a website containing articles, videos and blogs about bad science, produced by Dr Ben Goldacre [accessed 17 June 2022].

You can find out more about the use, abuse and misuse of statistics in the news and everyday life by listening to *More or Less*. This is a radio programme that is broadcast on BBC Radio 4 in the UK, produced together with the Open University. Downloads and podcasts are available from the BBC website (www. bbc.co.uk/programmes) [accessed 17 June 2022].

WHERE DOES RESEARCH START?

In Activity 1.1 Liyana's research started with an observation. But there are other ways that research can start. Figure 1.4 and Activity 1.5 help you to think about them in more detail.

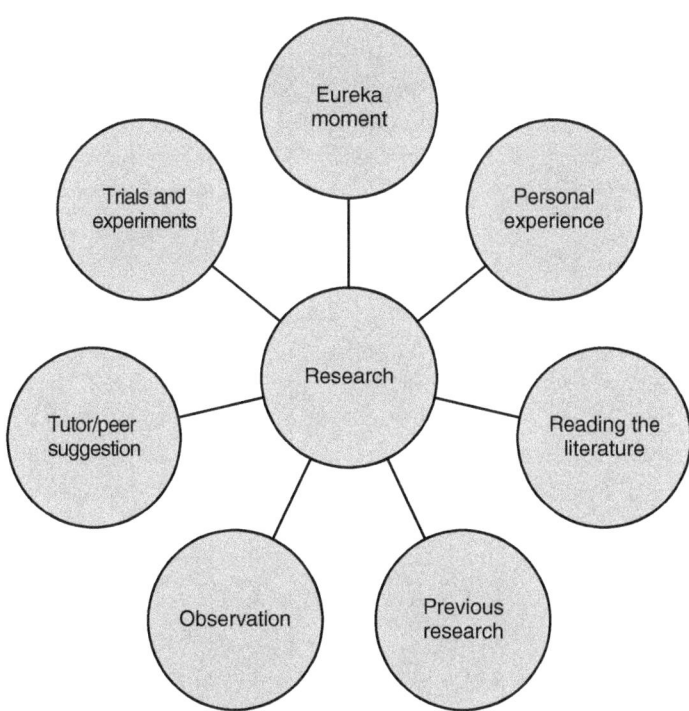

Figure 1.4 Research origins

Activity 1.5: Reflection

The items in Figure 1.4 are not exhaustive. Can you think of any other ways in which research can start? How will *your* research start? Jot down, or make a voice note of, any other ways you can think of. We return to this issue in more depth in Chapter 6, where specific examples of research projects and their origins are given in Activity 6.6.

WHAT DOES RESEARCH DO?

Research answers a research question. This is a specific and actionable question around which the research is centred. It develops from the initial idea, which could have arisen from any of the starting points given in Figure 1.4, or from somewhere else.

Let's look again at Liyana's story in Activity 1.1 and consider how she might develop a research question. Activity 1.6 will help you to do this.

Activity 1.6: Practical examples

Read and digest the following examples to get a better understanding of how Liyana's observations lead to different research questions, depending on what she is studying. Once you have done this, try thinking about other subjects and consider how they might generate different research questions from Liyana's observations.

Example 1

Liyana is studying a course on Fashion Buying and Merchandising. Her observations lead her to think about whether it might be possible to understand and perhaps predict dress-buying behaviour by women in the UK. Her first try at a research question is: 'How do women in the UK behave when making decisions about which dress to buy?' This can be described as exploratory research.

Example 2

Liyana is studying Sociology. Her observations lead her to think about what might influence the way people perceive women wearing dresses. Her first try at a research question is: 'What are the sociological, psychological and structural factors that have an influence on the way people perceive women wearing dresses in the UK?' This is exploratory research, but it could also be theory-building research, if Liyana goes on to develop theory from her findings (this could be for postgraduate study, for example).

Example 3

Liyana is studying a course on Textile and Design. She is interested in finding out whether different types and colours of fabric can enhance mood. Her first try at a research question is: 'What effect does the colour and type of fabric have on the mood of the wearer?' In this research Liyana intends to develop different types and colours of fabrics, which will then be tested on participants. This is experimental research in which variables are measured, calculated and compared.

Example 4

Liyana is studying Social Psychology. Her observations lead her to contemplate the possibility that people treat women with more respect if they are wearing a dress. Her first try at a research question is: 'Are women who wear dresses treated with more respect than women who wear trousers?' This is theory-testing research. Liyana has developed a hypothesis that she wants to test to see whether it is correct.

GO FURTHER 1.2

Straightforward, clear and simple advice about producing a research question can be obtained from O'Leary, Z. (2018) *Research Question (Little Quick Fix)*. London: Sage.

For more comprehensive coverage of the topic, consult White, P. (2017) *Developing Research Questions*, 2nd edition. London: Red Globe Press.

Liyana's examples illustrate that the same observation leads to different types of research, and these different types of research can be influenced by a number of factors, including discipline, subject of study, previous experience and personal interest. You will see, later in this book, that these different types of research give rise to, or require, different ways of doing research.

Figure 1.5 gives some more real-life examples from a variety of disciplines, to help you understand this a little better. Note that they have been written as statements rather than questions, which is often easier for students to undertake. If you struggle to develop a research question, try producing a statement first, then turn it into a question. Activity 1.7 will help you to do this.

I'm going to carry out exploratory research. I want to find out how images are used in computer games to engage and motivate players. I don't have any prior assumptions or hypotheses to test. **Adam: exploratory research**

I am interested in the potential dangers of synthetic dyes in baked foods sold in India. I intend to find out whether there are any adverse effects on health from these dyes. **Marsha: experimental research**

My research is going to test the theory that violent films lead to aggressive behaviour in adults in the US. I want to find out if this theory provides a plausible explanation for aggression and violence. **Jamil: theory-testing research**

I want to predict the output of a new type of solar panel by using modelling and simulation techniques. I will be able to model output power and approximate generated power. **Jenny: predictive research**

My research is about coping strategies of people with respiratory illnesses in Singapore. I want to describe their experiences, instabilities and vulnerabilities and show how they cope with these from day to day. **Olek: descriptive research**

Figure 1.5   Research project examples

Activity 1.7: Application

Once you have read the examples in Figure 1.5, practise turning each one into a research question.

More information about producing a research question is provided in Chapter 6, where you can find out the qualities of a good research question and consider what constitutes a good or bad research question.

WHO DOES RESEARCH?

All sorts of people do research. These people might work or study in universities or research centres, or they might work in industry, the charitable sector or private companies, for example. Activity 1.8 will help you to think more about who these people are.

Activity 1.8: Word search

Fifteen words are listed below. They refer to types of people who do research. Find them in the puzzle (see p. 16) before checking the answers, which can be found at the end of the chapter.

analyst

artist

businessperson

chemist

doctor

entrepreneur

historian

layperson

musician

nurse

physicist

scientist

student

teacher

technician

WHERE DOES RESEARCH END?

The simple answer is that research ends when the research question has been answered and the research has been written up and/or reported. This is the case for most student projects. We will discuss these aspects of the research process later in the book.

However, research never really ends. It's a continual process of refining, adding, learning, reviewing, developing and growing. One researcher might finish their project, but another might choose to continue the work at a later date. Or they might feel that the work needs improvement. Or that the work is incorrect. Research builds from research. This is why it is important to think about how your research could be improved and expanded at a later date. It also shows that you are aware of the wider

M U S I C I A N R P P K I L
L A Y P E R S O N L H P J D
O F X J T F A N A L Y S T J
P W X M V V N N U R S E G O
X S T U D E N T F Z I E B S
T C G L T E C H N I C I A N
J I T E A C H E R J I N D J
Z E S T R K Q O X U S R M K
W N W Y Y U T V A R T I S T
C T E T O C H E M I S T G P
H I S T O R I A N F B V L Q
Y S J D W V L N Y U C E D Q
Q T E N T R E P R E N E U R
B U S I N E S S P E R S O N

picture and that you understand that there are limitations to what you can do in the time that you are given. Activity 1.9 will help you to consider these issues in more depth.

─────── TIP 1.1 ───────

Think about the wider picture as you start to design your project and progress through your research. Keep written or recorded notes as you go. It is useful to refer back to them when you produce your thesis or dissertation. Examiners want to see that you understand the wider picture, know the limitations and are able to suggest ways to improve or expand your work.

Activity 1.9: Matching

Three words to consider when thinking about how research can be expanded, improved, scrutinized or checked are given at the top of the following page, along with three definitions. Match each word with the most appropriate definition. Answers can be found at the end of this chapter.

Words	Appropriate Definition (See below: 1, 2 or 3)
Replicate	
Repeat	
Reproduce	

Definitions

1 The original researcher follows the same methods and procedures within the same conditions to achieve the same results.
2 A different researcher duplicates the results of a study through using the same data and same methods as the original study.
3 A different researcher achieves the same (or similar) results using the same methods with new samples (from the original population) and new data.

Pause for thought ...

As you work through this matching activity, you might consider these definitions to be contentious, or you might disagree with them. If so, explain why. (Remember, as a student you should analyse and critique what you are told: if something doesn't seem right to you, question what you are told, develop your own argument and find evidence to back up your argument.) Once you have given your explanation, consult the answers at the end of this chapter to find out more.

WHY DO UNDERGRADUATES HAVE TO DO RESEARCH?

That is a good question. Why do *you* think undergraduates have to do research? Activity 1.10 will help you to think about this in more detail.

Activity 1.10: Reflection

Write down, or make a voice note of, five succinct reasons why you think undergraduates have to (or choose to) do research, then read the answers at the end of this chapter.

1

2

3

4

5

It might help you to get a clearer understanding of the benefits if you consider some practical examples from students studying different subjects. Activity 1.11 will help you to do this.

Activity 1.11: Practical examples

The following examples from undergraduate students help to explain why they were required (or chose) to conduct research. They also illustrate the benefits that can be gained from research and offer advice or tips to other undergraduates.

Rose, chemical engineering

I had to do research for my final assessment to show I was capable. It was fun working in a scientific team. I worked with others who were really enthusiastic and knew what they were doing. Of course, there were problems, but we got them worked out. Doing the research shows I can solve problems and work in a team. Be nice to team members. Help each other. Make friends. You learn so much.

Manaia, ecology

I was well aware of the lack of Indigenous researchers in New Zealand. I chose my course because it really interested me and I knew I'd get the opportunity to do research that'd give a voice to my family and community. We've been overlooked for so long. My grandparents told me the importance of where we come from and how we need to work hard to keep our environment safe. I really wanted to do the research for them. It showed I was able to succeed in a place where there's still not many people like me. If I think about it, it also helped me open other people's eyes to our way of life. I'm not saying it was easy though. You have to straddle two very different lives, especially when you're the first to go to university and experience a different way of learning.

Jeff, nursing (mental health)

I want to work in mental health nursing and doing the research gave me loads of experience. To be fair it was quite daunting to start. Getting to interview people was a bit scary. But I got into it. I've learnt how to talk to people I don't know and get them to trust me so they tell me things without feeling uncomfortable. That sort of skill will help me in work. I probably also learnt to organize and plan. So don't feel daunted or scared. My tutor helped – yours will as well.

Jia-Yi, ceramic design

Our whole final year involves research – it's just part of the course and I knew that when I signed up. I developed a project to work collaboratively with a local gallery. They were really keen to get involved. It was a learning curve for me because I can get too taken up with my work and not look at what is going on around me. It's made me become more critically aware of what I do and of visual language and discourse. It's also opened me up to possible professional development opportunities.

Now that you have a better idea of what research is and why it is important, we can move on. However, before we continue to the next chapter, let's test your understanding of what has been covered in this chapter with a short multiple-choice quiz.

Activity 1.12: Multiple-choice quiz

Read each question and choose the correct answer. The topics in all three of these questions have been covered in this chapter, so if you can't answer any of the questions, return to some of the activities to refresh your memory. Answers can be found at the end of the chapter.

1   A researcher wants to test their idea that watching advertisements for highly processed food on television leads children to eat more of this type of food. What type of research is this?

    a   Exploratory research.
    b   Theory-testing research.
    c   Descriptive research.

2   What is a research question?

    a   An open-ended question used in interviews.
    b   A closed-ended question used on paper questionnaires.
    c   A specific and actionable question around which the research is centred.

3   What is 'research integrity'?

   a   The ethical codes that govern and guide all types of research.
   b   The professional standards, codes and practice, along with moral
        principles, required to conduct research to the highest standards.
   c   Specific standards set by national governments to ensure all research is
        conducted to the highest standard.

ACTIVITY ANSWERS: CHAPTER 1

Activity 1.2: Word search

Activity 1.3: Missing-word puzzle

Research is an intellectually stimulating process that helps us to answer *questions*,
solve *problems*, improve decision-making and tackle many of the issues faced in

the world today. It is an innovative and creative process that enables us to generate, build and advance *knowledge* and ideas.

Research inspires us to work together on a national and *international* basis. It facilitates the cross-fertilization and generation of ideas and encourages us to transfer and *share* skills, techniques, equipment and knowledge.

Research benefits *individuals*, communities, society, industry, the economy and the environment. It enables us to combat disease, increase life expectancy, become more energy efficient and understand how to stop wasting precious resources. Through research we can improve our mental health, understand how people interact and work out what makes us tick. It is a way to combat lies and provide evidence for the *truth*.

Activity 1.4: Checklist (right and wrong answers)

Researchers must identify and declare conflicts of interest: Yes. There are a number of conflicts of interest that can occur at different stages of a research project. Often, they are related to funding and political or financial interests of researchers or grant-awarding bodies. If research is to be trusted and respected, researchers should avoid conflicts of interest. If this is impossible all conflict should be declared in a clear and transparent way.

It is not necessary to declare who has funded a research project: No. All researchers must declare who has funded a research project. This enables others to see that there has been no undue pressure placed on the researcher to carry out research and report in a particular way and that there are no strings attached to the funding.

Researchers should not criticize other science without justification and evidence: Yes. Research builds on research. If researchers find that another project is flawed, they can prove this with evidence. If criticism seems to be unjustified and is not backed up by evidence, there is usually another cause for the criticism, such as political, financial or personal gain.

Researchers should allow their political opinion to influence their research: No. This is a form of bias. All research should endeavour to be free from bias, but if this is not possible, bias should be identified and acknowledged. There are methods and procedures in place that enable researchers to reduce bias in scientific work and they should be understood and followed carefully. If you believe that it is impossible to eliminate bias (we are human) then a careful and systematic account of possible or potential bias should be provided. More information about recognizing and addressing bias when analysing data is provided in Chapter 10.

Media and social media can misrepresent good research: Yes. When this occurs, it can be very frustrating for experienced and conscientious researchers. They can struggle to get their research reported in an unbiased way. As consumers of different types of media, we should ensure that we are sceptical of sensationalist headlines and that we check original sources to verify information.

It is important to know the original source of research: Yes. This is related to the point above. Respectable journalists and bloggers should make sure that a link or reference to the original source is provided so that readers and viewers can check the information for themselves.

Researchers must back up statements with evidence. Yes. For research to be respected and trusted, all arguments should be well reasoned and backed up with evidence. This is the case for all academic work you complete as a student.

All research methods must be well documented and clear to see. Yes. Research is seen to be reliable and trustworthy if all documentation of methods and analysis is clear and transparent. It enables others to see how the research was conducted. It also helps others to reproduce or replicate the research at a later date (e.g. to build on the research or to verify original findings).

Researchers should use conjecture when reporting their results: No. Conjecture can be defined as an opinion or stance that has been formed without reference to evidence. It is based on incomplete information. When researchers are reporting their results, they should include all the information required, backed up with evidence. Conjecture has no place in research.

Politicians quote research that goes against their political beliefs: No. Have you ever seen this happen? No, politicians pick and mix research, choosing findings that back up their political beliefs, argument or ideology. On occasions they can misuse statistics in an appalling way, believing that if statistics are complex enough, or if they are convincing in their speech, no one will question them. As researchers it is important that we look out for this type of abuse and set the record straight.

Tabloid newspapers prefer research that has a sensationalist or newsworthy headline: Yes. They most certainly do; after all, their job is to sell newspapers. However, be critical when reading this type of coverage. Research can be misreported or reported in a biased way (e.g. to sensationalize or to back up a particular agenda, political view or moral stance). Think about why certain research results have been chosen and others omitted (bias by omission) or why the story has been placed where it has (placement bias).

Research findings should be placed in context: Yes. It is important that all research findings are placed in context, with a clear and accurate description of the circumstances in which the research was conducted. This should include an assessment of what contributed to the success of the project (or led to particular findings) and what hindered the research. This makes it harder for others to use findings inappropriately (e.g. transferring findings to a different setting or country in which the findings are inapplicable).

Researchers should stretch findings to make them a little more publishable: No. It is important that all findings are backed up with appropriate evidence. Sometimes, there is a temptation to stretch positive outcomes, or useful findings, to make them more interesting in the hope that they will be accepted for publication (or help you to pass your course). Researchers might also face pressure from funding bodies to talk up the results to give them more significance. Researchers must work with integrity and avoid this type of activity if their work is to be trusted. More information about reporting findings ethically is provided in Chapter 12.

Activity 1.8: Word search

```
M U S I C I A N R P P K I L
L A Y P E R S O N L H P J D
O F X J T F A N A L Y S T J
P W X M V V N N U R S E G O
X S T U D E N T F Z I E B S
T C G L T E C H N I C I A N
J I T E A C H E R J I N D J
Z E S T R K Q O X U S R M K
W N W Y Y U T V A R T I S T
C T E T O C H E M I S T G P
H I S T O R I A N F B V L Q
Y S J D W V L N Y U C E D Q
Q T E N T R E P R E N E U R
B U S I N E S S P E R S O N
```

Activity 1.9: Matching

Words	Appropriate definition (1, 2 or 3)
Replicate	3. A different researcher achieves the same (or similar) results using the same methods with new samples (from the original population) and new data.
Repeat	1. The original researcher follows the same methods and procedures within the same conditions to achieve the same results.

| Reproduce | 2. A different researcher duplicates the results of a study through using the same data and same methods as the original study. |

These definitions could be considered contentious when approached from different subjects (e.g. in biology, where an exact copy of a sample that is being analysed is defined as a replicant, or in statistics, where replication is the repetition of an experimental condition).

GO FURTHER 1.3

Detailed information which illustrates how these definitions might differ between disciplines can be obtained from Fidler, F. and Wilcox, J. (2021) 'Reproducibility of scientific results', *The Stanford Encyclopedia of Philosophy* (Summer 2021 Edition), Zalta, E.N (ed.), https://plato.stanford.edu/archives/sum2021/entries/scientific-reproducibility [accessed 7 January 2022].

Activity 1.10: Reflection

There are a number of reasons why undergraduates are required to conduct research:

- You are able to pursue a topic that is of personal, community, political and/or cultural interest. This helps to engage and motivate.
- You can contribute to knowledge and build understanding on a particular topic. It enables you to discover something new and make an impact.
- It demonstrates that you are able to think and work independently, plan a project, manage your time, organize your work and complete your project to a specified deadline. These are useful transferable skills that are valued by employers if you are hoping to obtain employment after your studies. More information about the skills that are developed during a research project is provided in Chapter 13.
- Undertaking research provides valuable experience if you want to continue with postgraduate research or pursue a research career. It is useful preparation for doctoral programmes.
- You are able to gain experience in justifying and defending choices, methods and results.
- Outputs in the form of long reports, dissertations or theses enable you to be assessed and illustrate how well you are able to integrate and apply your skills, knowledge and understanding.
- You can gain academic credit for future studies, careers and personal satisfaction.

- You are able to work together with peers and more experienced researchers, developing abilities to collaborate, cooperate and network, and building friendships that can last a lifetime.
- You can take advantage of university hardware and software, at no cost to yourself, and learn to use materials and equipment effectively, with help and advice from experts.
- Undertaking research provides a sense of purpose and satisfaction, while encouraging personal development and growth.

Activity 1.12: Multiple-choice quiz

1   A researcher wants to test their idea that watching advertisements for highly processed food on television leads children to eat more of this type of food. What type of research is this?

    a   Exploratory research.
    b   Theory-testing research (correct answer).
    c   Descriptive research.

2   What is a research question?

    a   An open-ended question used in interviews.
    b   A closed-ended question used on paper questionnaires.
    c   A specific and actionable question around which the research is centred (correct answer).

3   What is 'research integrity'?

    a   The ethical codes that govern and guide all types of research.
    b   The professional standards, codes and practice, along with moral principles, required to conduct research to the highest standards (correct answer).
    c   Specific standards set by national governments to ensure all research is conducted to the highest standard.

2

EXPANSION – BEFORE WE BEGIN, LET'S CONSIDER THE PHILOSOPHY OF RESEARCH ...

CHAPTER CONTENTS

CHAPTER ACTIVITIES

CHAPTER OBJECTIVES

By the end of this chapter, you will be able to:

- Discuss and evaluate what you know about your research topic and methods
- Summarize the sources of your knowledge
- Evaluate, critique and justify your knowledge and assumptions
- Discuss what is meant by truth and consider whether finding the truth is the primary goal of your research
- Define epistemology and theoretical perspective and discuss how they relate to each other
- List and define a number of epistemologies and theoretical perspectives
- Discuss the relevance, importance and impact of epistemology and theoretical perspective in relation to your research

---

Some students conduct research without considering the underlying philosophy that frames their work. They decide on a topic, find out about methods and procedures, collect their data, analyse their data, write up their results and, hopefully, pass their course. Fair enough. If you are interested in research only as a means necessary to passing your course, you might not be interested in this chapter. However, I urge you to wait a moment and think again. If you take time to think about the philosophy of research it increases your understanding, enables you to feel more engaged with your work and will help you to produce better research. This applies to students from all disciplines.

The philosophy of research considers the beliefs and assumptions we have about the sources and nature of our knowledge. How do we know what we know? Where does this knowledge come from? It also considers the methods that we use to gather and develop our knowledge, methods that you will use for your research.

It's always good to consider the wider picture. Research does not take place in a vacuum. It is historically, culturally, socially, academically and politically situated, as is our prior knowledge and the knowledge that we might generate from our research. This might sound complicated, but it's not. The activities presented in this chapter help you to think about these issues and deepen your understanding about how they relate to your research. Let's start with three reflection activities to get you thinking more about what we mean by beliefs and assumptions relating to your research.

TIP 2.1

The topics presented in this chapter can be daunting and you might feel overwhelmed. Even so, work your way through the chapter because you will find that the issues become clearer as you read more. However, if you are really struggling, move on to other chapters and then return to this one once you feel more confident about research methods.

WHAT DO I KNOW ABOUT MY RESEARCH METHODS AND TOPIC?

Students are sometimes surprised when they are asked, early in the planning stages of their research, to describe what they know about their research methods and topic. They ask: 'Why is this important?', 'Why do I need to think about this, especially now?' The answers to these questions will become clear as you work your way through this chapter.

Activity 2.1: Reflection

Write down, or make a voice note of, five things you know about your research methods and topic. Think specifically about what you know. Take a little time to distinguish between what you know, what you think you know and what you assume you know.

1

2

3

4

5

HOW DO I KNOW WHAT I KNOW?

Now that you have noted five things you know about your research methods and topic, return to each one to analyse it a little more deeply.

Activity 2.2: Reflection

For each of the five things you noted in Activity 2.1, think about how you know what you know. Write down or record your thoughts. At this stage you might decide to modify, alter or delete one or more of the items you have listed.

1

2

3

4

5

WHAT ARE THE SOURCES OF
MY KNOWLEDGE?

For the third part of this activity return again to each of the things you know about your research methods and topic, listed in Activity 2.1.

Activity 2.3: Reflection

Now, think about the source of this knowledge. Where has your knowledge come from? You might already have touched on this in Activity 2.2. Consider whether the sources you identify are valid, reliable and trustworthy, and record your thoughts for each item listed.

1

2

3

4

5

HOW DO I JUSTIFY MY KNOWLEDGE AND
ASSUMPTIONS?

Activities 2.1, 2.2 and 2.3 help you to think more about what you know, how you know it and where your knowledge comes from. Activity 2.4 gives two practical examples of this process. This will help you to understand a little more about how to reflect on what you know, how you know it and how your knowledge and assumptions can be justified.

Activity 2.4: Dialogue

Read through the following dialogues. Each piece shows how a student and supervisor work through some of these issues. Once you have read these two pieces of dialogue, you might decide that you need to change or modify some of the answers you have given in Activities 2.1, 2.2 and 2.3.

Research into infection control and prevention

Prof. Anderson: Tell me what you know about your research methods and topic.

Shelly: I know about standard infection control precautions, what they are and how they work. I know that interviewing people is a good way to get information about what they do to stop passing on infection.

Prof. Anderson: Okay. Let's take those one at a time. How do you know about standard infection control precautions?

Shelly: I learnt about them on this course.

Prof. Anderson: So now you know that the information is correct?

Shelly: Yes.

Prof. Anderson: Do you know that the information is correct, or do you assume it to be correct?

Shelly: I guess I assume it to be correct because my tutors told me. They wouldn't tell me the wrong information, would they?

Prof. Anderson: I would hope not. But how can you be sure that what you've been told is correct? Perhaps we need to think about what we mean by 'correct'. When we consider infection control and prevention, what was seen as correct in the 19th century would be very different from what is considered to be correct in the 21st century. And how might this translate to different contexts, situations and countries?

Shelly: I'd not thought about that.

Prof. Anderson: This is why we're having this chat. Find more information from reliable and varied sources. Don't just consider a traditional Western approach: go beyond Eurocentric evidence.

Shelly: Become broader and more inclusive? Think about context?

Prof. Anderson: Excellent. Yes. Now let's also look at your statement about interviewing people being a good way to get information about what they do to stop passing on infection. Do you know that this is the case?

Shelly: I guess I'm presuming again, or making an assumption that this is the case?

Prof. Anderson: You're getting it! It might well be that interviewing people is a good method for this project. But you need to think more about this. Think about other methods that could be used. Find out more about different types of interviews. Build your knowledge. Develop your argument. Assumptions might be accepted as true, but there is no proof. You need proof. Evidence. Then you can justify your choices.

Research into earthquakes around nuclear facilities

Dr Parry: So, your research involves testing sensors for earthquakes around nuclear facilities?

Olena: Yes.

Dr Parry: Let's start at the beginning. What do you know about earthquakes?

Olena: Earthquakes are caused by seismic waves that are released as a result of sudden movements along fault lines caused by the movement of tectonic plates.

Dr Parry: Is that the case for all earthquakes?

Olena: Yes, I think so.

Dr Parry: What about seismic events caused by human action, such as fracking?

Olena: I'd not thought of that and I don't know about that.

Dr Parry: Don't just think about what you know but think also about what you don't know. What do you know about tectonic plates?

Olena: They're constantly moving slabs that divide the earth's crust. They're different rocky sections. When they rub together it leads to earthquakes.

Dr Parry: Do they really exist?

Olena: What do you mean?

Dr Parry: Well, perhaps you're basing your research on the assumption that tectonic plates exist.

Olena: Everyone knows they do!

Dr Parry: Do they? Or is it a scientific theory that says they exist? Okay, it is a well-established, credible and well-supported theory that explains observations about the earth successfully, but it's a theory, nevertheless. I'm just pointing this out so you start to think about what you know, where you get your information from, whether the information is true or correct and whether it even matters if the information is true and correct. Tell me about your research methods.

Olena: I'm going to use sensors in my research that'll help me detect ground displacement so I can see how far the ground moves. I learnt how to do this on my university course and because I've read about it in books.

Dr Parry:	Good. Good. And I hope we've taught it well! But think about whether sensor-based methods are objective and true. You'll also need to think about validity and reliability. Just because you assume your sensors will work in the way that you intend, it doesn't mean that this is the case. Would your measurements be the same in repeated trials? How well do sensor-based methods measure what you assume they'll measure, or what they purport to measure?
Olena:	There's a lot to think about.
Dr Parry:	Yes, but it's important to consider these issues early when you're thinking about the design of your research project. Your initial thoughts will help you to think about how you actually do your research. If you think about it now, it'll save you having problems later and it'll help your research run smoothly.
Olena:	Okay, thanks. I think!
Dr Parry:	Come back and have a chat when you've had chance to think about all this. You'll find it really helps to talk through your ideas.

IS FINDING THE TRUTH THE PRIMARY GOAL OF MY RESEARCH?

In the second piece of dialogue in Activity 2.4 Dr Parry asks whether sensor-based methods are objective and true. This is a question that can be asked about all research methods: we will return to this later in the book. Another question concerns whether we are looking for the truth in our research: some researchers believe that finding the truth is the primary goal of their research; others believe that this is not a goal. Some believe that truth does not even exist and others believe that truth means different things to different people.

Before you can begin to consider whether finding the truth is the primary goal of your research, we need to unpick what we mean by truth. Activity 2.5 encourages you to think about the definitions given and Figure 2.1 gives some common definitions of truth. Once you have considered these definitions and thought more deeply about what is meant by truth, we will look more closely into your thoughts about truth. This will help you to consider whether finding the truth is the primary goal of your research.

Activity 2.5: Judgement

Read each definition given in Figure 2.1 and think about whether any of them are problematic, or whether they could be questioned or contested. Once you have done this, we will go on to think more about what is meant by truth.

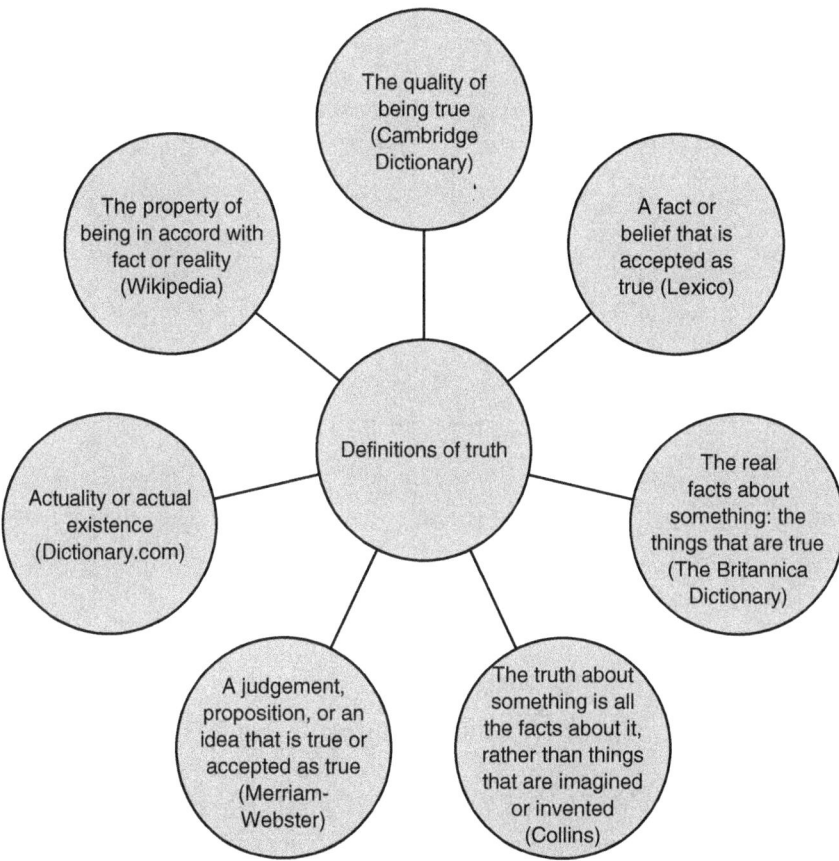

Figure 2.1 Definitions of truth

WHAT IS TRUTH?

As we touched on in the previous section, people have very different ideas about what truth actually is, or what is meant by truth (see Figure 2.2). Figure 2.1 provides standard, simple answers. Now we need to unpick this a little more. Activity 2.6 will help you to do this.

Activity 2.6: Statement organization

Below are some statements that have been made about truth. Read through these statements and order them into a list, with the top of the list closest to your stance

(Continued)

on what you think is meant by the truth, and the bottom of the list with the statement that is furthest away from your stance. There are no right or wrong answers to this: people have very different views. However, once you have done this, go to the end of this chapter for an indication of what the order of your list might mean for your proposed research.

Every individual has their own truth.

There are absolute truths.

Truth is contingent on the social, political, cultural and technical norms of a particular era.

Truth is constructed by individuals.

Truth is subjective.

A truth is a fact.

Truth is relative to language or culture.

Objective truth can be found through systematic investigation.

Truth is highly contextual.

There is no single source or origin for truth beyond the individual.

Objective truth can be approached through revision and critique.

Truth is partial.

The traditional notion of truth is used by those in a position of power to oppress others.

Truth is negotiated through dialogue.

The discussion at the end of this chapter gives you an idea of what the order of your list might mean for your research. In this discussion, which touches on the philosophy of research, there are some terms that can be rather overwhelming and off-putting. They include positivism, post-positivism, relativism, postmodernism and interpretivism. However, don't worry about these terms. Go to the end of this chapter and read how the ranking you have given above relates to these terms. You might be surprised to see that your answers suggest a leaning to one of these terms, even though you are unclear as to what they mean. We will return to these terms later in the chapter.

If I See something with my own eyes, does that mean it is true?

Figure 2.2 Eyes image

WHAT IS EPISTEMOLOGY?

Epistemology is a great word. It is pronounced ih-pis-tuh-mol-o-jee. It sounds good and, once you understand what it means, it can be used to impress and inspire others. Also, in certain circumstances, knowledge of the word can lead to positive change. Let me tell you a story that really did happen ....

Activity 2.7: Story

There's a particular part of Northern England that had some of the country's richest and biggest coal mines. Generations of the same families worked in and around the mines: girls and women and boys under the age of ten worked underground until 1842. The work was incredibly dangerous: many lives were lost through mining accidents and many more through different types of lung disease caused by coal mine dust. Yet, as time moved on into the 20th and 21st centuries, the people were proud of their coal mining heritage: they told stories of their parents, grandparents and great grandparents. Yes, they talked about the hardship they went through, but they also looked back fondly on the sense of community, belonging and purpose that went with it.

Then the mines began to close. Families were devastated. Unemployment hit record levels. Communities began to break down.

Joan was in her early forties. She was worried and anxious about the future. Her husband couldn't find work and was taking it very badly. He had spent his whole working life in the mines and now he had nothing. Some of his friends had moved away to find work, others couldn't afford to socialize. Knowing she had to do something, Joan enrolled on a university course run by her local college. No one in her family had ever gone to college or university. She was scared but desperate. Four children needed food, heating and clothing, and her family needed to build hope for the future.

She didn't receive much support: further and higher education seemed a world away from her community. He husband thought she was wasting her time and her children didn't really understand what she was doing. Then, one evening, everything changed.

The family were sitting together watching their usual television popular quiz show. Answers were shouted out: some were right, some were wrong, as usual. Questions usually involved popular culture or music and could be answered by both children and adults. Then the family were stunned into silence by the following question:

What is epistemology?

a   The study of social inequality
b   The theory of knowledge
c   A contextual framework for research
d   A description of cultural phenomena

Joan shouted out the correct answer. Her husband almost fell off his chair. Her children stared at her with mouths wide open.

'How did you know that, mum?' the eldest asked.

'We're doing it on my course at college. Last week, on my research methods course.'

The youngest child looked up: 'What's research methods?'

'It's how you find out about things. Like experiments. Or when you ask questions. It's very exciting because you keep on finding out new things.'

The family turned back to the television to wait for the next question. Joan was curious and hopeful: her children had displayed real interest in what she was doing and saying. Perhaps things were going to improve?

Joan graduated with a first-class honours degree in 2019 after five years of part-time study. Her husband and children were all at the graduation ceremony. Her oldest son is in his second year of university, one child is working as an apprentice, another is in the final year of college and the youngest is just beginning A-level study at school. All now believe in the value of education. There are many reasons for this transformation in her family, but Joan still puts it down to the fact that she knew what was meant by epistemology.

Do you know the answer to the question Joan got right? The answer, along with a fuller definition of what is meant by epistemology, can be found at the end of the chapter.

WHAT IS EPISTEMOLOGICAL POSITION?

Crotty (1998) identified three distinct epistemological positions: objectivism, constructionism and subjectivism. Let's take a little time to think about what these words mean. Activity 2.8 will help you to do this.

Activity 2.8: Matching

Consider each of these words carefully and think about what they might mean. Think about what we covered earlier in this chapter relating to truth, knowledge and assumptions. Match each epistemological position with the definition you believe is correct (clues are in the definitions). Go to the end of this chapter for answers.

Epistemological position   **Appropriate definition (See below: 1, 2 or 3)**

Objectivism

Constructionism

Subjectivism

Definitions

1   Truth and reality are only what we perceive them to be. Everything is relative. There is no objective or external truth to be discovered. Knowledge is acquired subjectively.
2   Human knowledge exists. It can be discovered through systematic and diligent scientific methods. Truths can be uncovered through observation, experimentation and the elimination of personal biases.
3   Knowledge is created and built collectively by scientists: it is not discovered. As scientific facts are social constructions, they cannot make claims to truth and reality.

Some disciplines have deep-rooted epistemological positions (e.g. sciences, where the scientific method is used to observe, experiment and find an objective truth). However, try not to locate yourself within one position just because it is expected, or even required, in your discipline. If you are open to different or alternative perspectives, you broaden your options while increasing your chance of completing successful research and finding out something new.

WHAT IS THEORETICAL PERSPECTIVE?

Now that you have been introduced to epistemology, let's turn our attention to theoretical perspective. 'Theoretical' involves theory – ideas or principles that help explain something. Theories have been developed and tested over time. 'Perspective' is a way of looking at something, or a point of view about an issue. Therefore, 'theoretical perspective' is a framework, or a lens, through which we make explanations or view the world.

In the answer given to Activity 2.6, you were introduced to positivism, postpositivism, relativism, postmodernism and interpretivism. As the answer explained, they are called theoretical perspectives, theoretical stances or research paradigms. Other theoretical perspectives include structuralism, post-structuralism and critical inquiry. Let's try a quick game in Activity 2.9 that helps to reinforce what you have learnt so far and introduces you to some other theoretical perspectives.

Activity 2.9: Spot the odd one out

Spot which of the following terms is the odd one out in the list. You have been introduced to some of these terms, but not all of them. Therefore, you might need to spend a little time looking up what the new terms mean before you are able to spot the odd one out. Once you have done this, explain why it is the odd one out. The answer can be found at the end of the chapter, where you can also find descriptions of the words you have not yet been introduced to.

Functionalism

Postmodernism

Constructionism

Structuralism

Symbolic interactionism

Positivism

Interpretivism

HOW DOES THEORETICAL PERSPECTIVE RELATE TO EPISTEMOLOGICAL POSITION?

Think about your epistemological position as the foundations to a house (see Figure 2.3). This is the supporting frame for your house, providing stability and strength. There are different types of foundation, depending on the type, size and weight of the building, and on the underlying geology (and, of course, there are different epistemological positions, depending on your beliefs, assumptions and experiences). Next, think about your theoretical perspective as the walls of your house. They are the building blocks that provide the structure, and they are sturdy and durable. They can be made of a variety of materials, depending on preference, cost and practicalities (just as there are a variety of theoretical perspectives depending on your epistemology, beliefs and assumptions). Walls support roofs: think of the roof as your methodology, which is the framework that guides your research. We will discuss this in Chapter 7, but you might find it useful to start to think about how methodology fits with epistemology and theoretical perspective at this stage of your research journey.

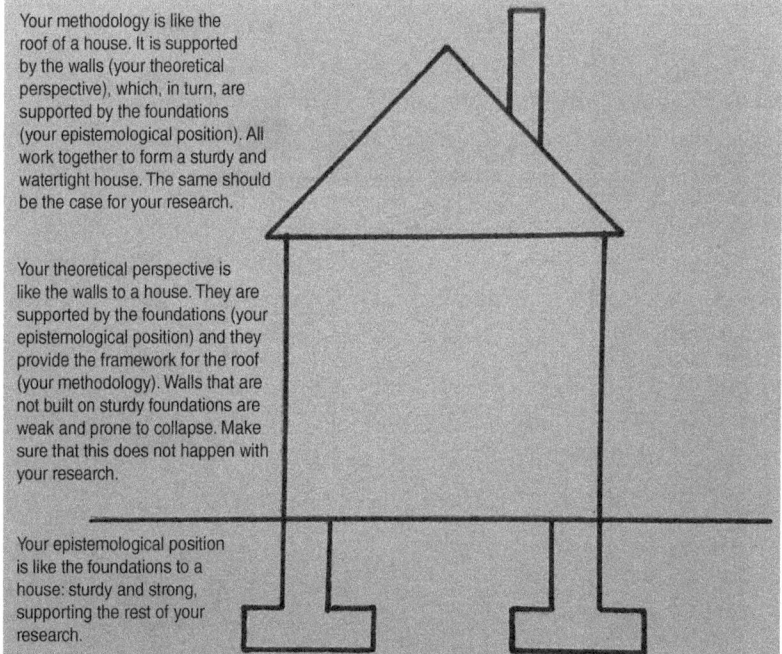

Your methodology is like the roof of a house. It is supported by the walls (your theoretical perspective), which, in turn, are supported by the foundations (your epistemological position). All work together to form a sturdy and watertight house. The same should be the case for your research.

Your theoretical perspective is like the walls to a house. They are supported by the foundations (your epistemological position) and they provide the framework for the roof (your methodology). Walls that are not built on sturdy foundations are weak and prone to collapse. Make sure that this does not happen with your research.

Your epistemological position is like the foundations to a house: sturdy and strong, supporting the rest of your research.

Figure 2.3 House image

We have seen that Crotty (1998) identified three distinct epistemological positions: objectivism, constructionism and subjectivism. Now, let's think about how different theoretical perspectives fit with each of these positions. Activity 2.10 and Figure 2.4 help you to do this.

Activity 2.10: Missing relationships

Read the following descriptions of theoretical perspectives. (If you need a fuller description, go to the end of this chapter and read the answer given for Activity 2.6.) Read each one carefully. Think about them and how they might relate to epistemological position. Then fill in the boxes in Figure 2.4 by entering a theoretical perspective into each empty space (or record their position as a voice memo). Clues can be found in the descriptions to help you with your choices and it doesn't matter which order you place them in the relevant boxes. Answers can be found at the end of the chapter.

Descriptions

Critical inquiry. As reality is socially constructed by institutions, society and the media, researchers gather, analyse and evaluate ideas, assumptions and evidence from a wide range of perspectives, while considering the social, political, economic and cultural contexts in which they occur.

Postmodernism. As there is no such thing as objective truth, knowledge and science portray the perspective of a particular culture. Therefore, researchers uncover hidden meanings within text and discourse: they are able to discover a particular reality but are also involved in the creation of that reality.

Positivism. As reality exists independently, outside the mind, it can be studied objectively. Researchers do this using the scientific method; through observation, experimentation, reason and logic, they can develop reliable and consistent knowledge and causation can be established.

Interpretivism. As reality is determined by personal perspectives, researchers access that reality through analysis of social constructions such as language, images and shared meanings. Researchers focus on meaning and understanding, employing naturalistic approaches of data collection, such as interviews and observations.

Structuralism. As human nature can only be understood in relation to existing social structures or systems, researchers study activities and behaviours that help them to discover the structures that produce and reproduce meaning within a particular culture.

Post-positivism. Although there is an objective truth to pursue, researchers can influence their observations and this, in turn, has an influence on their conclusions. Researchers follow set procedures but recognize that bias exists.

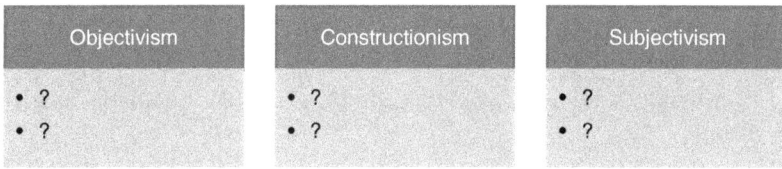

Figure 2.4   The relationship between epistemological position and theoretical perspective

WHY DO I NEED TO KNOW ABOUT EPISTEMOLOGY AND THEORETICAL PERSPECTIVE?

Your research is framed and guided by epistemology and theoretical perspective. Having an understanding of both these terms will help you to understand more about your research, the methods you use and the knowledge you generate. It will also help you to justify and defend your research approach and choice of methods. Some students need to undertake a viva, or oral examination, in which they discuss their research and defend their methods. This is easier if you get to grips with what is meant by epistemology and theoretical perspective.

An understanding of epistemology and theoretical perspective will help you to think more about your research results and the assumptions you make. When you understand more about the type of knowledge your research will generate, you can begin to see whether assumptions and/or conclusions are flawed. Before we continue, let's think a little more about what we mean by flawed assumptions or conclusions. Activity 2.11 will help you to do this.

Activity 2.11: Checklist (right and wrong answers)

Consider each of the examples below. Work through them, putting 'Yes' next to examples in which you think statements, assumptions and/or conclusions are correct and 'No' next to those you think are wrong. This will help you to think about flawed assumptions and conclusions. Answers and explanations can be found at the end of the chapter.

Example 1 (yes or no)

For my research I carried out in-depth interviews with ten teachers in a school in Canada who had been in the job more than ten years. My results show that they are suffering more stress now than they were ten years ago. I have concluded that teaching is becoming more stressful. Teachers need more support in the way of counselling and stress-management courses, and they need more support from their head teacher. More funding should be made available to support teachers.

Example 2 (yes or no)

I have produced and tested my hypothesis about back pain and physiotherapy. I have stated and rejected my null hypothesis. My results are valid and can be repeated. I understand that I cannot say my hypothesis is a 100% correct, but I believe it forms a reasonable basis for action by physiotherapy services and others who work with back pain sufferers.

Example 3 (yes or no)

I have conducted three online focus groups to discuss attitudes to police officers carrying guns. I understand that this research has taken place in one country at one point in time. I also understand that participants in my groups were volunteers and may have had a specific motive for taking part in the focus groups. I know that I cannot generalize my findings to the whole population, but this is not my goal. I want to get a better idea of what individuals think about police carrying guns in our country. It's their personal perceptions and attitudes that are of interest and I will write up a descriptive account of them.

HOW DO EPISTEMOLOGY AND THEORETICAL PERSPECTIVE RELATE TO MY RESEARCH?

As we have seen in the previous sections, epistemology and theoretical perspective frame and guide your research. They have an influence on the approach you adopt, the methods you choose and the knowledge you generate. It is important to note that your epistemological position and theoretical perspective lead to different types of research question and different types of research output. Once you understand more about them, activities such as analysis and writing-up become easier: you understand where your research is heading and what is important in your findings and outputs.

┌─────────────── THINK INTEGRITY 2.1 ───────────────┐

Consider the term 'epistemic research integrity'. Epistemic relates to knowledge. Research integrity relates to values of honesty, rigour, transparency and openness. Therefore, epistemic research integrity relates to the production of knowledge (and the goals of our research), the values we place on the knowledge we produce and the values we place on the research that has produced that knowledge. It is important to pay attention to epistemic research integrity as it enables us to convince others of the value and authenticity of our research. It helps to build epistemic trust, which is the belief that new knowledge is trustworthy and relevant.

└──┘

Now that you understand a little more about the philosophy of research, we can move on. However, before we do, let's test your understanding of what has been covered in this chapter with a short multiple-choice quiz.

Activity 2.12: Multiple-choice quiz

The topics in all three of these questions have been covered in this chapter, so if you can't answer any of the questions, return to some of the activities to refresh your memory. Answers can be found at the end of the chapter.

1 What is the epistemological position of a scientist who believes that knowledge exists and can be discovered through systematic and diligent methods?

   a   Constructionism.
   b   Subjectivism.
   c   Objectivism.

2 If a researcher tells you that they believe there is no objective or external truth to be discovered, and that truth and reality are only what we perceive them to be, what is their epistemological position?

   a   Constructionism.
   b   Subjectivism.
   c   Objectivism.

3 What is interpretivism?

   a   An epistemological position.
   b   An assumption.
   c   A theoretical perspective.

ACTIVITY ANSWERS: CHAPTER 2
Activity 2.6: Statement organization

If you have placed statements such as 'a truth is a fact', 'there are absolute truths' and 'objective truth can be found through systematic investigation' at the top of your list, you are indicating that you think there is a truth to be found and that the way to do this is through the use of scientific method and procedures. This is *positivism*, which is the term that has been given to the scientific study of the physical and social world. Positivists believe that truth can be found through observation, experimentation and measurement. If this is what you believe, then the purpose of your research might be to search for cause-and-effect relationships, make explanations, and acquire and report knowledge, for example.

If you have placed the statement 'objective truth can be approached through revision and critique' near the top of your list, along with some of those listed for positivism above, perhaps you should explore *post-positivism*. This suggests that there is an objective truth to be sought, but researchers can have an influence on observations, experiments and measurements. Observation is fallible and can contain errors, and all theory is revisable and can be improved. If this is what you believe, then you might be interested in careful experimentation, triangulation (combining methods, theories and observers to overcome bias), academic scrutiny and theoretical criticism.

If you have placed the statement 'truth is relative to language or culture', 'truth is highly contextual' or 'every individual has their own truth' at the top of your list, you might be interested in exploring more about *relativism*. There are a number of slightly different forms of relativism, but they are all connected by the view that there is no such thing as objectivity (or objective knowledge that is independent of the observer) and no such thing as an absolute truth. If you have prioritized statements that suggest a leaning towards relativism, you might have placed those that suggest a learning towards positivism towards the bottom of your list ('a truth is a fact' and 'there are absolute truths', for example).

If you have placed 'there is no single source or origin for truth beyond the individual', 'truth is contingent on the social, political, cultural and technical norms of a particular era' or 'truth is partial' near the top of your list, you might be interested in finding out more about *postmodernism*. For postmodernists there are no objective or absolute truths: it is not possible to obtain one particular view of the world. Postmodernists emphasize concrete experience over abstract principles, which can be considered through interpretations or the deconstruction of existing concepts, belief systems or commonplace social values and assumptions. If you have also placed 'the traditional notion of truth is used by those in a position of power to oppress others' near the top of your list, then you might be interested in finding out more about *feminist postmodernism*. This recognizes multiple explanations of reality and looks for social processes that lead to variations in behaviour within the conditions imposed by structures within society.

If you have placed 'truth is negotiated through dialogue', 'truth is constructed by individuals' and 'truth is subjective' near the top of your list, you might be interested in finding out more about *interpretivism*. This can be aligned with the relativist and/or postmodern statements above, so you may find that they also appear near the top of your list. Interpretivists emphasize the importance of multiple meanings and ways of knowing, which can only be studied by immersing themselves into the social context under study to observe from the inside.

This answer has introduced you to positivism, post-positivism, relativism, postmodernism and interpretivism. They are called theoretical perspectives, theoretical stances or research paradigms. As you read more, you might find that other positions become important in your research (e.g. structuralism, post-structuralism or critical inquiry). If you are interested in finding out more, useful sources are given in the Go further 2.1 box. We will also return to this topic later in these answers.

Activity 2.7: Story

What is epistemology?

a   The study of social inequality
b   The theory of knowledge (correct answer)
c   A contextual framework for research
d   A description of cultural phenomena

Epistemology is the theory of knowledge (the study of the nature of human knowledge and how it is acquired). It involves an assessment or evaluation of the origin, nature, validity and scope of knowledge. It considers how we know what we know and how we obtain and build knowledge. It is also concerned with what constitutes valid knowledge and the difference between belief and knowledge.

TIP 2.2

Take time to consider epistemology. A well thought-out epistemological position, at the start of your research, will help your research to run smoothly and help to avoid problems and confusion as your research project moves forward. Epistemology is important because it has an influence on your research design, your choice of methodology and the way that you build knowledge and generate theory. It influences your research question and your research outcomes.

GO FURTHER 2.1

Although the following book is quite old now, it is still extremely useful for helping you to understand more about the issues covered in the answer above: Crotty, M. (1998) *The Foundations of Social Research: Meaning and Perspective in the Research Process*. London: Sage.

Wi-Phi is a website run by philosophers and educators. There is an interesting video on the nature of truth, along with a variety of other videos on epistemology that you might find interesting:

www.wi-phi.com/videos/the-nature-of-truth [accessed 3 November 2023]
www.wi-phi.com/series/epistemology [accessed 3 November 2023]

Activity 2.8: Matching

Epistemological position	Appropriate definition (1, 2 or 3)
Objectivism	2
Constructionism	3
Subjectivism	1

Activity 2.9: Spot the odd one out

Constructionism is the odd one out in this list as it is an epistemological position. All the others are theoretical perspectives. The two theoretical perspectives that you have not yet been introduced to are *functionalism* and *symbolic interactionism*. Functionalism, as a social theory, suggests that a social structure exists independently of the individual: this structure has shared norms and values that bind society together. Researchers look for general laws that explain human action and behaviour, using scientific methods at the macro level (they look at the whole of society, rather than at individuals).

Symbolic interactionism is a strand of interpretivism. It suggests that our social world is constructed through the everyday interaction of individuals and the shared symbols that are used to communicate (e.g. language, objects, concepts and images). Researchers tend to use qualitative methods, such as participant observation (see Chapter 9) to research social interaction and the meaning of actions, although some use a mix of research methods in an attempt to gain deeper understanding (see Chapter 7).

GO FURTHER 2.2

A useful podcast, if you are new to symbolic interactionism and want to find out more, can be found at https://podtail.com/en/podcast/the-sociology-show/an-introduction-to-symbolic-interactionism-student [accessed 3 November 2023].

    A video that covers three sociological perspectives (functionalism, symbolic interactionism and conflict theory) can be found at www.youtube.com/watch?v=VnF9lei8BTM [accessed 3 November 2023].

Activity 2.10: Missing relationships

The correct answers, illustrating the relationship between epistemology and theortical perspective, are provided in Figure 2.5.

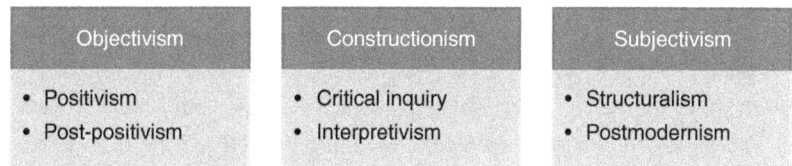

Objectivism	Constructionism	Subjectivism
• Positivism • Post-positivism	• Critical inquiry • Interpretivism	• Structuralism • Postmodernism

Figure 2.5 The relationship between epistemological position and theoretical perspective: answers

Activity 2.11: Checklist (right and wrong answers)

Example 1: No

This conclusion is flawed. This student has only interviewed ten school teachers in one school in Canada. They go on to generalize their findings by talking about all teachers. It may be correct that the one school visited had a particular problem with stress among teachers; however, other schools might not have the same problem. It may also be that only the teachers interviewed had a problem with stress, whereas others in the same school might not have similar problems (perhaps those with more stress volunteered to be interviewed). Making an assumption that all teachers suffer from stress after conducting ten interviews is wrong. This student should have thought more about epistemology and theoretical perspective, and how they relate to research aims and objectives. If they believe generalizations can be made (there is an objective truth to be sought), their approach and methods would be different (a large survey of school teachers, with careful sampling, for example; this is quantitative research and we will discuss this in Chapter 7). In-depth interviews with only ten participants can generate interesting and useful information about their behaviour, attitudes and coping strategies. This is a qualitative study that can be used to provide descriptive accounts or explanations, but it cannot be used to make generalizations. We will return to this topic in Chapter 7.

Example 2: Yes

This statement is correct. The student has performed all the required procedures and statistical tests but understands that, even though this has been done, it is not possible to say that the hypothesis has been confirmed, is true or is 100% correct. Future tests and experiments may, in time, prove the hypothesis false, or they may modify and develop the hypothesis. The relationship here to epistemology and theoretical perspective is the nature of scientific inquiry adopted: this student is following the scientific method that sets out a number of rules and procedures to follow in order to complete the research.

Example 3: Yes

This student has made correct assumptions: it is not possible to generalize from this type of research and a descriptive account of attitudes and perceptions would work well for this type of qualitative research (three focus groups that look in depth at the attitudes and perceptions of those taking part: we will return to this in Chapter 7). This student is suggesting that there is not one single truth to be found, but that individuals have different truths, depending on their personal experiences, motivation and standpoint. This understanding makes it easier for the student to write up their descriptive account.

Activity 2.12: Multiple-choice quiz

1 What is the epistemological position of a scientist who believes that knowledge exists and can be discovered through systematic and diligent methods?

   a   Constructionism.
   b   Subjectivism.
   c   Objectivism (correct answer).

2 If a researcher tells you that they believe there is no objective or external truth to be discovered, and that truth and reality are only what we perceive them to be, what is their epistemological position?

   a   Constructionism.
   b   Subjectivism (correct answer).
   c   Objectivism.

3 What is interpretivism?

   a   An epistemological position.
   b   An assumption.
   c   A theoretical perspective (correct answer).

3

COLLABORATION – LET'S THINK ABOUT WORKING TOGETHER ON RESEARCH ...

CHAPTER CONTENTS

CHAPTER ACTIVITIES

CHAPTER OBJECTIVES

By the end of this chapter, you will be able to:

- Explain what is meant by research collaboration
- List the benefits to be gained through collaboration
- Describe how to collaborate between disciplines, cross-culturally and ethically
- Summarize how to start a collaboration project
- Discuss potential problems when collaborating and identify possible solutions
- Provide examples of undergraduate and postgraduate collaboration projects
- Consider whether to get involved in a collaboration project

There are many opportunities for you to work with others on research: it is a great way to learn more, remain motivated and enjoy your work. Collaboration opportunities can be at course, departmental, institutional, local, regional or international level, and can be in person, online or through a hybrid approach (using a mix of in-person and online methods and tools). For example, you might be asked to work with your peers on a group research project for an assessed piece of work for your course. Or you might decide to join a research team on a voluntary basis, to gain valuable research experience and pursue a particular interest of yours. Perhaps you will choose to undertake a collaborative dissertation or thesis with an external partner organization, enabling you to gain practical experience and build networks for future employment. Or maybe you will have the opportunity to join a research team undertaking interdisciplinary and/or international research.

With collaboration comes exciting opportunities. This chapter takes you through the important issues involved with collaboration, helping you to understand what it is, why it is important, who you can collaborate with and how to go about collaborating successfully and ethically.

WHAT IS COLLABORATION?

To answer this question, let's first consider how the word 'collaboration' is defined. Activity 3.1 encourages you do this.

Activity 3.1: Definitions and develop your own checklist

Have a look at Figure 3.1, which gives some common defintions of the word 'collaboration'. Once you have read and digested each of these defintions, write or record as a voice memo a list of what you consider to be the main points to note about collaboration, then read the list given below.

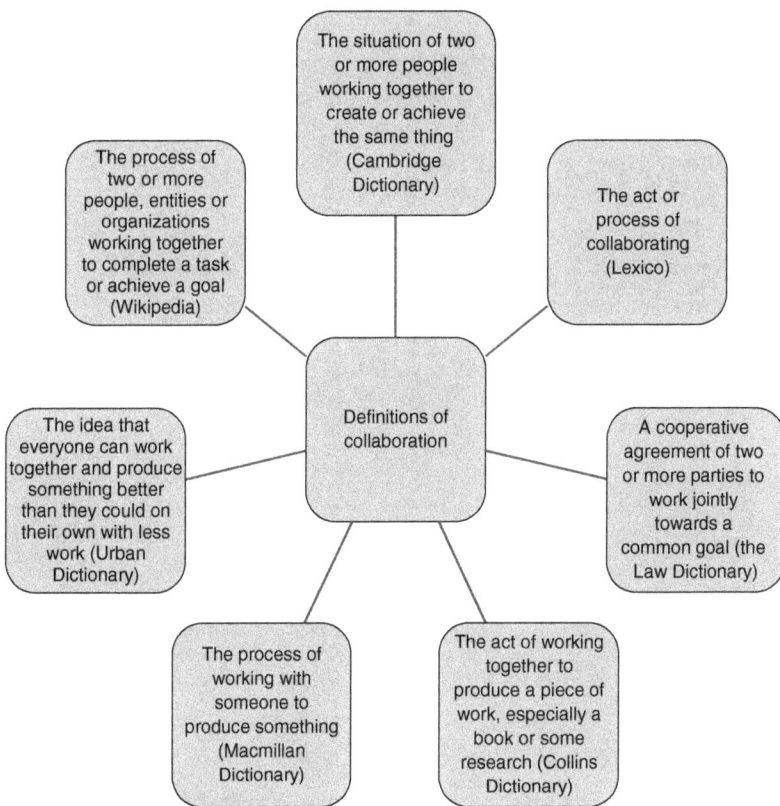

Figure 3.1 Definitions of collaboration

Points to note about collaboration

The definitions given in Figure 3.1 raise the following points about collaboration:

- It takes place between two or more people, entities or organizations.
- The purpose is to achieve a common goal.
- It involves cooperation and working jointly together.
- More can be achieved through collaboration than can be achieved by working alone.

Now that you have thought more about what is meant by collaboration, let's think about how you have collaborated in the past. Activity 3.2 will help you to do this.

Activity 3.2: Reflection

Think back through your studies and life in general. Identify five different types of collaboration that you have been involved with in the past and list them below or as a voice note. You might think that you have not collaborated but you have. Think about what has taken place during your studies: student projects, groups discussions, peer teaching, role play or field work, for example. Or you might consider hobbies or extra-curricular activities: drama, online games, sports or voluntary work. Perhaps you have been involved in some type of project or teamwork in full- or part-time employment, or had to work with family members caring for a relative or arranging a social event. There are many types of collaboration; thinking about what you have done in the past will help you to understand the relevance of what we are discussing in this chapter.

1

2

3

4

5

WHY SHOULD I COLLABORATE?

There are many reasons why you should collaborate. Work through Activity 3.3 to find out what they might be.

Activity 3.3: Reflection

Return to the list you produced in Activity 3.2. Taking each item in turn, give a reason why you embarked on the type of collaboration you have listed. Write them down or record a voice note. This will give you five reasons for collaborating. Go to the end of this chapter to find a comprehensive list of reasons given by other students.

1

2

3

4

5

WHY SHOULD I COLLABORATE IN RESEARCH?

The list you have produced in Activity 3.3 provides five reasons why you have collaborated in the past. Let's now consider the relevance to research of what you have listed. Activity 3.4 will help you to do this.

Activity 3.4: Application

Consider whether any of the reasons you have listed relate to collaboration in research: you might find that some do and some don't. Once you have done this, consider the reasons given by other students in the answer to Activity 3.3. Go through each one, identifying those you feel are relevant to research.

Now that you have a better idea of the relevance to research of what you have listed, let's look at collaboration in research in more detail. Activity 3.5 will help you to do this.

Activity 3.5: Missing-word Puzzle

Complete this missing-word puzzle by filling in the blanks from the list of words provided. It will help you to think about why you should collaborate in research. Answers can be found at the end of the chapter.

Collaboration in research facilitates the cross-fertilization of ideas and enables us to generate, build and advance [_____]. We are able to solve complex [_____], generate fresh ideas and cultivate greater awareness.

Through collaboration we can consider [_____] perspectives, adjust to different world views, learn new methods and build [_____] for other disciplines. We can transfer, share and exchange knowledge, skills and experience.

Collaborating with others expands our research [_____], raises our research profile and increases our understanding and experience of research methods. It also enables us to develop our [_____] skills for employment and life beyond: communication, [_____], negotiation and diplomacy skills, for example. Collaborating enables us to build lasting friendships and develop professional [_____].

interdisciplinary

knowledge

networks

output

problems

respect

teamworking

transferable

TIP 3.1

Think about collaborators as partners in the learning process: you help each other to utilize your experiences and draw out each other's knowledge. It is a two-way process in which responsibilities are shared.

WHO CAN I COLLABORATE WITH?

There are a wide variety of people who researchers can collaborate with. These collaboration opportunities tend to be influenced by the level at which you are studying, your discipline, the topic of your research, the type and structure of your course, the preferences of your tutor, requirements set out by your university and your personal motivation. Activity 3.6 will help you to think about who these people and organizations might be.

Activity 3.6: Word search

Fourteen words are listed below. Each provides an example of who you can collaborate with. They can be individuals, organizations or sectors. Find them in the puzzle on the following page before checking your answers at the end of the chapter.

academic

alumni

charity

employer

engineer

industry

mentor

peer

practitioner

researcher

scientist

stakeholder

student

supervisor

IS IT POSSIBLE TO COLLABORATE ACROSS OR BETWEEN DISCIPLINES?

Yes, it is possible to collaborate across or between disciplines. Activity 3.7 is a game of chance and imagination for you to play. It encourages you to think outside the box and mix and match academic subjects that you might think could not work together. It will help you to think about the strengths, skills, knowledge and understanding developed within different subjects and to work out how they might be of benefit in a collaboration project. It also encourages you to think about interdisciplinary subject areas and research topics. This game does not have to be too serious: even outlandish suggestions still make the intended point (see Example 4 in Activity 3.8).

```
M  C  B  G  H  L  L  L  K  R  V  P  K  N
U  I  C  H  A  R  I  T  Y  D  W  E  R  K
R  E  S  E  A  R  C  H  E  R  I  E  S  T
F  G  T  T  C  M  P  U  Q  K  N  R  U  A
E  L  E  A  A  J  E  X  C  O  D  X  P  O
K  M  N  H  D  K  O  N  I  J  U  G  E  D
X  W  G  L  E  O  E  T  T  T  S  P  R  J
B  F  I  Z  M  T  I  H  N  O  T  F  V  A
X  S  N  M  I  T  G  E  O  Q  R  W  I  L
H  Z  E  J  C  H  D  Y  H  L  Y  P  S  G
X  R  E  A  L  U  M  N  I  P  D  V  O  K
Z  D  R  W  T  E  M  P  L  O  Y  E  R  T
J  P  B  S  C  I  E  N  T  I  S  T  R  V
Q  D  F  B  Q  S  B  Z  V  Y  F  R  R  Y
```

Activity 3.7: Game of chance and imagination

This game can be played by yourself, with a friend or with several friends. Write each of the following academic subjects onto a separate piece of card or paper or record them as a voice memo (you can add, change or delete subjects if you wish). Place them on a table, face down, or play your voice memo. The first person picks two, three or four subjects without letting the rest of the players know what they have chosen (unless you are playing this game by yourself). The first person must then imagine a research project that incorporates all two, three or four subjects that have been picked at random. If you are playing by yourself, try to think of a research project that would incorporate all the academic subjects you have chosen. If you are playing with others, the player describes their research project without mentioning the academic subjects they have chosen. The other members of the group must then try to guess what academic subjects have been chosen from the description that has been provided. A point is awarded for each correct answer and the person with the most points at the end wins the game. If you don't want to play this game, undertake Activity 3.8 instead.

Anatomy

Anthropology

Archaeology

Biology

Business studies

Chemistry

Computer science

Data analytics

Dentistry

Development studies

Earth science

Ecology

Economics

Ergonomics

Film studies

Fine art

Geology

Human geography

Law

Mathematics

Mechanical engineering

Medicine

Nursing

Photography

Physics

Psychology

Sociology

Sports science

Statistics

Visual arts

Zoology

Activity 3.8: Practical examples

Read these examples of research projects imagined by students when this game has been played on previous occasions. Try to guess which academic subjects make up each of the research projects described. Go to the end of this chapter to find the answers.

Example 1

This research project looks at factory environments with the aim of improving working conditions for employees and thus improving productivity. It considers building structure, ventilation, lighting, furniture and facilities, while also looking at employee behaviour and perceptions. Researchers from which subject areas would be useful for this project?

Example 2

Researchers re-imagine depictions of animals in folklore to produce an exhibition of modern-day interpretations of images. The exhibition includes textual descriptions of the evolution of both animal and image. Researchers from which subject areas would be useful for this project?

Example 3

A nurse notices that children on her ward need mental stimulation. She works with a couple of researchers from different subject areas to devise some games that will help children to develop their numerical and digital skills, while keeping their minds occupied and stimulated. Researchers from which subject areas would be useful for this project?

Example 4

Aliens from the planet Researchosis arrived two months ago to find out more about the earth's biosphere, hydrosphere, atmosphere and geosphere. They also wanted to collect evidence to take back to their leaders to explain why the planet Earth should be invaded. They wanted a visual representation to illustrate what was desirable about Earth and data that would be able to predict the outcome of such an invasion. Researchers from which subjects would be useful for this research project?

CAN I COLLABORATE WITH EXTERNAL PEOPLE OR ORGANIZATIONS?

Yes, you can, and you will have found some examples in Activity 3.6 (e.g. stakeholder, employer, engineer, charity and practitioner). An interesting and useful way for undergraduate students to become involved in a research project with an external organization is through a collaborative dissertation. Postgraduate students may also choose to collaborate with external organizations on their thesis (thesis collaboration). The case studies in Activity 3.9 give examples of this type of collaboration.

Activity 3.9: Case studies

Case study 1: Javier

Javier was in his second year of an undergraduate course on Business Administration and Management at Barcelona University, Spain. He chose an optional module on Business Analytics. He really enjoyed the course and, realizing the huge potential for small businesses in his home town, he started to develop the idea of working with a local company for his dissertation. He spoke to his personal tutor, who said that it was an excellent idea. Javier was told to put together a proposal that would explain his idea, discuss his research methods and illustrate the benefits to be gained by both Javier and the organization that he chose to work with.

Javier spent some time thinking about who he would like to work with and how they could both benefit from the project. He was passionate about sustainability and wanted to work with people who had similar ethical values and beliefs. He found a local social enterprise that had been set up for social and environmental good, rather than for the generation of profit. He worked out how business analytics might be of benefit to the enterprise, put together a proposal document and organized a meeting with the partners who had set up the enterprise. He also checked with his tutor that the work would be of the required standard and that it would meet university ethical approval.

The meeting went well and an agreement was made for a collaborative dissertation. Both parties could see that they had similar ethical values and beliefs, could see the benefits and were willing to put in the time and effort required to produce a useful piece of research. The social enterprise partners realized that business analytics would help them to refine their business strategy, develop and improve their product, make comparisons with competitors, improve public relations and retain staff. Javier felt that the research would give him practical, real-world experience; improve his research, communication and business skills; and help him to build networks with like-minded people.

Javier took four months to complete his research and write his dissertation. He obtained his degree, went on to study for a Masters' degree and then set up his own social enterprise in his home town. He is friends with the people who he collaborated with for his dissertation and offers business advice when asked.

Case study 2: Efia

Efia studied in the School of Arts at the University of Ghana. Her doctoral research was in folk art and personal adornment. She attended an exhibition put on by a local gallery where she had the opportunity to talk to a museum curator and a contemporary artist. She realized that both these people would be useful collaborators in her arts-based research where she hoped to bring together folk art and personal adornment, contemporary art and adornment and art curation in an exhibition that would blur boundaries and merge roles.

The museum curator was happy to come on board: she could see that the proposed exhibition had real potential in terms of expanding the work of her museum and increasing public interest in the exhibitions. The artist realized that it would be a great opportunity to get his work known and exhibited, while increasing his knowledge and understanding of folk art and the work of museum curators.

Efia's supervisor thought that the collaboration was a good idea. However, she told Efia that she must take time to work out issues surrounding intellectual property (IP). She suggested that Efia visit the university IP advisor to talk through issues such as copyright ownership (which nearly always rests with the artist) and reaching agreement on the publication of artwork before, during and after the exhibition (we will return to IP issues later in this chapter and it is also discussed in Chapter 4).

The exhibition was a success for all involved and was popular with visitors. Efia was awarded her PhD and has now set up a consultancy working with other artists who want to exhibit their work.

CAN I COLLABORATE INTERNATIONALLY?

Yes, you can collaborate internationally. There are huge benefits to be gained by bringing collaborators together across international borders. Collaborators can:

- Share resources, expertise and data
- Access new research funds
- Learn from different cultures
- Get to know different higher education and research systems

- Maximize scientific output and increase research profiles
- Provide or receive mentorship
- Travel, meet people and make new friends

As a student, you might have the opportunity to work within an international research team. This will provide interest, varied work and lasting friendships, perhaps with the opportunity to travel internationally.

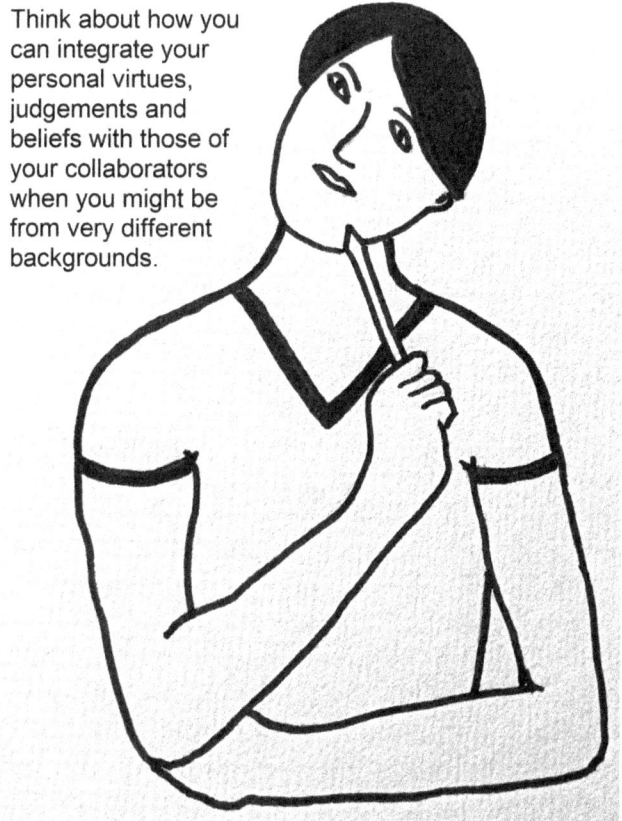

Think about how you can integrate your personal virtues, judgements and beliefs with those of your collaborators when you might be from very different backgrounds.

Figure 3.2   Integrating beliefs image

HOW DO I START ON A COLLABORATION PROJECT?

There are several questions to consider when thinking about how to start a collaboration project (see Figure 3.3).

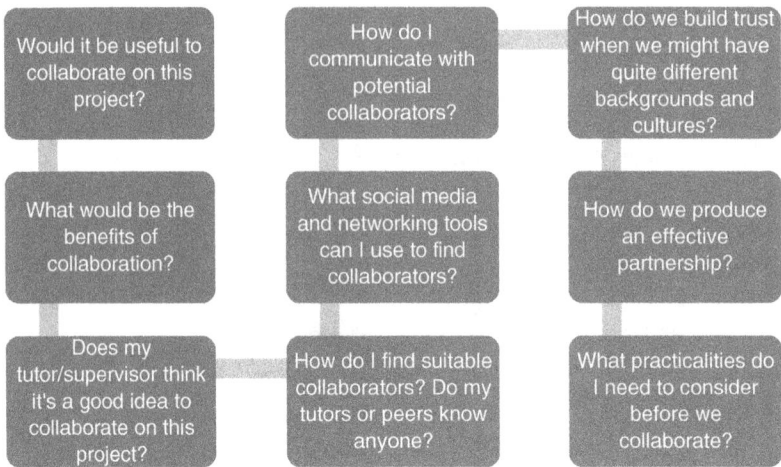

Figure 3.3 Collaboration questions to consider

Let's consider each of these columns in turn. First, take a step back to think about whether collaboration is a good idea for this particular project. Think about the benefits: would it help to generate fresh ideas, solve problems, increase understanding and bring new perspectives, for example? Discuss your ideas with your tutors, supervisor and/or interested peers. Find out what they think about your collaboration idea before you move forward.

Second, think about how you might find suitable collaborators and, once found, the best way to communicate with them. Social media and networking tools provide a useful way to make contact (e.g. ResearchGate, Academia, LinkedIn, Facebook and X), and academic networking events such as workshops, seminars, webinars and conferences all provide useful ways to meet potential collaborators. Sometimes, they are attended by professionals and industry representatives and, therefore, provide a useful way to meet external collaborators. Choose the most appropriate communication method (e.g. in person, email, phone or online) and be courteous, respectful and polite when contacting people.

Third, think about how people with different backgrounds and experiences might have different viewpoints, perspectives, working cultures and beliefs about ethics (see Figure 3.2). Think about how you can work with this difference, build trust and produce an effective partnership. This involves being open, honest and transparent, and careful thought about the paperwork and documentation required (e.g. a code of ethical conduct and non-disclosure agreements). Read on for more information about this paperwork and documentation.

WHAT ARE THE PRACTICAL ISSUES INVOLVED WITH A COLLABORATION PROJECT?

There are various practical issues involved in a collaboration project, depending on the type of collaboration (e.g. a student project, a small team working on a science project, a large team working with industry or an international research team). Activity 3.10 will help you to think about what they might be.

Activity 3.10: Brainstorm

Take a few minutes to brainstorm a list of the practical issues associated with collaboration. Consider different types of collaboration project when you do this. Try to list as many items as possible, as soon as they come into your mind, and write them down, or record them as a voice note, without analysis or judgement. Once you have spent a few minutes brainstorming, go to the end of the chapter for some examples given by other students.

You will see from the examples given at the end of this chapter that not all practical issues are relevant to undergraduate student collaboration projects. However, if you decide to move on to postgraduate study, or if you are thinking about pursuing some type of research for a career, it is important that you get a good grasp of some of the issues listed in the brainstorm answers. The resources in the Go further 3.1 box at the end of this chapter provide information and advice for those of you who want to find out more.

HOW DO I WORK EFFECTIVELY WITH OTHER STUDENTS AND/OR RESEARCHERS?

To answer this question let's turn it on its head: thinking about the mistakes people make will be an entertaining and memorable way for you to think about how to work effectively with other students and/or researchers. Activity 3.11 will help you to do this.

Activity 3.11: Spot the mistakes

Read through each of the scenarios and spot the mistakes in behaviour, attitude or practicalities made by the characters that led to ineffective or problematic collaboration. Describe each mistake and then give a short description of how you think the mistakes could be rectified to make the collaboration more effective. Go to the end of the chapter to find the answers and some suggested solutions.

Example 1

Harry had to work on a student project with three of his peers. He knew one member of the group was particularly keen. Therefore, Harry was happy to stand back, letting this person take the lead and do most of the work.

Example 2

Lanying joined an international research team as an undergraduate student. When the Covid pandemic struck all interaction went online. Lanying was unable to attend several Teams meetings because they took place at 3am in her home country. Once travel restrictions were lifted the researchers arranged an in-person workshop, but Linyang's university refused to provide funding for her to travel. As she could not afford to pay herself, she did not attend the event.

Example 3

Seynabou was collaborating with industry for her doctoral thesis. The research went really well, therefore towards the end of the data collection stage, Seynabou decided to publish interim findings in a podcast and YouTube video. Her industry partner severed all links and refused to participate in the research any further.

HOW DO I COLLABORATE ETHICALLY?

A useful way to consider the issues involved in ethical collaboration is to produce a code of ethical cooperation. This is a document that sets out how collaborators should act and behave ethically so that the project can move forward successfully. Activity 3.12 will help you to do this.

Activity 3.12: Practical example

This list provides an example of issues that can be included in a code of ethical cooperation. Read through the list and decide whether you would add, modify or delete any of the points for a collaboration project in which you might become involved.

- All team members must be trustworthy and accountable and must act with mutual respect and fairness.
- All team members must be treated with respect and courtesy. Requests for help, information, meetings, and so on should be dealt with promptly and efficiently.
- An overall communication routine should be established, with team members encouraged to take part in personal and informal exchange.
- All researchers must act with integrity. If conflicts of interest arise, they must be disclosed and managed, following the relevant institutional guidelines.
- All team members must treat participants with dignity, privacy and autonomy. Informed consent must be sought and harm and risk must be minimized.
- Roles and functions within the project should be made clear from the outset and every team member should understand, and meet, their commitments. There should be a healthy balance in duties such as mentorship and grant writing.
- Management and leadership issues must be addressed from the outset. All team members must know their manager and to whom they are accountable. Special attention must be given to problems that can arise, in particular, when different management cultures are merged.
- Budgets need to be clear and transparent so that all team members understand what money is available, where it has come from and what is available for their use.
- Ownership issues must be addressed from the outset. This can include ownership of equipment that was bought via grant funds for use on the research project. It can also include ownership of research output:
  - All team members must adhere to accepted author protocols concerning published material, including parity in first authorship.
  - Agreement must be reached concerning data-release, IP, the sharing of potentially sensitive information, patents and copyright.
- A suitable data management and sharing plan must be established and all team members must understand, and adhere to, the plan.
- Credit should be shared appropriately.

Source: Dawson, C. (2016) *100 Activities for Teaching Research Methods*. London: Sage, pp. 230–1.

THINK ETHICS 3.1

Ethical collaboration involves treating all parties with dignity, courtesy and respect. Care must be taken to build trust between students and researchers from different disciplines, backgrounds and cultures. To do this, all parties need to be honest, open and transparent. You may need to bring together ethical practice or standards from different disciplines. This involves reconciling research approaches and methodologies that might focus on different aspects of ethical practice, and balancing different cultural, social and political perceptions and beliefs about research ethics, for example.

WHAT DO I NEED TO KNOW ABOUT COLLABORATING CROSS-CULTURALLY?

Many collaborations involve two or more different cultures that bring with them different ideas, customs, norms, standards and beliefs. These cultures can be organizational, management, disciplinary, class, social, ethnic or Indigenous, for example. In cross-cultural collaboration it is important to recognize and acknowledge difference, seek commonality, work to build trust and develop new skills, attitudes and behaviour. All these skills are transferable and will be useful for life beyond your studies. Activity 3.13 illustrates how this works in practice.

Activity 3.13: Notes from the field

Read the following notes from the field and think about the takeaway points that might be relevant to your own cross-cultural collaboration project.

Preparation for collaboration

It is with a certain amount of discomfort that I note, analyse and address my preconceptions and bias. In doing so, I hope to be able to undertake equitable collaboration where all parties are recognized for the work that they do.

A thought niggles at me: I cannot find the expertise required for this project on the small island in which I am working. Why do I have this thought? I am from a high-income country, working at a well-endowed, research-intensive university. No such universities exist on this island. But why does that mean there is not the expertise required for this project? In fact, there is a great deal of knowledge and expertise for many different parts of the project and I am finding local communities and individuals not only willing, but very able, to work with me in a variety of ways.

My idea of knowledge needs a rethink. I also need to think about this thing called research. What am I doing? How do I do it? How might what I think I should be doing differ from what local people think I should be doing? Why is there this difference? What do they know? What do I know? Where do we get this knowledge from? Who is the expert here?

It's never occurred to me to understand the social, physical and spiritual understandings that local communities have about the world in which they live. I am a scientist: I observe, predict and test. I rely on certain principles and laws and I hope, in doing so, that my research will be reliable and valid and provide solutions to improve the health of local people.

Another thought niggles: I can only work with people who are trained in my discipline. Yet I can see that local people have their own kind of science, different from mine, but science nonetheless. They have built systematically their knowledge of their natural environment and applied this knowledge practically to overcome problems and achieve positive outcomes. I need to consider how two different systems of knowledge and science can complement each other within this collaboration and look at how we can all make a meaningful contribution.

I also need to think about our different world views, cultural values and hopes for the future. And I need to think about whether we might have different priorities for the project: I need to analyse my priorities and think about whether they can be adapted for the benefit of the collaboration. This is a lot to think about for my first day of preparation, but these issues have to be addressed from the start if this collaboration is to be successful.

THINK INTEGRITY 3.1

Working with a high level of integrity improves cross-cultural collaboration. This involves respecting local knowledge, understanding, beliefs, values and customs; communicating appropriately (with collaborators and participants); building trust among collaborators and in the research, data sharing and publication process; addressing and overcoming misunderstandings, preconceptions and/or bias; developing cultural sensitivity in method; and adhering to local rules, regulations and laws.

WHAT IF SOMETHING GOES WRONG?

It is possible, in all collaborative projects, that something could go wrong. If you are able to anticipate what might go wrong, and deal with the problem before it escalates, your collaboration will be more successful and you will learn from the experience (see Figure 3.4). Activity 3.14 will help you to think about this in more detail.

Activity 3.14: Matching

Match the problem with the appropriate solution. Answers can be found at the end of this chapter.

Problem

1   The collaborative project is taking up too much time and you are unable to complete other work required for your course.
2   The collaborative project has lost its way and work has stalled, even though individuals are enthusiastic about the project.
3   Individuals are demotivated but have no choice but to continue with the project.
4   Two team members have clashed badly and find it difficult to work together.

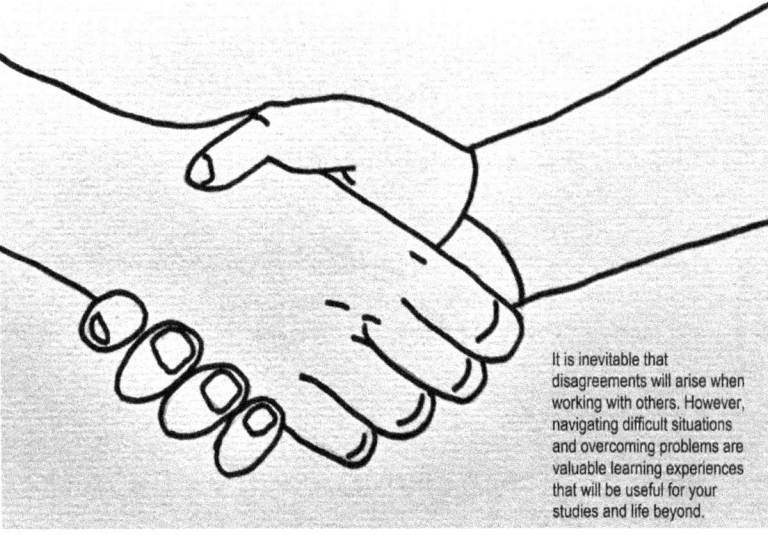

It is inevitable that disagreements will arise when working with others. However, navigating difficult situations and overcoming problems are valuable learning experiences that will be useful for your studies and life beyond.

Figure 3.4   Navigating difficult situations image

Solution

a   Make sure everyone understands the benefits to be gained from the collaborative project and that they are rewarded appropriately. Make sure that the reward system is balanced.

b   Arrange a meeting with all collaborators to discuss problems. Find out if everyone wants to continue with the project. If so, set new goals with specific deadlines. Reallocate roles and responsibilities. Create a feedback loop to discuss and overcome problems further down the line.

c   Speak to collaboration partners. Negotiate a reduced workload, set boundaries, delegate, and be honest and upfront about workload pressures.

d   Allocate different roles within the group so that members do not have to work together. If this is not possible, arrange for a conciliation meeting or some other type of mediation.

GO FURTHER 3.1

Podcasts of first-hand accounts of social scientists working collaboratively across disciplines can be accessed at www.ucl.ac.uk/research/domains/collaborative-social-science/podcasts/collaborative-social-science-domain-podcasts [accessed 12 January 2024].

Methods and tools for co-producing knowledge are provided by the Swiss Academy of Sciences: https://naturalsciences.ch/co-producing-knowledge-explained [accessed 12 January 2024].

Repko, A. and Szostak, R. (2017) *Interdisciplinary Research: Process and Theory*, 3rd edition. Thousand Oaks, CA: Sage.

Kater, I. (2022) 'Natural and Indigenous sciences: reflections on an attempt to collaborate.' *Regional Environmental Change*, 22 (109), published online 03 September 2022, doi:10.1007/s10113-022-01967-3.

Reeves, J., Starbuck, S. and Yeung, A. (2020) *Inspiring Collaboration and Engagement*. London: Sage.

Now that you understand more about how to collaborate in research, we can move on to the next topic. Before we do, let's test your understanding of what you have learnt so far, with a short quiz.

Activity 3.15: Multiple-Choice Quiz

Read each question and choose the correct answer. The topics in all three of these questions have been covered in this chapter, so if you can't answer any of the questions, return to some of the activities to refresh your memory. Answers can be found at the end of the chapter.

1   What is a collaborative dissertation?

   a   The final report of a research project carried out by an undergraduate student with their tutor.
   b   The final report of a research project carried out by an undergraduate student with an external organization.
   c   The final report of a research project carried out by a doctoral student with their supervisor.

2   What is a code of ethical cooperation?

   a   A document that describes how certain information within the collaboration will be kept confidential.
   b   A document that explains how materials will be transferred between collaborators.
   c   A document that sets how collaborators should act and behave ethically together so that the project can move forward successfully.

3   What is the term used to describe working with two or more different cultures that bring with them different ideas, customs, norms, standards and beliefs?

   a   Interdisciplinary collaboration.
   b   Transdisciplinary collaboration.
   c   Cross-cultural collaboration.

ACTIVITY ANSWERS: CHAPTER 3
Activity 3.3: Reflection

There are many reasons why we might have collaborated in the past. The following are examples of answers given by students previously, when they have been asked to undertake this activity:

- Wanting to feel part of something
- Needing support and encouragement
- For the enjoyment of working with others
- For personal satisfaction
- For personal and moral support
- For the friendship and camaraderie
- To solve a problem
- To come up with new ideas
- To achieve a common goal
- Wanting to help others
- Being told to by tutors, teachers or employers
- Necessity/no choice
- Wanting to win a game or an award
- To beat competitors/other players
- Wanting to achieve good marks
- Wanting to succeed in a job
- Too nervous to do it by myself
- To learn from people who have more experience
- To have the opportunity to work with people from other countries
- To work with people from different backgrounds and cultures
- To increase the visibility of my culture/have our voices heard
- To build networks

Activity 3.5: Missing-word puzzle

Collaboration in research facilitates the cross-fertilization of ideas and enables us to generate, build and advance *knowledge*. We are able to solve complex *problems*, generate fresh ideas and cultivate greater awareness.

Through collaboration we can consider *interdisciplinary* perspectives, adjust to different world views, learn new methods and build *respect* for other disciplines. We can transfer, share and exchange knowledge, skills and experience.

Collaborating with others expands our research *output*, raises our research profile and increases our understanding and experience of research methods. It also enables us to develop our *transferable* skills for employment and life beyond: communication, *teamworking*, negotiation and diplomacy skills, for example. Collaborating enables us to build lasting friendships and develop professional *networks*.

Activity 3.6: Word search

```
M  C  B  G  H  L  L  L  K  R  V  P  K  N
U  I  C  H  A  R  I  T  Y  D  W  E  R  K
R  E  S  E  A  R  C  H  E  R  I  E  S  T
F  G  T  T  C  M  P  U  Q  K  N  R  U  A
E  L  E  A  A  J  E  X  C  O  D  X  P  O
K  M  N  H  D  K  O  N  I  J  U  G  E  D
X  W  G  L  E  O  E  T  T  T  S  P  R  J
B  F  I  Z  M  T  I  H  N  O  T  F  V  A
X  S  N  M  I  T  G  E  O  Q  R  W  I  L
H  Z  E  J  C  H  D  Y  H  L  Y  P  S  G
X  R  E  A  L  U  M  N  I  P  D  V  O  K
Z  D  R  W  T  E  M  P  L  O  Y  E  R  T
J  P  B  S  C  I  E  N  T  I  S  T  R  V
Q  D  F  B  Q  S  B  Z  V  Y  F  R  R  Y
```

Activity 3.8: Practical examples

Example 1. Sociology, psychology, business studies and ergonomics

Example 2. Fine art and zoology

Example 3. Computer science, nursing and mathematics

Example 4. Earth sciences, data analytics and photography

Activity 3.10: Brainstorm

Practical issues involved in collaborative projects, suggested in brainstorms with other students, include the following (they have been edited, amalgamated and expanded, where required):

- Deciding whether a leader is required and if so, choosing a leader
- Delegating tasks
- Establishing communication protocols/methods and keeping everyone in the loop
- Finding a suitable venue if meeting in person
- Finding and agreeing a suitable time and date for online synchronous (real-time) meetings
- Obtaining funding
- Making sure everyone has the time to spare
- Choosing materials, software and tools suitable for collaborative projects
- Sourcing and paying for materials, equipment and tools used on the project
- Reaching agreement on who owns equipment if research grants have been used to purchase it
- Reaching agreement on intellectual property (who owns ideas, creations and research outputs)
- Producing required agreements (e.g. non-disclosure agreements, materials transfer agreements and code of ethics)
- Chasing up and/or dealing with those who don't do their work
- Keeping everyone happy and motivated
- Finalizing the work
- Disbanding at the end of the project

Activity 3.11: Spot the mistakes

Example 1

Harry's mistake is that he is relying on one group member to do the work. This can lead to resentment or ill-feeling, or work might not be completed successfully if that person is unable or unwilling to take on the workload. It is important that all members agree on roles and contribute to the work. Behaviour should be courteous and respectful, and all team members should ensure that they make the required (and agreed) contribution.

Example 2

There are two main mistakes in Lanying's example: 1) video meetings were arranged at a time when Lanying could not attend; 2) there was an assumption that everyone could afford or would receive funding to attend the workshop. Synchronous video meetings must be arranged at a time that is suitable for everyone, and this must take into account differences between time zones if the team is crossing international borders. The person arranging these meetings had not taken this into account, which meant that Lanying could not join in. Instead, some type of asynchronous meeting (e.g. text, email or video message) could have taken place, where participants could join at a time convenient to them. Alternatively, another Teams meeting could have been arranged for those in different times zones.

For the second mistake the person organizing the workshop had not taken into account the issue of funding, especially for undergraduates who are often unable to secure funding from their university. Funds could be made available for team members to travel or online workshops could be arranged (at a time suitable for all participants – if this is not possible, two or more workshops could be arranged for different time zones).

Example 3

Seynabou's mistake was not to agree on author and publishing protocols, and on IP, when she started the collaboration project. There could have been several reasons why the industry partner pulled out, perhaps because the research was considered to be commercially sensitive and it did not want the findings to reach the public domain, or wanted an embargo on data release. Perhaps the partner thought that it should have been consulted before Seynabou published or wanted to publish itself or jointly with Seynabou. All these issues should have been considered at the start and written into a collaboration agreement.

GO FURTHER 3.2

If you are entering into any type of collaboration with individuals or organizations outside your university, you must seek expert advice. This will help you to avoid the types of mistakes outlined in Activity 3.11. Speak to your tutor or supervisor and contact the relevant university department. This might be your university IP office or the enterprise unit, for example. You will be able to speak to an adviser and obtain templates or guidance on the paperwork required. More information about IP internationally can be obtained from the relevant IP office:

- Africa: www.aripo.org
- Australia: www.ipaustralia.gov.au
- Canada: https://ised-isde.canada.ca/site/canadian-intellectual-property-office/en
- China: https://english.cnipa.gov.cn
- EU: https://euipo.europa.eu/ohimportal/en
- India: www.ipindia.gov.in
- New Zealand: www.iponz.govt.nz
- UK: www.gov.uk/intellectual-property-an-overview/protect-your-intellectual-property
- USA: www.wipo.int/portal/en/index.html
- World Intellectual Property Organization: www.wipo.int/portal/en/index.html

---

Activity 3.14: Matching

Problem	Solution
1	c
2	b
3	a
4	d

Activity 3.15: Multiple-choice quiz

1   What is a collaborative dissertation?

   a   The final report of a research project carried out by an undergraduate student with their tutor.

   b   The final report of a research project carried out by an undergraduate student with an external organization (correct answer).

   c   The final report of a research project carried out by a doctoral student with their supervisor.

2   What is a code of ethical cooperation?

   a   A document that describes how certain information within the collaboration will be kept confidential.

   b   A document that explains how materials will be transferred between collaborators.

   c   A document that sets how collaborators should act and behave ethically together so that the project can move forward successfully (correct answer).

3   What is the term used to describe working with two or more different cultures that bring with them different ideas, customs, norms, standards and beliefs?

   a   Interdisciplinary collaboration.

   b   Transdisciplinary collaboration.

   c   Cross-cultural collaboration (correct answer).

4

REGULATIONS – LET'S CONSIDER (AND ADHERE TO) POLICY, RULES AND REQUIREMENTS ...

CHAPTER CONTENTS

CHAPTER ACTIVITIES

CHAPTER OBJECTIVES

By the end of this chapter, you will be able to:

- Identify regulations and legislation that are relevant to your research
- Describe the ethical approval process
- Consider whether you need to make an application for ethical approval
- Illustrate how to prepare and submit an application for ethical approval
- Explain what is meant by a risk assessment
- Discuss the different types of risk that could be encountered when conducting research and consider whether any have relevance to your research
- Discuss data protection legislation and its relevance to your research
- Illustrate how to prepare and submit a data management plan
- Define intellectual property (IP) and explain how IP and data ownership relate to your research

---

An important part of research that you can't skip, however much you might want to, is adherence to policy, rules and requirements. Some students are daunted by all the rules and regulations that seem to surround research. However, don't worry about them: your tutor, supervisor and members of staff at your university want you to succeed in your research and, therefore, provide all the support, information, guidance and templates required. Advisors are available to talk you through some of the more complex legislation, if required, and your tutor can offer advice about where to go for further help and information.

When you plan and undertake research, it is important to build trust and confidence in your work. This encourages people to take part in your research. Once people have agreed to take part you need to ensure that you protect their rights, welfare, safety, dignity and data. There are rules, regulations and requirements put in place to ensure that you do this, and it is important that you understand them before you embark on your research project. The policy, rules and requirements that are relevant to you depend on a number of factors, such as the type of research, your research methods, your subject area, the level of study and the country in which you are studying. For example, if your research is with human beings, you need to consider issues such as human rights, data protection, consent, and health and safety.

Members of staff at your university need to check that you have considered the relevant policy, rules and requirements before you begin your research, and the way that they do this is by asking you to make an application for ethical approval. For many students this is a simple process, so don't be daunted: your tutor or supervisor can offer support and guidance, and you can obtain all the information you require from your university research ethics office or equivalent. The ethical approval process is covered later in this chapter but, first, let's start, at the beginning …

HOW DO I FIND OUT WHAT REGULATIONS AND LEGISLATION ARE RELEVANT TO MY RESEARCH?

This is a good question that Activity 4.1 will help you to answer. Once you have worked your way through this activity, consult the Go further 4.1 box for information about where to find out more about the issues you have identified. Then speak to your tutor or supervisor to find out if there is anything you have not considered, or anything you have missed.

Activity 4.1: Classification

Consider each of the items contained within the following list. Classify them according to whether the item is relevant to your research, not relevant to your research, or you don't know (and perhaps need to find out more). There are no right or wrong answers to this as the way that you complete this classification is unique to your research project.

This is relevant	This is not relevant	I don't know
Human rights law		
Data protection law		
Clinical trials law		
Human tissue law		
Animal research law		
Indigenous law		
Law relating to consent		
Mental capacity law		
Health and safety law		
Equality and diversity law		
Safeguarding requirements		
Risk assessment requirements		
Duty of confidentiality common law		
Telecommunications law covering recording, privacy and protection		

Privacy and electronic communications regulations

Intellectual property law

Law relating to security-sensitive research materials

Freedom of information law

Conflict of interest regulations

GO FURTHER 4.1

UK legislation can be found on the government legislation website. Searches can be made by title, year, number and type: https://www.legislation.gov.uk [accessed 11 January 2023].

Information about legislation in force, and legislation under preparation, in the EU can be obtained from the official website of the EU: https://european-union.europa.eu/institutions-law-budget/law/find-legislation_en [accessed 11 January 2023].

The Federal Register of Legislation is a government website for Commonwealth legislation and related documents in Australia: www.legislation.gov.au [accessed 11 January 2023].

Information about legislation in the US can be obtained from Congress.gov, which is the official website for US federal legislative information: www.congress.gov [accessed 11 January 2023].

Information about legislation in India can be obtained from the Legislative Department of the Ministry of Law and Justice: https://legislative.gov.in [accessed 11 January 2023]

The Office of the High Commissioner for Human Rights (UN Human Rights) 'represents the world's commitment to the promotion and protection of the full range of human rights and freedoms set out in the Universal Declaration of Human Rights': www.ohchr.org/en/ohchr_homepage [accessed 11 January 2023].

The European Convention on Human Rights can be accessed at: www.coe.int/en/web/human-rights-convention [accessed 11 January 2023].

WHAT IS ETHICAL APPROVAL?

Any research that involves human participants or use of their tissue or data, or involves animals, must receive ethical approval before data collection can begin (see Figure 4.1). This is to protect research participants and animals from harm. It also serves to protect students and researchers from harm and helps to shield institutions from legal action (e.g. if a research participant is harmed, they could make a claim against the researcher and/or the university).

The type of ethical approval depends on the type of research, the research methods and the level of study. If your research is at undergraduate level and deemed low risk, ethical approval is a simple process, carried out at school, department or faculty level. If it is deemed higher risk, ethical approval needs to be obtained from a research ethics committee (or review board) at your university. If your research involves animals it needs to be reviewed by a specialized committee at your university (e.g. an Animal Welfare and Ethical Review Body in the UK). Consult your university website/VLE (virtual learning environment) and speak to your tutor or supervisor to find out more about what is required for your research.

In certain cases, outside ethical approval is also required. Medical research in the UK requires approval from an NHS research ethics committee and research involving UK Armed Services personnel requires Ministry of Defence research ethics committee approval, for example. Your tutor or supervisor can offer advice specific to your research and to your country.

Is ethical review required? If it is, your data collection cannot begin until approval has been granted.

Figure 4.1 Stop image

DOES MY RESEARCH NEED ETHICAL APPROVAL?

Although most undergraduate and postgraduate research projects require some form of ethical approval, there are some types of research that do not. Activity 4.2 will help you to decide whether or not your project requires approval. Note that this list is not exhaustive: your university might require you to answer more detailed questions to find out whether your research needs approval. Once you have completed the activity, seek clarification from your tutor or supervisor.

Activity 4.2: Checklist (yes or no)

Work your way through the checklist, answering each question with 'yes' or 'no'. Once you have done this, go to the end of the chapter to find out what your answers might mean.

Section 1 (yes or no)

Does your research involve human participants?

Does your research involve the collection, use and/or storage of human tissue?

Does your research involve the collection of personal identifiable data?

Does your research involve the collection of sensitive data?

Does your research involve the collection of confidential data?

Does your research involve the use of audio and/or video recordings?

Does your research involve children?

Does your research involve adults with special needs?

Does your research involve the administration of drugs?

Does your research require participants to test medical devices?

Does your research involve psychological tests or interventions?

Does your research involve risk to participants?

Does your research involve socially sensitive topics?

Could your research harm participants?

Could your research cause your participants distress or anxiety?

Section 2 (yes or no)

Is your research an evaluation (an assessment of a programme or service)?

Does your research involve information freely available in the public domain?

Are you undertaking secondary data analysis?

Was informed consent obtained at the original time of data collection?

Are data completely anonymous?

Can you ensure that you do not collect sensitive or personal identifiable data?

Can you ensure that vulnerable or dependent groups are not included?

Do you have express permission to use secondary data for the required purpose?

Can you prove that data use falls within the remit that data subjects consented to?

HOW DO I APPLY FOR ETHICAL APPROVAL?

Your tutor or supervisor should be your first contact when finding out how to apply for ethical approval. They will be able to offer advice about whether you need to make an application. This process is illustrated in Figure 4.2.

Although procedures vary, in general, your tutor or supervisor decides whether your research is high or low risk. If it is deemed to be low (or minimal) risk, you need to complete a standard form and your tutor or supervisor can sign off using the correct university procedures. This means that you can proceed with your project. If your work is deemed high (or more than minimal) risk, you need to complete a full application that is sent to your faculty, school or university research ethics committee (or institutional review board). You will not be able to start your research until your application has been reviewed and approval granted (see Figure 4.1). This can take a few weeks, so it is important to apply early.

--- **TIP 4.1** ---

Remain positive about ethical review: it is an important part of your project that leads to better research with greater impact. It will help you to think about why your research is important, analyse your chosen methods, anticipate and overcome problems, and ensure that your research is sound ethically.

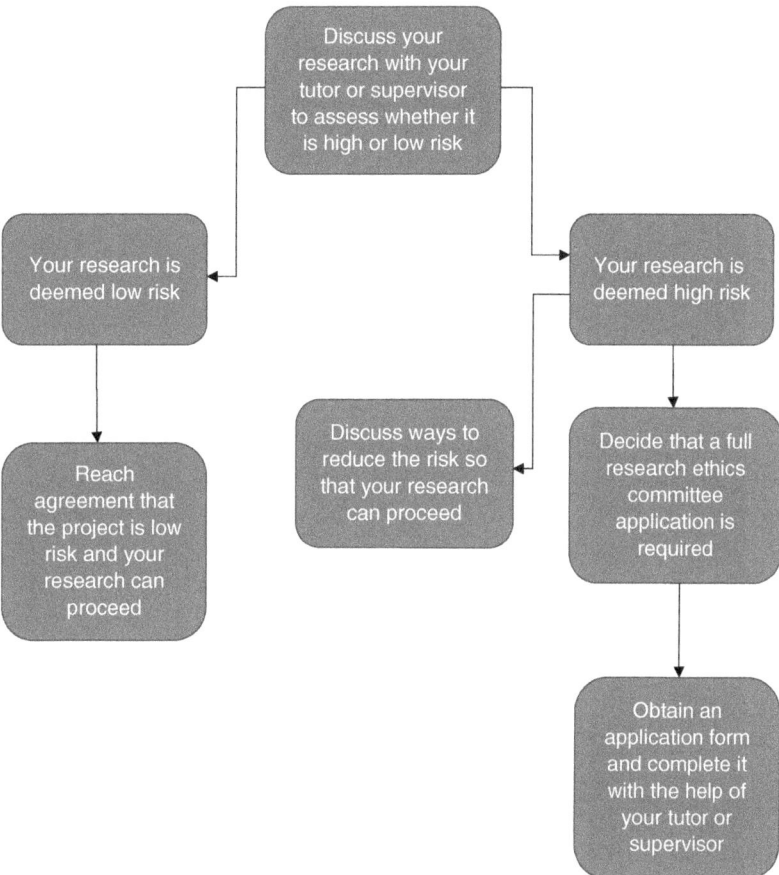

Figure 4.2 Ethical approval application

WHO IS RESPONSIBLE FOR SEEKING ETHICAL APPROVAL?

Responsibility for obtaining ethical approval varies between universities so it is important that you seek clarification from your tutor or supervisor. As we have seen in the previous section, if your research is deemed low risk your tutor or supervisor is able to sign it off, following correct procedures. However, some universities might require students to complete an online form that is then sent directly to the ethics committee coordinator, to determine whether the research is deemed high risk or low risk. In these cases, you, rather than your tutor or supervisor, need to ensure that you complete and send the required form. You will be informed of the decision and will be given instructions as to what you should do next.

In cases where there is a high risk and a full application form is required, again, procedures vary. At some universities your tutor or supervisor works with you to complete the necessary forms, and then submits them on your behalf (in these cases, your tutor or supervisor is called 'the approver'). At other institutions, you are required to submit the forms yourself. Check your university website/VLE to find out what procedures you need to follow.

Activity 4.3: Action

Now that you understand a little more about what is meant by ethical approval and the process involved, visit your university website/VLE to find out more about ethical approval at your university. Do this now, while it is fresh in your mind. This helps to reinforce your learning and increases your understanding of the process required at your university.

WHAT IS A RISK ASSESSMENT?

A risk assessment is a detailed examination of what could cause harm during your research. It considers the type of harm, to whom, how and when, and determines the type of risk control measures that need to be put in place. The aim is to ensure the health and safety of participants, researchers and anyone else who might be affected by the research. A risk assessment is required as part of the ethical approval process described previously. There are different types of risk that you need to consider when undertaking your assessment and they are illustrated in Figure 4.3. Once you have consulted Figure 4.3, complete Activity 4.4, which will help you to think about the types of risk in more depth.

Activity 4.4: Application

Consider the types of risk given in Figure 4.3. Go through each and provide an example of that type of risk. Then think about whether any of them are relevant to your research. Examples of the different types of risk can be found at the end of the chapter.

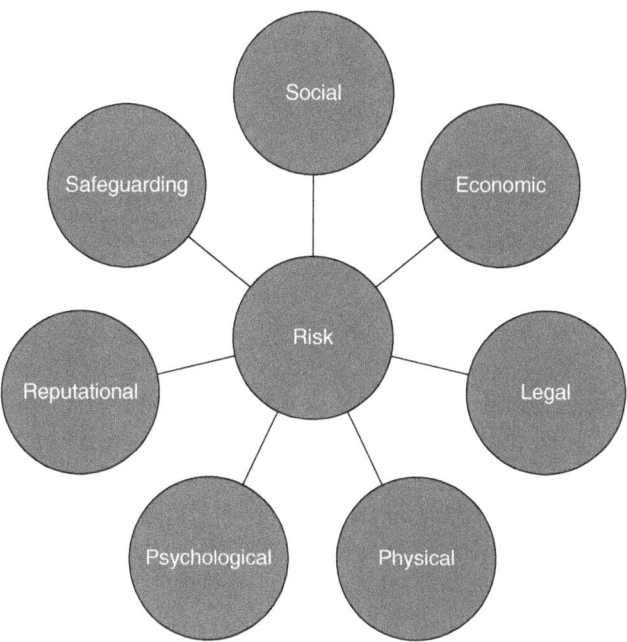

Figure 4.3 Types of risk

HOW DO I COMPLETE A RISK ASSESSMENT?

Procedures vary, depending on your university. In most cases, you are expected to work with your tutor or supervisor to complete the required risk assessment forms. The forms that you need to complete depend on your research and the types of risk present. If your research is low risk the form will be simple. If it is higher risk, you need to complete additional forms (e.g. event risk, travel abroad risk, microscope-based risk and computer-based risk). They can be found on your university website/VLE and contain all the advice and guidance required to complete them. Other information on your university website/VLE might include flowcharts that illustrate the risk assessment process; examples and case studies of risk; risk estimation toolkits; examples of completed risk assessment forms; and university risk policy and procedures. Your risk assessment forms, once completed, are included in your ethical approval application.

Activity 4.5: Action

Now that you understand a little more about what is meant by a risk assessment and the process involved, visit your university website/VLE to find out more about

(Continued)

the procedures at your university. Don't skip this activity as it helps to reinforce your learning and increases your understanding of the risk assessment process.

WHAT DATA PROTECTION LEGISLATION DO I NEED TO ADHERE TO?

The data protection legislation to which you need to adhere depends on where you are studying and conducting your research. It also depends on what type of data you are collecting. At the time of writing (January 2023), on a worldwide basis, 71% of countries have data protection and privacy legislation, 9% of countries have draft legislation, 15% of countries have no legislation and 5% of countries have no data available, perhaps due to conflict, crisis or low statistical capacity. These figures are available on the United Nations Conference on Trade and Development (UNCTD) website (https://unctad.org/page/data-protection-and-privacy-legislation-worldwide). You can find an interactive map on this site that helps to determine whether the country in which you are researching and studying has relevant legislation. Activity 4.6 will help you to explore this in more depth.

Activity 4.6: Action

Visit the UNCTD website (https://unctad.org/page/data-protection-and-privacy-legislation-worldwide). Click on the country in which you are researching and studying. If legislation is available, click on the country to find a list of all the relevant legislation to which you must adhere. Follow the links to the relevant pages to find out more about the legislation.

WHAT IS A DATA MANAGEMENT PLAN?

A data management plan (DMP), or a data management and sharing plan, is a detailed document that provides information about the type of data you hope to generate and the methods you intend to use to collect or create data. It is submitted as part of the ethical review process. A DMP includes information about how you intend to store, preserve, share, transfer, disseminate and dispose of original and/or secondary data. It can also include, depending on the nature of your data, information about security (e.g. encryption, passwords and controlled access) and restrictions on data (e.g. embargos or limits on sharing to protect intellectual property or safeguard research participants). Activity 4.7 will help you to think about what you might need to include in your DMP.

Activity 4.7: Word search

Fourteen words are listed below. They are items, issues or procedures that you need to consider when thinking about your DMP. Find them in the puzzle before checking your answers, which are found at the end of this chapter. This list is not exhaustive: can you think of other items, issues or procedures you might need to consider for your plan?

anonymization

confidentiality

consent

disposal

encryption

key

lock

password

permission

preservation

privacy

restriction

security

storage

HOW DO I PRODUCE A DATA MANAGEMENT PLAN?

Plans can be very simple, perhaps one page in length (for an undergraduate project), or very detailed and several pages in length (e.g. for a postgraduate thesis). Universities provide information and guidance about producing a DMP, so visit your university website/VLE and speak to your tutor or supervisor. Some universities provide templates, whereas others request that you use templates produced by outside organizations such as the Digital Curation Centre (DCC) in the UK (see Go further box 4.2). If you are studying at postgraduate level and need a more detailed plan, find out whether your university provides workshops, training or information sessions.

```
S P A S S W O R D S X L C N O N
L T N S W X A S D I S P O S A L
V K O F U U R A Q T T F N C W C
E T N R N R V P S R G N S C K N
Q X Y O A H V Q R V S U E L O C
D V M V V G M K B H M B N I K E
K T I Y B R E S T R I C T I O N
B H Z H B P W C D X D A T V C C
C K A E I S R J Y W V Z T G G R
E G T Q P S E C U R I T Y K E Y
M D I N W P A P E N L S W F A P
S Y O R T V P S Y F C W C R B T
C O N F I D E N T I A L I T Y I
O E B R N R B V K Q M N K Z F O
Y M P M P E R M I S S I O N W N
T P W L J E B C N Q F A N T J L
```

Activity 4.7 introduced you to a number of issues or procedures that you need to consider when thinking about producing your DMP. Activity 4.8 provides a practical example that helps to make this a little clearer.

Activity 4.8: Dialogue

Consider the following piece of dialogue in which three undergraduate students talk about producing a DMP. As you read, think about whether any of the points mentioned in the dialogue are relevant to your own research.

DMP workshop, third year undergraduate students

Jess: So, I'm guessing we need to produce this plan asap?
Obuya: Yes. It's got to be done before we start anything.
Alana: Yes, as part of that ethical review thing. So, where to start?

Jess: I guess we've got to think about the data we're collecting?

Obuya: Well, I'm going to record interviews and I'm going to produce transcripts from all of them.

Jess: So, that's data and how we collect data. So, you're going to do interviews? You're going to have recordings and transcripts? How are you going to make sure people can't be identified? Or stop people who're not supposed to listen to them?

Obuya: Well, they'll be digital recordings so I guess voices could be identified even if there's not any personal information in them. So that means I've got to think about storage and security and what happens when I carry recordings around with me. [Name of tutor] told me about encrypted digital recorders. She also told me to look into encryption and password protection of written files. Wow, it's a lot to think about.

Alana: And it's not just now. What do you do with all your recordings and transcripts once you've finished your research?

Obuya: Yes, I've been looking into that. They've got to be destroyed in a certain time. I could argue the recordings are important and argue for archiving for research in the future, but I don't think I'll do that.

Alana: I think a big issue for me is to make sure I don't lose any of my data. That'd be a nightmare. I've got to back everything up and do it securely. Computer services can help, apparently. They'll help with encryption and password protection as well, which might help you Obuya.

Jess: Most of my research is online. I wonder if software companies and other ones like search engines take care? I guess I've got to look into their privacy policies. We're going to try our best to look after data, but what about them? Do they have the same morals as us?

Alana: What do you mean?

Jess: You know, like internet service providers, search engines, cloud file syncing, email providers, video tools. Do they protect data? Do they protect privacy?

Alana: I see what you mean. So, you'll have to think about that for your plan?

Jess: Yes. And I'll have to think about what I'm finding online and what I do with it. Are people happy for me to use their information? Did they say I could use it? Can stuff be misused? Can people be harmed? And I've got to watch out for hacking and theft, you know, viruses and trojans and things. And, of course, the other thing I've got to do is think about who owns the information I'm going to use. You know, copyright and stuff like that.

Obuya: You know what you're touching on here? It's also how we report what we find. Obviously, we've got to write our dissertation so we'll be sharing what we've found with other people. How do we make sure people who are part of our research are kept safe? There's a big thing about anonymization to keep our research people safe. And who do we share our data with?

Alana: And confidentiality. We can't talk about what we find out in our research or share our data with everyone.

Jess: Well, we can talk to our supervisors.

Alana: That's true. I think that's the next step from here. Talk to our supervisors before we move on.

THINK INTEGRITY 4.1

The FAIR principles (findable, accessible, interoperable and reusable) for data management were proposed by a consortium of scientists and organizations to support the sharing and reusability of digital assets. These principles provide useful guidance for students and researchers, encouraging them to be transparent and open, while leading to greater collaboration and better decision-making. Start to think about how you can make it easier for others to find, access and use your research data. This can include making sure you have detailed metadata (which gives information about your data) and clear identifiers. It also includes using trusted repositories and clear usage licences. More information can be obtained from the Go FAIR initiative (www.go-fair.org/go-fair-initiative).

HOW IS MY DATA MANAGEMENT PLAN REVIEWED?

How your DMP is reviewed depends on the requirements at your university and on the type and level of your research. If you are studying at undergraduate level and need only to produce a simple DMP, it can be reviewed and signed off by your tutor or supervisor. This is part of the ethical approval process if your research involves collecting data from human participants. If you are studying at postgraduate level or are part of a larger research project, the DMP is a more complex document that needs to be reviewed by the relevant university committee. Again, this is part of the ethical approval process if the research involves data from human participants. Many universities have a research data manager (or equivalent) to offer advice, guidance and reviews of DMPs. If you are applying for funding for your research, your DMP needs to be submitted as part of the grant application and is reviewed by the funding body. Activity 4.9 provides a list of questions that are considered when your DMP is reviewed. Your DMP will be more useful and effective if you are able to answer yes to most or all applicable questions.

Activity 4.9: Checklist (yes, no or n/a)

Once you have produced your DMP, work your way through the following checklist, putting a 'yes', 'no' or 'not applicable' next to each question.

Yes, no or n/a

Have I shown where existing data will come from?

Have I described the software I will use to analyse existing data?

Have I illustrated that no new data will be generated?

Have I explained why I need to collect new data?

Have I provided a justification for collecting new data?

Have I shown how I will collect/produce new data?

Have I provided a clear description of the methods I will use to collect data?

Have I described the type of data I will collect (e.g. audio, visual, textual)?

Have I described the way I will store different types of data?

Have I explained how I will convert data?

Have I provided an estimation of the volume of data?

Have I discussed metadata that will accompany data?

Have I explained how data will be organized?

Have I shown how I will share data?

Have I explained how data can be reused?

Have I explained how data will be kept safe and secure?

Have I illustrated back-up procedures?

Have I explained how sensitive data will be kept safe?

Have I demonstrated how all data protection policy will be adhered to?

Have I discussed restrictions on data?

Have I demonstrated that there are no restrictions on data?

Have I included details of the repositories that will be used?

Have I explained how data will be preserved?

Have I provided a justification for the preservation of data?

Have I described how data will be disposed of?

Have I discussed the data management costs involved?

Have I illustrated that there are no costs involved?

TIP 4.2

Make sure that you take time to maintain and review your DMP as your research progresses. It is a dynamic, living document. It can develop and alter as your research progresses, perhaps due to advances in technology, institutional requirements or changes in the direction of your research, for example.

GO FURTHER 4.2

The Digital Curation Centre (DCC) in the UK has useful information about producing a DMP, including a summary of funders' expectations, FAQs, a useful checklist, templates and examples: www.dcc.ac.uk/resources/data-management-plans [accessed 18 January 2023].

The DCC also has an online service that enables students to create, review and share DMPs that meet funder and institutional requirements. Some universities in the UK require students to use this service instead of providing their own university templates: https://dmponline.dcc.ac.uk [accessed 18 January 2023].

If you are studying elsewhere, check to see whether your country has a similar organization. For example, information about producing a DMP in Australia can be obtained from the Australian Research Data Commons (https://ardc.edu.au/resource/data-management-plans/) [accessed 03 May 2024].

WHY IS DATA OWNERSHIP IMPORTANT WHEN RESEARCHING?

When we talk of data ownership in research there are two important areas to consider. The first is to do with possession and the legal right to own data (e.g. protected by copyright and database rights). This is intellectual property (IP), which is discussed later and in Chapter 3. The data owners have control over data and this includes the ability to create, modify, edit and share data. The second is to do with responsibility and the stewardship of data. Here, data owners must ensure that all data are used in accordance with institutional, professional, ethical and legal rules, regulations and policy.

Therefore, as a student conducting research, you need to consider who owns the data that you intend to use in your research. Any data that is protected by copyright or database rights cannot be used without the owner's permission. However, many researchers believe that data should be made freely available and attach a licence, such as a Creative Commons licence, which sets out how data can be re-used. This is something that you can consider when generating your own data (information about licences and sharing data can be included in your DMP). Universities have different rules about who owns data generated by students and researchers: speak to your tutor or supervisor to find out whether you own data generated in your research.

TIP 4.3

Seeking permission to use data can take time and it might not always be granted. Therefore, begin seeking permission early and include a contingency plan that outlines the action you will take if you are unable to secure permission.

GO FURTHER 4.3

Visit the websites of the relevant national and international organizations for information about copyright and copyright permissions [accessed 23 January 2023]:

- Australia: www.copyright.com.au/about-copyright/permission
- Canada: https://ised-isde.canada.ca/site/canadian-intellectual-property-office/en/copyright
- China: https://en.ncac.gov.cn
- Global: www.wipo.int/copyright/en
- India: https://copyright.gov.in
- UK: www.gov.uk/copyright
- US: www.copyright.gov

Information about Creative Commons licensing can be obtained from https://creativecommons.org/licenses [accessed 23 January 2023].

WHAT IS INTELLECTUAL PROPERTY AND HOW IS IT RELEVANT TO MY RESEARCH?

We have seen in the previous section that data ownership and IP are important issues to consider when conducting your research. Let's think a little more about what is meant by IP and how it is relevant to your research. Activity 4.10 will help you to do this.

Activity 4.10: Missing-word puzzle

Complete this missing-word puzzle by filling in the blanks from the list of words provided. It will help you to think about what is meant by IP and how it relates to your research. Answers can be found at the end of the chapter.

The term 'intellectual property' (IP) refers to intangible assets (not [_____] in nature) owned by an individual or a company. IP has legal [_____] that prevents others from using it without [_____].

Students generate various types of IP as part of their studies and research. This includes artistic creations, [_____], materials, research findings, data, software, music and literary works. Students also use IP owned by other [_____], creators and designers, but they can only do this if permission has been granted.

IP ownership has implications for how students use and share ideas, [_____], data and creations. This includes how research is disseminated and [_____].

However, it is important to note that even if a student has created or generated IP, they might not, necessarily, own it. If IP has been created [_____] or has used significant university [_____], for example, it might be owned by the university and not the student.

consent

designs

jointly

knowledge

physical

protection

published

researchers

resources

THINK ETHICS 4.1

There are a variety of ethical questions you need to ask when thinking about data ownership. For example, if research participants give their personal details voluntarily, does this mean that students own that data? Should participants retain ownership over your research outputs? If so, how can you ensure that they retain ownership? Might students and research participants come into conflict about who owns research data? Who owns data collected from the internet or from social media research? If we use images of research participants, or images produced by them, who owns them? When students want to use these data or images in their dissertation, can they do so? What permission needs to be gained? If you have questions such as these, seek clarification from your tutor or supervisor.

Now that you understand more about policy, rules and requirements, we can move on to the next topic. Before we do, let's test your understanding of what you have learnt so far, with a short quiz.

Activity 4.11: Multiple-choice quiz

Read each question and choose the correct answer. The topics in all three of these questions have been covered in this chapter, so if you can't answer any of the questions, return to some of the activities to refresh your memory. Answers can be found at the end of the chapter.

1   What is the purpose of ethical review?

   a   To check that students work with integrity.
   b   To protect human participants and/or animals.
   c   To check that methods are suitable for the topic.

2   What is the purpose of a risk assessment?

   a   To ensure the health and safety of participants, researchers and others.
   b   To ensure that research is not dangerous.
   c   To ensure that ethical review is successful.

3   Who owns student-generated IP?

   a   The student who created or generated the IP.
   b   The university at which the student studies.
   c   It depends on a number of factors, including university policy.

ACTIVITY ANSWERS: CHAPTER 4
Activity 4.2: Checklist

Section 1

If you have answered 'yes' to *any* of the questions listed in Section 1 of this activity, you need to obtain ethical approval for your research. As we have seen, this might be a simple process that can be sorted out by your tutor or supervisor, if your research is deemed low risk. However, if you have answered 'yes' to most or all of these questions, your research might be deemed higher risk. Therefore, an application for ethical approval needs to be made to your research ethics committee/review board. Consult your university website/VLE and speak to your tutor or supervisor to find out how to proceed.

If you have answered 'no' to *all* of these questions you might not need to obtain ethical approval. Section 2 of this activity helps to clarify the issue, but you should still seek advice from your tutor or supervisor.

Section 2

If you have answered 'yes' to most of these questions you might not need to obtain ethical approval for your research. If you have answered 'no' to most of the questions, you probably do need to obtain ethical approval (unless your research is an evaluation of a programme or service). Seek further advice from your tutor or supervisor and consult your university website/VLE as requirements might vary slightly between universities.

Activity 4.4: Application

The following are examples of the different types of risk listed in Figure 4.3. This list is not exhaustive and your list might differ significantly: there are no right or wrong answers. The important point to note is that you must try to consider all eventualities when undertaking your risk assessment.

Social risk:

- Job losses (for researchers or participants)
- Arguments and disputes (among participants, friends, family, colleagues or researchers)
- Loss of respect (for participants, researchers or the research process)
- Loss of standing in the community (for participants, gatekeepers or stakeholders)

Economic risk:

- Decrease in wages, bonuses or incentives due to research findings
- Increased financial burden on participants (e.g. paying for technology used in the research)
- Financial harm to researcher or university (e.g. disclosure or financial conflict of interest)

Legal risk:

- Disclosure of criminal acts
- Participation in criminal acts (participants and/or researcher)

- Civil claims for compensation
- Action taken against the researcher or university
- Expulsion, deportation, detention or arrest of researchers by semi-authoritarian or authoritarian regimes

Physical risk:

- Risk of infectious disease or illness
- Entering areas of armed conflict, war zones or dangerous neighbourhoods
- Dangerous situations when meeting participants for face-to-face interviews (e.g. unsafe venues, meeting alone and dangerous pets)
- Actual or perceived physical violence when in the field

Psychological risk:

- Loss of self-esteem through research going badly
- Participants and/or researchers suffer sexual or other types of harassment
- Emotional distress when researching distressing situations or harrowing accounts
- Abuse and threats from activists who disagree with the research results or project
- Abuse and threats from online trolls

Reputational risk:

- Tabloid newspapers twist and manipulate results, ruining a researcher's reputation
- Prolonged and bitter disputes with other researchers
- Damage to public perception of researcher or university

Safeguarding risk:

- Risks to young or vulnerable people from improper behaviour, abuse or exploitation
- Risk of compromising situations
- Risk of accusations of improper behaviour
- The influence of power, hierarchy and authority (of gatekeepers and researchers: actual or perceived)
- Dangerous environment or situations for young or vulnerable people

Activity 4.7: Word search

Activity 4.10: Missing-word puzzle

The term 'intellectual property' (IP) refers to intangible assets (not *physical* in nature) owned by an individual or a company. IP has legal *protection* that prevents others from using it without *consent*.

Students generate various types of IP as part of their studies and research. This includes artistic creations, *designs*, materials, research findings, data, software, music and literary works. Students also use IP owned by other *researchers*, creators and designers, but they can only do this if permission has been granted.

IP ownership has implications for how students use and share ideas, *knowledge*, data and creations. This includes how research is disseminated and *published*.

However, it is important to note that even if a student has created or generated IP, they might not, necessarily, own it. If IP has been created *jointly* or has used significant university *resources*, for example, it might be owned by the university and not the student.

Activity 4.11: Multiple-choice quiz

1 What is the purpose of ethical review?

   a   To check that students work with integrity.

   b   To protect human participants and/or animals (correct answer).

   c   To check that methods are suitable for the topic.

2 What is the purpose of a risk assessment?

   a   To ensure the health and safety of participants, researchers and others (correct answer).

   b   To ensure that research is not dangerous.

   c   To ensure that ethical review is successful.

3 Who owns student-generated IP?

   a   The student who created or generated the IP.

   b   The university at which the student studies.

   c   It depends on a number of factors, including university policy (correct answer).

5

ETHICS – LET'S MAKE SURE WE CONSIDER ETHICAL AND MORAL ISSUES ...

CHAPTER CONTENTS

CHAPTER ACTIVITIES

CHAPTER OBJECTIVES

By the end of this chapter, you will be able to:

- List a variety of ways to treat research participants sensitively, with courtesy, dignity and respect
- Plan how to take account of equality, diversity and inclusion, and consider how to conduct discrimination- and fairness-aware research
- Describe how to conduct research with vulnerable groups and children
- Assess whether to collect data on sexual orientation and gender identity
- Explain what is meant by informed consent
- Outline the steps required to obtain informed consent in your research
- Discuss potential problems and dilemmas when obtaining consent in online and digital worlds, and suggest possible solutions
- Explain how to meet the ethical needs of stakeholders

In the previous chapter you found out about rules, regulations and requirements that must be considered when you start your research. We saw that making an application for ethical approval is an important part of this process. Now we are going to look in more detail at the ethical and moral issues you need to consider as a researcher. They are essential in responsible research, regardless of whether they need to be included in an application for ethical approval.

The term 'research ethics' refers to the moral principles that govern and guide research. The rules and regulations we saw in the previous chapter have been shaped by these principles and they provide standards and guidelines for the conduct of responsible research. Now you need to think more closely about your own behaviour and actions, and how they might affect people who take part in your research and/or your research results. While there are standards and guidelines that help you to conduct responsible research, you also need to evaluate your own behaviour and actions. For example, you want to pass your course. You need participants for your research: if you don't get them, you are worried that you won't pass. So, you persuade people to take part. You cut corners. You offer incentives. You choose others who aren't really in your sample (this is a smaller group of your research population that has been defined at the beginning of your research, which makes your research more manageable: we will discuss samples in Chapter 9). These actions might seem harmless, but are they? What might be the consequences of such behaviour?

The activities in this chapter help you to think more about the ethical and moral issues that are relevant to your research. They encourage you to think about your own actions and behaviour and assess how they might have an influence on your research, your participants and/or the success of your project.

HOW DO I TREAT PARTICIPANTS WITH DIGNITY AND RESPECT?

Treating people with dignity and respect is important in all areas of life, but it is especially so when we are conducting research. People give up their time willingly to help us, often with no incentive or reward. They might be nervous, anxious or worried about what will happen to the information they give us. We have a moral duty to treat them with dignity and respect. But what does this actually mean? Activity 5.1 will help you to think about this in more depth and Activity 5.2 encourages you to consider how this relates to your research.

Activity 5.1: Role reversal

Imagine that you are a research participant. How would you like to be treated? Write down or make a voice note of five ways that you would like (or expect) to be treated by a researcher, then go to the end of the chapter to find suggestions from other students.

1

2

3

4

5

Activity 5.2: Application

Once you have read the answers to Activity 5.1, think about how they might relate to your research. How can you ensure that you cover all the issues listed to ensure that you treat your participants with dignity and respect? Consider each of the answers listed and write down or make a voice note of some ideas about how each point can be addressed in your own research.

HOW CAN I ENSURE I TAKE ACCOUNT OF EQUALITY, DIVERSITY AND INCLUSION?

Equality, diversity and inclusion (EDI) should be embedded into all parts of the research process. Put simply, equality means that all should be given the same or equal opportunities and resources. They should be treated fairly and not discriminated against. Diversity covers recognizing, respecting and valuing human differences, cultures, backgrounds, conditions and mindsets. Inclusion ensures that everyone feels valued, included and welcomed. EDI recognizes individuality, aims to eradicate prejudice and ensures social justice. At an institutional level, universities are committed to supporting EDI: visit your university website/VLE for more information. However, there are many factors that stand in the way of EDI, including structural racism, systemic bias and unconscious bias. The first step in ensuring that you take account of EDI in your research design is to recognize and reflect on bias with reference to EDI. Activity 5.3 will help you to do this.

Activity 5.3: Media observation

Spend two days observing the media, paying particular attention to EDI (some brief definitions of the term are given in the paragraph above). Choose any media types that suit you, perhaps because you use them every day, find them interesting or know little about them. You can include social media, newspapers, television, video games, events, websites, radio, virtual reality, videos, messaging apps and email, for example.

As you observe your chosen media types, reflect on the content in relation to EDI. What is being said or portrayed? What assumptions are being made? Who is included/excluded? Are all viewers/members treated equally? Are opinions based on stereotypes, generalizations or one-off experiences? Can you identify biases against people with certain characteristics? Are some media types much better in relation to EDI than others? Why do you think this is the case?

Make written or voice notes as you undertake this activity. This raises your awareness of EDI and enables you to think more deeply about EDI in relation to your research. When you have completed this activity, go to the end of this chapter to find examples of what other students observed.

Now let's think about how what you have found in Activity 5.3 relates to your research. Activity 5.4 will help you to do this.

Activity 5.4: Application

Read through each of the answers to Activity 5.3 given at the end of this chapter. For each, decide how it relates to your research, and think about the steps you can take to overcome the problems identified. Then read the answers provided.

Activities 5.3 and 5.4 raise your awareness of EDI and help you to think about your own bias with reference to EDI. In Figure 5.1, all the strands from these two activities are drawn together to provide a simple diagram of the action you can take to work towards taking account of EDI in your research.

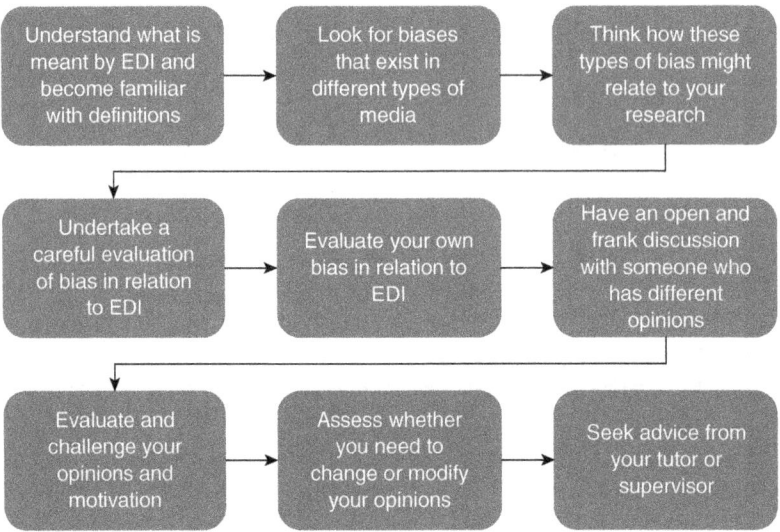

Figure 5.1   Taking account of EDI

HOW CAN I ENSURE MY METHODS ARE DISCRIMINATION- AND FAIRNESS-AWARE?

Evaluating your bias, and the bias of others, with reference to EDI is one step you can take towards ensuring that your methods are discrimination- and fairness-aware. Another is to take steps towards ensuring that you collect and analyse data with reference to EDI. It might seem odd to talk about data collection and analysis at this stage of the book as these topics appear later. However, it is important that you start to think about the ethics of data collection and analysis at the planning stages of your work. This will help you to predict, prepare for and understand how to overcome ethical problems that may occur as you proceed with your research. Activity 5.5 will help you to think about how to work towards making your methods discrimination- and fairness-aware when using data collected by others. We will look at your own data collection methods in Chapter 9 and data analysis methods in Chapter 10.

Activity 5.5: Scenarios

Read through the following scenarios, answering the question for each. Then go to the end of this chapter to find suggestions.

Scenario 1

Mariana's research involves data mining. Using this method, she intends to examine existing datasets to uncover hidden patterns, trends and relationships. She believes that datasets are discrimination-free and fair. Therefore, if she follows correct proce- dures when mining data, she believes that her results will also be discrimination-free and fair. Are her assumptions correct?

Scenario 2

Hinata intends to use statistics generated in a number of different countries for her comparative research. She thinks that all countries have similar systems for collect- ing, analysing and reporting statistics, and that all are guided by similar ethical principles. Therefore, if she adheres to the research methods she has been taught on her course, she assumes that her results will be discrimination-free and fair. Are her assumptions correct?

Scenario 3

Luke intends to use a well-known search engine to find useful resources for his research. He also intends to use a popular online tool to design and administer an online questionnaire, along with data analysis software that is used by other researchers in his discipline. As all tools and software are widely known and used by other researchers, he assumes that his research will be discrimination-free and fair. Are his assumptions correct?

THINK INTEGRITY 5.1

Although you try to work with integrity, others might not. Think about software, codes and algorithms developed by others and consider whether there might be problems written into them. Some might be genuine mistakes, perhaps made due to lack of knowledge or training. Others might be due to unconscious or structural bias. Some might be deliberate and could be due to personal, political, ideological or financial factors, for example. Working with integrity should be both an individual and collective responsibility. If you encounter problems, consider working with others to get them addressed and rectified.

HOW DO I CULTIVATE SENSITIVITY IN METHOD?

In Activity 5.1 you were asked to imagine that you were a research participant. Let's return to this as it enables you to understand how to cultivate sensitivity in method. Activities 5.6 and 5.7 help you to do this.

Activity 5.6: Role reversal

Go back to imagining that you are a participant in a research project. You can choose the type of project, the topic and the methods used. As the research progresses you start to realize that the researcher is acting insensitively and/or using insensitive methods. But what, exactly, does this mean? What is the researcher doing to make you think that they are acting insensitively and/or using insensitive methods? Write down or make a voice note of all the things you can think of, then go to the end of the chapter to find a list of things mentioned by other students.

Activity 5.7: Application

Once you have read the answers to Activity 5.6, think about how they might relate to your research. Using the list of answers as a guide, produce a written or verbal checklist that will enable you to act sensitively when you carry out your research.

HOW DO I RESEARCH PEOPLE WHO ARE VULNERABLE?

Researching people who are vulnerable has additional ethical implications that must be considered before you begin your research. People who are vulnerable include those who are, or have been, exposed to harm, attack or influence (physically, mentally or emotionally); those who are in need of special care, support or protection because of disability, age, neglect or risk of abuse; those who find it difficult to give free and voluntary informed consent; and/or those who have only a rudimentary understanding of the language that is written or spoken by the researcher, for example. If you intend to conduct research with people who are vulnerable, there are a number of steps you need to take. They are illustrated in Figure 5.2.

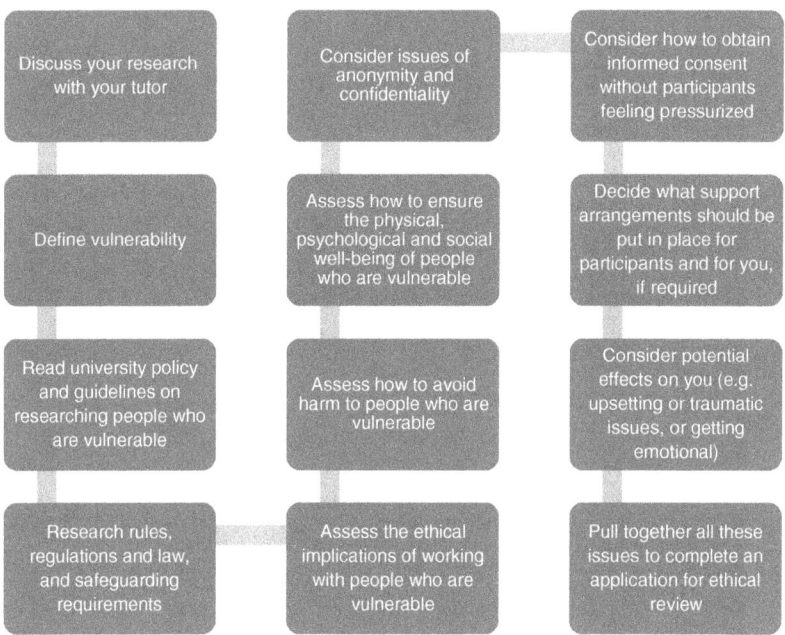

Figure 5.2   Researching people who are vulnerable

TIP 5.1

You might find it useful to develop distress protocols before you begin your data collection. A participant distress protocol describes how you can recognize distress in participants and outlines what will happen if a participant becomes distressed during your research. It covers issues such as recognizing signs, pausing interviews

(Continued)

and providing information about support services. A researcher distress protocol discusses the physical and psychological harm that you might experience as a researcher and outlines action that can be taken to minimize harm.

WHAT DO I NEED TO KNOW ABOUT RESEARCHING CHILDREN?

Children are classed as vulnerable; therefore you should consider the issues discussed above when researching children. There are other issues you also need to consider and Activity 5.8 will help you to do this. Note that some of these issues relate to consent; we will return to this topic later in the chapter.

Activity 5.8: Checklist (right and wrong answers)

Consider each of the statements below. Work through them, putting a 'yes' next to the statements you think are correct and a 'no' next to those you think are wrong. Answers can be found at the end of the chapter.

Statement 1 (yes or no?). I must obtain informed consent from parents, guardians or carers for *all* children under the age of 18 who are going to take part in my research.

Statement 2 (yes or no?). I must consider whether a child is mature enough to give their consent to take part in my research.

Statement 3 (yes or no?). I must find out about, and adhere to, all legal requirements when conducting research with children.

Statement 4 (yes or no?). I must not offer incentives for children to take part in my research because this will be viewed as coercive.

SHOULD I COLLECT DATA ON SEXUAL ORIENTATION AND GENDER IDENTITY?

The simple answer to this question is provided in Figure 5.3. Take time to think. If you feel you have to collect this data, produce a justification and discuss with your supervisor or tutor.

Sexual orientation and gender identity data should be collected only if they are vital to your research, they are relevant to your research question and there is a valid and justifiable reason to collect the data.

Figure 5.3 Stop to think image

WHAT IS INFORMED CONSENT?

Informed consent is one of the main components of research ethics and is an ethical and legal requirement for all research. Put simply, informed consent refers to consent given by participants to take part in your research, based on an understanding of what is involved. Consent must be given freely and voluntarily by participants who have been informed fully about the risks and implications of taking part. Participants must have the mental capacity to make the decision for consent to be valid.

Universities have comprehensive information, guidance, forms and templates relevant to obtaining informed consent. They include guidance on whether oral or written consent is required; how to obtain consent for photos, videos and images (in accordance with data protection legislation); guidance on participants' capacity to consent (e.g. relevant mental health legislation); and information about collecting, storing and sharing sensitive personal data in line with university policy and relevant legislation. They will become more familiar to you as your work your way through Activity 5.9.

Activity 5.9: Action

Now that you understand a little more about informed consent, visit your university website/VLE to find out about rules, regulations and procedures at your university. Do this now, while it is fresh in your mind. Don't skip this activity as it is an extremely important part of your research.

Seeking informed consent can be a simple process for some research projects. However, it can also be a little more complicated, depending on the type of research and the methods you intend to use. Activity 5.10 illustrates some of the problems that can arise when seeking informed consent and starting your research. Although interviews are covered later in this book, it is important to start to think about these issues in the planning and design stages of your research.

Activity 5.10: Notes from the field

[Recording starts.] It's been an interesting week. My interviews have gone okay, but I need to record two problems. The first was when I turned up for an interview with a person in their own home. I could tell immediately that they were very drunk. I decided that the interview couldn't happen. This person had signed a consent form when I first made contact, but now I didn't think the interview could happen. I think consent has to be given by someone who is able to make a reasoned judgement about taking part in my research. They need to understand the risks and potential consequences according to our university website. Although this person had initially consented, I decided they were too drunk to know what they were saying. I don't know if I've done the right thing, I need to speak to my tutor to find out. I also need to consider what happens in cases where people lack capacity to be interviewed, but on a temporary basis. Do I get back in touch with this person later in my research?

The second situation was where a carer sat in on the interview and kept trying to answer for the participant, who was perfectly capable of answering themselves. It was a big problem. I kept trying to make eye contact only with the participant, and even ignoring what the carer was saying, but it didn't work. I feel that I didn't get much useful information as the carer kept interrupting. By the way, I did get informed consent for this interview, from the participant, but not from the carer! It was a difficult situation that I didn't handle very well. [Recording ends.]

TIP 5.2

You might find it useful to undertake a participant comprehension assessment. This enables you to assess a person's ability to understand, retain and weigh-up the risks and benefits, and ascertain their ability to communicate their consent. Develop some questions to test their comprehension; ask them to summarize or paraphrase information you have provided; or ask them to describe the risks and benefits of participation and what might be expected of them during the research, for example.

HOW DO WE OBTAIN INFORMED CONSENT IN THE DIGITAL WORLD?

When obtaining informed consent in the digital world there are a number of difficulties and/or dilemmas you might encounter. Deciding in advance how to overcome them is an important part of your project planning. Activity 5.11 will help you to do this.

Activity 5.11: Matching

Match each difficulty/dilemma with the appropriate solution. Answers can be found at the end of the chapter.

Difficulty/dilemma

1 A researcher wishes to access a discussion forum on drug abuse. It is a private group and all members expect their comments to remain private.
2 A researcher has received consent to use some digital images, provided by a participant, in their research project. However, there are some people captured within the images who have not given their consent.
3 When undertaking data analytics, a researcher is concerned that people providing their data might have consented to their data being used by the organization collecting them but have not consented to them being used for research purposes.

Solution

a Find out about the consent policies used by the organization that has collected the data. Check for regulatory, ethical and integrity compliance. If data are anonymized and there is no way of gaining consent, the researcher can consider going ahead if they are happy with the organization's compliance.
b Contact the group administrator to ask them to seek consent from the rest of the group. Once this has been given, the researcher can make themselves known to the group to discuss, in more detail, issues of consent, opting out and withdrawal.
c Ask the participant to obtain consent from those appearing in the images. If consent is not given, don't use the images.

WILL MY RESEARCH MEET THE ETHICAL NEEDS OF STAKEHOLDERS?

You can assess whether your research will meet the ethical needs of stakeholders first by understanding what a stakeholder is, second by thinking about why stakeholders are important in your research, and third by identifying their ethical needs. Activity 5.12 will help you to do this.

Activity 5.12: Missing-word puzzle

Complete this missing-word puzzle by filling in the blanks from the list of words provided. It will help you to think more about stakeholders and their ethical needs. Answers can be found at the end of the chapter.

A stakeholder is an [_____], a group of people, an organization or a community that has an interest in (or is implicated or affected by) your research [_____], methods, results and/or outcomes. Stakeholders can be engaged in your research (perhaps helping you to collect data) and/or you might share your data and outcomes with stakeholders.

There are various reasons that you might engage stakeholders in your research: it increases the [_____] of your research; enables your research to be aligned to the needs of people it relates to; increases collaboration; and shares knowledge, power and [_____].

Sharing your data and outcomes with stakeholders increases openness, transparency, fairness and respect; enables others to reproduce and [_____] your work; reduces the costs of further research; saves time and resources; reduces participant [_____]; and helps to build science.

You can meet the ethical needs of stakeholders by undertaking a stakeholder analysis at the [_____] of your research project. This enables you to identify key stakeholders, assess their interests and evaluate the way that these interests might affect your research.

beginning

burden

decision-making

impact

individual

replicate

topic

Now that you understand more about the ethics and moral issues relevant to research, we can move on to the next topic. Before we do, let's test your understanding of what you have learnt so far, with a short quiz.

Activity 5.13: Multiple-choice quiz

Read each question and choose the correct answer. The topics in all three of these questions have been covered in this chapter, so if you can't answer any of the questions, return to some of the activities to refresh your memory. Answers can be found at the end of the chapter.

1   What does a participant distress protocol do?

    a   It describes how participants have suffered from anxiety prior to their participation in a research project.

    b   It describes how to recognize distress in participants and outlines what will happen if a participant becomes distressed during a research project.

    c   It describes how a particular participant became distressed during an interview.

2   Which of the following must apply if consent is to be valid?

    a   Participants must be available at the time of data collection.

    b   Participants must have met with the researcher.

    c   Participants must have the mental capacity to make the decision.

3   What is a stakeholder analysis?

    a   A plan that identifies key stakeholders, assesses their interests and evaluates the way that these interests might affect a research project.

    b   A count of the number of stakeholders involved in a research project.

    c   A statistical analysis of stakeholder engagement on completion of a research project.

ACTIVITY ANSWERS: CHAPTER 5

Activity 5.1: Role reversal

Students, as research participants, would like:

- Their opinions to be valued and respected
- The researcher to take notice of what they say
- To be believed and taken seriously

- To be respected for who they are and where they come from
- Their background, experiences and knowledge to be acknowledged
- Not to be belittled, contradicted or made to look a fool
- Their personal details to be kept safe and secure
- Their information not to be passed on to others
- To be treated fairly
- Not to be discriminated against
- Respect for their cultural heritage and traditions
- Not to be forced, or feel forced, to take part
- Not to be bribed to take part
- To have some sort of acknowledgement for giving up their time
- To be thanked for their time
- To be told what will happen to the information they provide
- To be told how and where the research will be published

Some of these answers touch on other issues that will be discussed elsewhere in this book (e.g. anonymization, data protection and data security in Chapter 11 and publishing and reporting results in Chapter 12).

Activity 5.3: Media observation

The following list presents a summary of some of the important points raised by students when this activity has been undertaken in the past. (Note that this list is not exhaustive: there are many other areas that you might have identified.)

Observations

1 Media can be aimed at a particular group in society. Others are excluded. Images display certain characteristics, with viewpoints reflecting those of media owners or content makers.
2 The content displays ignorance about others. Stereotypes and generalizations are presented as truth and content is based on incomplete knowledge or partial experience.
3 There is a certain amount of censorship: people are afraid to say what they really think because they fear a social media backlash. Online bullying stops people from being themselves. People retreat from certain platforms: they become invisible and their voices are silent.
4 Media cherry pick what they cover. Content supports their political opinion or ideology and those who have differing opinions or ideologies are excluded.
5 Media sensationalizes: dramatic stories and shocking information can take centre stage to the detriment of less sensationalist information.

Activity 5.4: Application

Below are some suggestions about how the media observations listed above might relate to your research. If you have listed other observations, work through them in a similar way.

Observation 1

This observation suggests that a number of biases and types of discrimination could be evident, including elite bias, structural bias, unconscious bias, gender bias, ageism, racism or sexism, for example. Poor research can also be affected by these biases and types of discrimination: health research undertaken only with male participants and generalized to the whole population; exploitative research focusing on negative social issues within Indigenous communities; and researchers publishing only in elite scientific publications, for example. Steps to overcome these problems include a careful evaluation of bias in relation to EDI and an open and frank discussion with your tutor or supervisor.

Observation 2

This observation could relate, in part, to unconscious bias. We all have biases about which we are unaware, which can have a significant effect on the research process. Steps you can take to address this include a careful evaluation of your thoughts and opinions and how they might be based on one-off experiences or long-held values; an open and frank discussion with someone who has different opinions; increasing your understanding of how unconscious bias affects research; and taking steps to mitigate unconscious bias so that you can produce ethical and responsible research.

Observation 3

Some students think that there is no relevance to research here, but there is. Some people might not take part in research because they fear the consequences: perhaps their boss might find out what they say and they lose their job, or perhaps people worry that they might be misrepresented or not taken seriously. Researchers can be viewed as authority figures, which could influence how participants act or what they say. Or some participants might feel intimidated by other people who are taking part in the research, for example. Ensure that you consider all these issues in the design stages of your work. More information is provided in the following chapters.

Observation 4

Poor research or pseudo-science could be influenced by political opinion and/or ideology. Good research is not. Steps you can take to avoid this are to evaluate and challenge your opinions and motivations; consider what has influenced your decisions about topic and method; talk to others, including your tutor and peers, to find out whether they can detect political or ideological bias.

Observation 5

This observation, in relation to research, could concern research topics that are chosen (e.g. those that stand a better chance of being published due to their topical or sensationalist nature); the way that researchers try to publish (positive outcomes are highlighted and negative or null results are supressed); or an editor's choice of paper to publish (e.g. those with positive outcomes). Steps you can take to avoid this are a careful assessment of your research topic and why it has been chosen, and discussion with your supervisor about avoiding publication bias, if you choose to publish your work.

Activity 5.5: Scenarios

Scenario 1

No, Mariana's assumptions are not correct. You should never assume that datasets are discrimination-free and fair. Discrimination can arise through a number of factors, including bias in human and machine-based reasoning. We are all beginning to understand more about problems with algorithms: humans write the code and develop the systems, and humans, as we have seen previously in this chapter, are not bias-free. Biases can be magnified and exacerbated (machine learning bias). If you are interested in these topics, useful publications can be found in the Go further 5.1 box.

Scenario 2

No, Hinata's assumptions are not correct. She needs to consider that not all systems are the same: some are badly designed; others are restrictive, incomplete or nonexistent; some are not guided by ethical principles, for example. This can lead to disadvantage, perpetuate inequalities or cause harm to individuals and communities. She should think about political influence, the domination of people who are rich and powerful, and/or economic inequality on data collection and statistical analysis in different countries. If you are interested in these topics, useful publications can be found in the Go further 5.1 box.

Scenario 3

No, Luke's assumptions are not necessarily correct. He needs to evaluate the tools and software he intends to use to find out about the ethical practice of owners and companies. An area he could consider is compliance of software companies and third-party providers: regulatory compliance (to local, regional, national and international law), ethical compliance (to ethical codes and standards, or within ethical frameworks) and integrity compliance (to codes of organization, professional and/or research integrity). Another area he could consider is how certain tools might discriminate or be unfair (e.g. racial bias in search engines) and take action to mitigate this (e.g. raising personal awareness and using a variety of search engines and search techniques).

GO FURTHER 5.1

A series of podcasts with EDI practitioners across different sectors can be accessed at www.bath.ac.uk/guides/ed-i-videos-and-podcasts [accessed 12 January 2024]

Broussard, M. (2019) *Artificial Unintelligence: How Computers Misunderstand the World*. Cambridge, MA: MIT Press.

Criado Perez, C. (2020) *Invisible Women: Exposing Data Bias in a World Designed for Men*. London: Vintage.

Kearns, M. and Roth, A. (2020) *The Ethical Algorithm: The Science of Socially Aware Algorithm Design*. New York: Oxford University Press.

O'Neil, C. (2017) *Weapons of Math Destruction: How Big Data Increases Inequality and Threatens Democracy*. London: Penguin.

Information about ethics, safety and promoting inclusion when researching with children can be obtained from the NSPCC Learning website: https://learning.nspcc.org.uk/research-resources/briefings/research-with-children-ethics-safety-promoting-inclusion.

Activity 5.6: Role reversal

The following is a summary of the more common answers given by students when this activity has been undertaken on my courses. This list is not exhaustive; you might have given some different answers:

- Not giving me time to get my head around the research and whether I should take part
- Providing information about the research that I don't understand
- Presuming that I will give consent and I'm happy to take part, even though I have concerns

- Passing over my worries and concerns, or trivializing them
- Not understanding that I'm really scared about the research process
- Lack of sympathy or empathy shown by the researcher
- He didn't understand my cultural background
- I don't think he took my race into account
- He didn't respect me as a woman
- Not including a category that includes my gender identity
- Using complicated language
- Using racist, sexist, ageist, ableist, classist, transphobic or homophobic language
- Not paying attention to my feelings
- Not listening to me in interviews
- Expecting me to answer far too many questions
- Using up too much of my time and not compensating me
- Expecting me to use my own devices, even if it costs me money
- Asking personal questions without explaining why
- Looking bored when I'm speaking
- Fidgeting in interviews
- Not respecting my dignity in health research
- He didn't have a clue about my mental health needs
- Spying on me in my online space
- Not giving enough detail about how my answers and personal information will be kept safe
- Doing what they want with the results of the research and not thinking about how that might impact me
- Sharing my information with other researchers or organizations when I haven't given my permission
- Using me to further their research careers

Source: Adapted from Activity 58: Cultivating sensitivity in method, in C. Dawson (2022) *100 Activities for Teaching Research Ethics and Integrity*. London: Sage, p. 203.

Activity 5.8: Checklist (right and wrong answers)

Note that the information provided in these answers relates to the UK and, although legislation and guidance are broadly similar in the devolved nations of the UK, there are differences from one nation to another. If you are researching elsewhere, you must check national rules and regulations before you begin your research.

Statement 1: No

This statement is incorrect because it emphasizes *all* children under the age of 18. Parental consent is required when it is considered that a child is incapable of understanding the implications of participating in research. Therefore, for very young children, you do need to obtain informed consent from parents, guardians or carers for them to take part in your research: the National Society for the Prevention of Cruelty to Children (NSPCC) in the UK recommends under the age of eight, for example. It also recommends that this type of consent should usually be sought for research with children aged 8–15. For young people aged 16 and 17, however, the NSPCC recommends that researchers consider very carefully if consent from an adult is required (NSPCC Learning: see Go further 5.1). Think about issues such as whether obtaining parental consent might negatively impact your research (e.g. if it is on sensitive topics such as sexual health or drug use) or whether it might cause harm to the child (e.g. in cases of abuse). If you intend to work with children, you must take time to reflect on, and discuss, consent boundaries and dilemmas.

Statement 2: Yes

This statement is correct. You must consider whether a child is mature enough to give their consent to take part in your research. They should be able to understand what your research involves and consider the potential implications and risks. Therefore, it is up to you to present this information in a way that they can understand and to take time to assess whether the child has understood fully the information you have presented. Note that informed consent is not valid if a child is pressured or coerced into taking part by a parent, carer, guardian or teacher, for example. If you feel that a child is not mature enough to provide their own consent and you obtain it from a responsible adult instead, it is advisable to obtain agreement from the child as well. This is called 'assent'. Here a child shows that they are willing to take part, even though they may not understand fully what the research is and/or the implications of taking part. You must use your informed judgement to determine whether or not to seek assent from a child: obtain further advice, if in doubt.

Statement 3: Yes

This statement is correct. You must find out about, and adhere to, all rules, regulations and legislation before you begin your data collection. Some of them relate specifically to conducting research with children or adults who are vulnerable, such as safeguarding requirements (Disclosure and Barring Service checks in England and Wales and equivalents in Scotland and Northern Ireland); regulations concerning consent and assent; and requirements about reporting abuse or child maltreatment (they differ depending on the country in which you are researching).

Others are relevant for all research, such as data protection and human rights legislation. More information about these issues can be found in Chapter 4.

Statement 4: No

This statement is incorrect. You can offer incentives for children to take part in your research. It will not be viewed as coercive, as long as you are careful about the type of incentive and how it is offered. It is important to consider the social and cultural contexts, which can include levels of poverty, the financial burden of taking part in research and the value of participants' time, for example. Incentives can be monetary, or they can take the form of some kind of reward, such as certificates or vouchers. Reflect on what is best for your participants and seek further advice from your tutor or supervisor.

Activity 5.11: Matching

The answers are:

1b

2c

3a

Activity 5.12: Missing-word puzzle

A stakeholder is an *individual*, a group of people, an organization or a community that has an interest in (or is implicated or affected by) your research *topic*, methods, results and/or outcomes. Stakeholders can be engaged in your research (perhaps helping you to collect data) and/or you might share your data and outcomes with stakeholders.

There are various reasons why you might engage stakeholders in your research: it increases the *impact* of your research; enables your research to be aligned to the needs of people it relates to; increases collaboration; and shares knowledge, power and *decision-making*.

Sharing your data and outcomes with stakeholders increases openness, transparency, fairness and respect; enables others to reproduce and *replicate* your work; reduces the costs of further research; saves time and resources; reduces participant *burden*; and helps to build science.

You can meet the ethical needs of stakeholders by undertaking a stakeholder analysis at the *beginning* of your research project. This enables you to identify key stakeholders, assess their interests and evaluate the way that these interests might affect your research.

Activity 5.13: Multiple-choice quiz

1   What does a participant distress protocol do?

    a   It describes how participants have suffered from anxiety prior to their participation in a research project.

    b   It describes how to recognize distress in participants and outlines what will happen if a participant becomes distressed during a research project (correct answer).

    c   It describes how a particular participant became distressed during an interview.

2   Which of the following must apply if consent is to be valid?

    a   Participants must be available at the time of data collection.

    b   Participants must have met with the researcher.

    c   Participants must have the mental capacity to make the decision (correct answer).

3   What is a stakeholder analysis?

    a   A plan that identifies key stakeholders, assesses their interests and evaluates the way that these interests might affect a research project (correct answer).

    b   A count of the number of stakeholders involved in a research project.

    c   A statistical analysis of stakeholder engagement on completion of a research project.

6

PLANNING – LET'S CONSIDER THE PRACTICALITIES …

CHAPTER CONTENTS

CHAPTER ACTIVITIES

CHAPTER OBJECTIVES

By the end of this chapter, you will be able to:

- Recognize your existing skills and assess their relevance to research
- Identify what you know and what you need to know to complete your research successfully
- List sources of information that will help to build your knowledge
- Show when to start your research
- Describe a variety of methods that can be used to help choose, or decide on, a research topic
- Explain what is meant by a research question and provide practical examples of good and bad research questions
- Explain what is meant by research aims and objectives and begin to compose your own aims and objectives
- Consider university requirements about standards, format and style, and explain how to plan your project accordingly
- List assessment criteria for your research

Let's now start to think about planning your research. Some of you might have jumped straight to this chapter because you are eager to get going with your research (perhaps you have a deadline looming). This book has been written in a way that lets you jump to the topics you feel are most important. However, once you have worked your way through the activities in this chapter, you might find it useful to consider some of the earlier chapters as they are very relevant to your research and will help you to understand more about what is required. References to earlier chapters are given within this chapter. Try to follow them up if you have the opportunity as, again, it will help you to develop your knowledge and give you a more complete understanding of the research process.

It is important to take time to plan your research carefully as this helps to ensure that it is pitched at the right level, covers a suitable topic and meets your university requirements. Careful planning also involves reflecting on your understanding, skills and experience, and an assessment of how they need to develop to enable you to undertake effective and responsible research. If you take time at the beginning of your project to plan carefully you will be able to anticipate and avoid problems arising as your research progresses. Also, if you take a little time to understand what is required, and how research is assessed, it enables you to produce better and more successful research. This chapter will help you to consider these issues.

AM I CAPABLE?

Some students are concerned about their ability to undertake an independent research project. However, although you may not be aware of it, you have already developed a number of research skills, both inside and outside university. Look back on what you have done on your course so far: you will see that you have worked independently in a wide variety of ways and, as a result, have developed a number of skills that you can bring to your research project. Activities 6.1 and 6.2 help you to think about these issues in more depth.

Activity 6.1: Reflection

Think back through your studies and life in general. Identify up to ten different skills that you have developed that will be useful to bring to your research project. Write down your list or make a verbal memo. Provide a brief description of the experience or behaviour that helped you to develop the skills you have listed.

You might think that you do not have any relevant skills, but you have. Think about what has taken place during your studies: finding sources, background reading, producing assignments, student projects, group discussions, peer teaching or field work, for example. Or you might consider hobbies or extra-curricular activities and the skills that you have developed from them: voluntary work, sports, crafts, art, music, cooking and photography, for example. Perhaps you have had full-time or part-time jobs where you had to deal with difficult customers or negotiate with others (see Figure 6.1).

Think about the skills that you have developed from undertaking these different activities. Once you have produced your list, go to the end of the chapter for some examples given by other students (there are no right or wrong answers to this: your list is unique to you).

Skill	Evidence
1	
2	
3	
4	
5	
6	
7	
8	
9	
10	

Figure 6.1 Thinking head image

Activity 6.2: Application

Now that you have seen the examples given at the end of the chapter for Activity 6.1, think about whether you need to amend or add to your list. Once you have done this, go through each item, recording the relevance of each to your research topic (this can be a written or verbal record). Again, there are no right or wrong answers as they are unique to you. Go to the end of the chapter to find some examples given by other students.

Skill	Relevance
1	
2	
3	
4	
5	
6	
7	
8	
9	
10	

WHAT DO I NEED TO KNOW?

Now that you have identified the skills you already possess that are relevant to your research, you can go on to think about the knowledge and understanding you possess, and the knowledge and understanding that you need to develop. Activity 6.3 will help you to do this.

Activity 6.3: Classification

Consider each of the items contained within the list. Classify them according to whether you already know about it, whether you need to find out more about it or whether it is not relevant to your research. There are no right or wrong answers to this as the way that you complete this classification is unique to your research project.

I know about this   I need to find out about this   This is not relevant

How to produce a research proposal

Whether I need to obtain ethical approval

How to obtain ethical approval

Materials and resources I need for my research

The costs involved in my research

How long my research will take

How to find sources for my literature review

How to engage critically with the literature

The software and hardware required for my research

Where to source software and hardware

The data collection methods I intend to use

The data analysis methods I intend to use

How to manage my research data

How to keep research data safe and secure

How to structure my dissertation/thesis

How to structure my argument

The standards required for an undergraduate dissertation (or postgraduate thesis)

My university assessment/marking criteria for undergraduate dissertations (or postgraduate theses)

The list in Activity 6.3 provides a useful checklist for you to refer to, and tick off, as you proceed with your research planning. Now let's think a little more about action you need to take to proceed. Activity 6.4 will help you to do this.

Activity 6.4: Application

In Activity 6.3 you identified issues you need to know more about for your research. Go through each of the items you listed in this column and explain how you intend to find out about it. Be specific, identifying all the action you need to take, then go to the end of the chapter for some suggestions.

WHEN DO I START?

When you are new to research it is difficult to know when to start as you have no idea how long the research will take. The best piece of advice is to start as early as possible. That way, you will have plenty of time to choose a topic, develop your question, choose methods and conduct your research without feeling pressurized about meeting deadlines. Additional tips are provided in Activity 6.5.

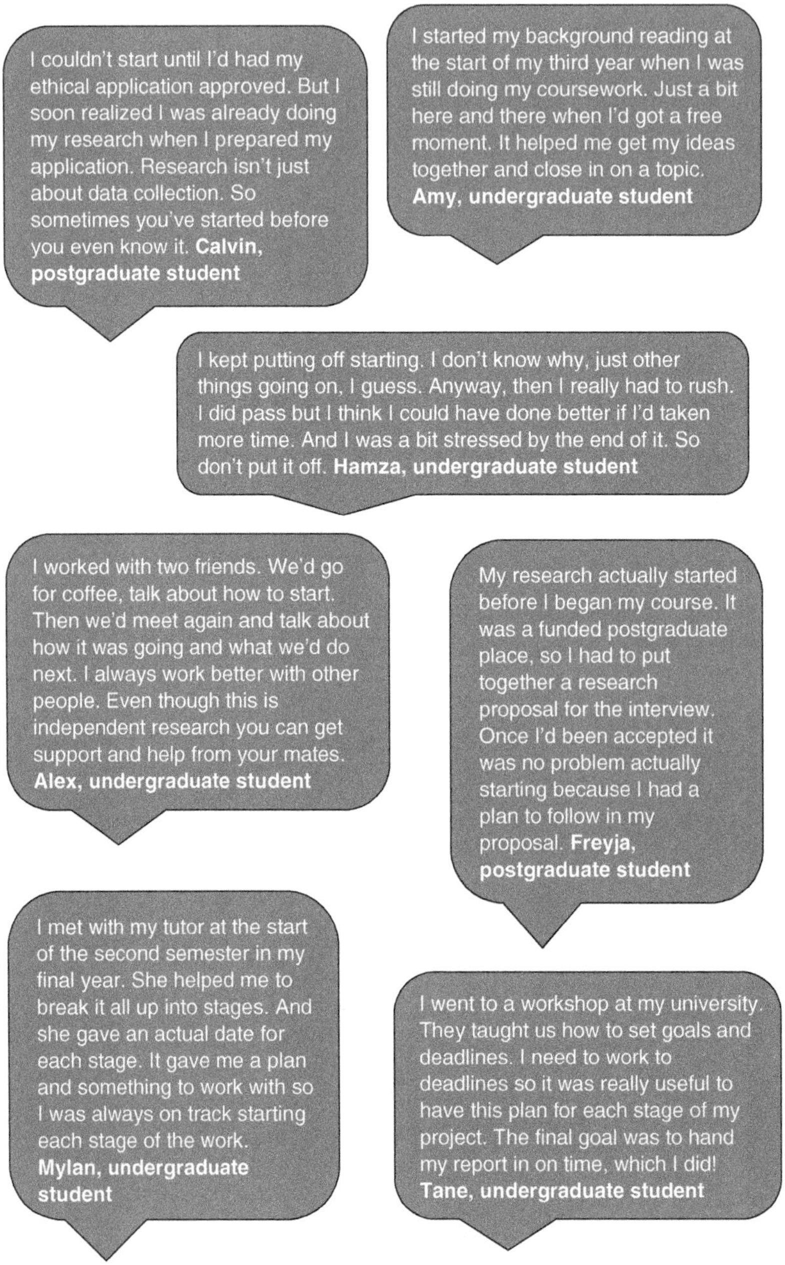

I couldn't start until I'd had my ethical application approved. But I soon realized I was already doing my research when I prepared my application. Research isn't just about data collection. So sometimes you've started before you even know it. **Calvin, postgraduate student**

I started my background reading at the start of my third year when I was still doing my coursework. Just a bit here and there when I'd got a free moment. It helped me get my ideas together and close in on a topic. **Amy, undergraduate student**

I kept putting off starting. I don't know why, just other things going on, I guess. Anyway, then I really had to rush. I did pass but I think I could have done better if I'd taken more time. And I was a bit stressed by the end of it. So don't put it off. **Hamza, undergraduate student**

I worked with two friends. We'd go for coffee, talk about how to start. Then we'd meet again and talk about how it was going and what we'd do next. I always work better with other people. Even though this is independent research you can get support and help from your mates. **Alex, undergraduate student**

My research actually started before I began my course. It was a funded postgraduate place, so I had to put together a research proposal for the interview. Once I'd been accepted it was no problem actually starting because I had a plan to follow in my proposal. **Freyja, postgraduate student**

I met with my tutor at the start of the second semester in my final year. She helped me to break it all up into stages. And she gave an actual date for each stage. It gave me a plan and something to work with so I was always on track starting each stage of the work. **Mylan, undergraduate student**

I went to a workshop at my university. They taught us how to set goals and deadlines. I need to work to deadlines so it was really useful to have this plan for each stage of my project. The final goal was to hand my report in on time, which I did! **Tane, undergraduate student**

Figure 6.2 When to start research: student experiences

Activity 6.5: Student experiences

Read through the experiences described by students who have completed their undergraduate dissertations and postgraduate theses successfully (see Figure 6.2). Consider the relevance to your own research.

HOW DO I CHOOSE MY TOPIC?

The origins of your research have an influence on the topic that you choose. Do you remember Figure 1.4: Research origins? If not, return to Chapter 1 to have another look at the diagram. Activity 6.6 helps to illustrate how research origins have an influence on choice of topic.

Activity 6.6: Practical examples

Read through the following examples of projects that stem from different origins. Consider the relevance to your own research.

Personal experience

Anna worked part time in a fast-food outlet in her local shopping centre. There were always queues of customers, which made the work quite stressful. Anna felt that food could be cooked in a better way, and that members of staff could work more efficiently to move through queues more quickly. Anna decided, first, to visit other fast-food outlets to see whether they had similar problems. She also spoke to her manager to find out their thoughts about the potential for a research project that might help to improve their service. The manager was very interested, so Anna approached her tutor to discuss the potential of the project.

Observation

Lixin was surprised to see that the amount of litter in his local town had increased since the Covid-19 pandemic. Why was this? He asked his friends if any of them had noticed similar problems in their towns: some had, some had not. Lixin didn't know whether this discrepancy was due to there being no difference in amounts of litter, or due to his friends not making the observation. He decided to search different types of media to see whether he could find any stories, articles, videos, podcasts or discussions about the problem. He found enough information about the topic to help him consider that it could be a viable research project.

Reading the literature

Sofia did not know what she wanted to research. She decided to go to the university library to read about subjects that interested her, related to her course. During this reading she came across a reference of a book about historical maps that she found intriguing. She put in an interlibrary loan request and received a copy of the book a week later. She found it fascinating as the maps were not literal, but were created based on the perceptions of the person creating the map. She thought it would be interesting to ask her peers to create maps of their local city, based on their knowledge and perceptions, which she would then compare and contrast. Her tutor thought it was a great idea and suggested she think a little more and put together a proposal.

Trials and experiments

In the second year of his undergraduate psychology course, Aziz had taken part in a group project that considered psychological differences between dog and cat owners. One experiment looked at emotional attachment to dogs and cats. Aziz felt that he would like to replicate this experiment and, depending on his new findings, expand the experiment for his research. He approached his tutor to find out whether this would feasible.

Eureka moment

Simone had been working with polymers for her undergraduate chemistry course. One night she awoke with a start: what if a polymer coating on medical gloves could be made to enhance tactile sensitivity, in addition to making them easier to put on? She took her idea to her tutor, who suggested she undertake some background research to find out what else had been done in this area. He advised she keep records of her reading as, if she decided to pursue this topic, the sources she found would be useful to her.

Previous research

Ashley had been part of a research team working on new antimicrobial agents. The project was funded by a charity, for a specific part of the work, for a specific length of time. Once the project was complete, Ashley met with the team leader to discuss the possibility of continuing with the research for their postgraduate study. The team leader agreed that there was scope to continue, suggesting that Ashley put together a proposal while the team leader looked into the issue of further funding for postgraduate study.

Tutor/peer suggestion

Daniel could not think of a research topic and time was moving on. The more he tried to think of something, the more his mind went blank. He arranged a meeting with his supervisor. During this meeting his supervisor suggested that Daniel create a list containing three topics that might be of interest and then have a chat with trusted peers about how the topics could be developed into a workable project. Daniel and his supervisor worked together to come up with three suggestions. Then Daniel chatted with some mates, informally, over a coffee. One of the suggestions (research into avatar choice) was popular and generated some interesting discussions. Daniel was able to develop a topic from the discussions.

The examples given in Activity 6.6 illustrate how students arrived at a particular topic, given the origins of their research. If you are still having trouble choosing a topic, Figure 6.3 will help.

HOW DO I DEVELOP AN ANSWERABLE RESEARCH QUESTION FROM MY TOPIC?

In Chapter 1 we saw that a research question is a specific and actionable question around which the research is centred. You were shown how a research question can be developed from your initial idea and given some examples of research questions. Return to this section in Chapter 1 to refresh your memory if you need to.

Now let's look a little more closely at what makes a good research question. Activity 6.7 will help you to do this.

- Observing phenomena or behaviours that need further investigation to explain patterns, behaviour or processes. Includes questions such as 'what' and 'why'

- Reflecting on, and thinking about, your experiences to stimulate your thoughts and develop your research topic

- Asking questions that stimulate reflection, introduce a problem, lead to critical thought or test existing assumptions and/or knowledge

- Visualizing, creating a picture or drawing a graph, diagram or mind map to clarify your thoughts and pull together your research topic

- Reading around the subject to deepen understanding, decide whether there is scope for research and to stimulate ideas

- Brainstorming without judgement, analysis or reflection to generate ideas and focus in on important issues

- Discussing your ideas with friends, family and tutors to stimulate thought and to test, modify and refine your ideas

- Logical thinking, working through ideas in a logical, sequential order, to organize your thoughts and focus in on your research topic

- Lateral thinking, approaching an issue through an indirect route, to create new ideas and develop your topic

- Producing a list of all the things that interest you, related to your course or subject of study, and choosing the most workable

Figure 6.3 Methods to help choose a research topic

Activity 6.7: Word search

Eighteen words are listed below. They describe the qualities of a good research question. Find them in the puzzle on p.134 before checking your answers, which can be found at the end of the chapter. These qualities of a good research question can be used as a guide to help you develop your own research question.

Accurate

Adaptive

Clear

Concise

Credible

Defendable

Elegant

Ethical

Feasible

Focused

Influential

Interesting

Relevant

Significant

Simple

Specific

Testable

Workable

A research question should focus on one concept or topic, rather than multiple concepts or topics. It should be a question rather than a statement, but make sure that it is not a closed question (one that can be answered with a simple yes or no). Useful words for starting your research question include 'What', 'How', 'Does', 'Has' and 'Is'. Your research question needs to be realistic in terms of what you are able to achieve in the time you have and with the resources that are available to you. Some examples of good and bad research questions are given in Activity 6.8 (you can also find some examples of research questions in Activity 1.6).

Activity 6.8: Checklist (right and wrong answers)

Consider each of the research questions below. Work through them, putting 'yes' next to the questions you think are examples of good research questions and 'no' next to those you think are examples of bad research questions. Answers can be found at the end of the chapter.

```
T  M  G  G  N  R  H  O  J  S  P  Z  R  Y  Q
D  O  Q  A  K  S  P  E  C  I  F  I  C  S  F
R  C  I  R  Y  L  V  G  Z  S  F  X  R  C  Y
F  F  O  E  C  C  L  E  A  R  I  Q  E  A  R
G  O  E  E  W  O  R  K  A  B  L  E  D  D  E
G  C  T  L  I  N  F  L  U  E  N  T  I  A  L
B  U  H  E  A  C  C  U  R  A  T  E  B  P  E
R  S  I  G  N  I  F  I  C  A  N  T  L  T  V
U  E  C  A  Z  S  I  M  P  L  E  X  E  I  A
Y  D  A  N  T  E  S  T  A  B  L  E  L  V  N
N  A  L  T  D  E  F  E  N  D  A  B  L  E  T
I  N  T  E  R  E  S  T  I  N  G  M  V  O  V
D  X  V  T  V  T  C  T  W  U  U  V  S  Y  Z
L  Y  B  C  Y  L  F  E  A  S  I  B  L  E  B
R  W  Y  N  X  V  L  S  T  B  O  C  B  R  I
```

Question 1 (yes or no). Have obesity levels been rising in the US?

Question 2 (yes or no). How effective are drug intervention programmes, aimed at secondary school students in the UK, at preventing illicit drug use?

Question 3 (yes or no). What effect do social media have on mental health?

Question 4 (yes or no). How significant is the availability of scholarships and bursaries when students make their university choice in Australia?

Question 5 (yes or no). What effect does loss of Arctic ice and melting permafrost have on arctic foxes?

WHAT ARE AIMS AND OBJECTIVES?

This question can be answered in a handout I have given to my students over the years. It gives a definition of 'aim' and 'objective' before going on to give advice about producing your aims and objectives.

Student handout

An aim is the overall driving force of your research. It is a simple and broad statement of intent that describes exactly what you want to achieve from your research. It should emphasize what is to be accomplished and address the outcomes of your project. Most research projects only have one aim, although it is possible to have more than one aim for certain types of research.

The objectives are the means by which you intend to achieve the aim. They are detailed and more specific statements that describe specifically how you are going to address your research question, building on the main issue that has been introduced in the aim. Five to ten objectives are usually a good number, but this can be flexible, depending on the type and level of your research. The main point is to make sure that your objectives show how you intend to meet your aim.

Take note of the following points when producing your aims and objectives:

- Your aims and objectives should give a clear indication of the five Ws of your research (what, who, why, when, where). They should not be stated explicitly but should be implicit within your aims and objectives.
- Your aims and objectives should provide an indication of how your project will proceed: this is not a specific statement of methods, but gives an indication through the terms used, for example 'identify', 'describe', 'explain' and 'observe'. It also gives an indication of your epistemological and methodological preferences.
- Your aims and objectives should support your methodology (e.g. you should only mention the intention to generalize when this is your methodological goal).
- Your aims and objectives should be clear, succinct and unambiguous, defining any technical terms used. They should also be concise.
- Your aims and objectives should provide an indication of the long-term outcome, such as 'produce an analysis' or 'develop associated theory'.
- Your aims and objectives must be realistic in terms of what you can achieve during your research (e.g. available resources, time, access to participants). Don't attempt too much or make your aims and objectives too ambitious.
- Your objectives should relate to your aim and you should ensure that each objective is distinct and does not merely repeat another using different terms. Number your objectives so that they are clear and distinct.
- Take care not to produce a list of issues that are merely related to your research topic and/or methods. Also, ensure that you do not mistake research objectives for project objectives (the latter is a list of practical steps involved in the day-to-day running of your research project).

If you are struggling to produce your aims and objectives, read around your subject, find other research that deals with similar issues and find out how the researchers have produced their aims and objectives.

Source: Dawson, C. (2016) *100 Activities for Teaching Research Methods*. London: Sage, p. 292.

WILL MY RESEARCH MEET REQUIRED STANDARDS?

This is an important question to ask in the planning stages of your research. You must make sure that your research question is suitable and enables you to produce a piece of research at the required level and to the required standards. Your research question enables you to understand whether your proposed topic is workable and feasible, and it leads to a research design that has credibility. Therefore, once you have developed your research question it is important that you discuss it with your tutor to make sure that it will help you to meet the required standards in terms of research expectations, research design, credibility and coursework requirements. The tutor tips provided in Figure 6.4 help you to think more about these issues and Activity 6.9 helps to reinforce your learning.

GO FURTHER 6.1

National frameworks provide a useful general guide about the standards you should be meeting for undergraduate and postgraduate courses. For example, in the UK consult:

QAA (2024) *The Frameworks for Higher Education Qualifications of UK Degree-Awarding Bodies*, 2nd edition. Gloucester: QAA. www.qaa.ac.uk/docs/qaa/quality-code/the-frameworks-for-higher-education-qualifications-of-uk-degree-awarding-bodies-2024.pdf?sfvrsn=3562b281_11

Activity 6.9: Action

Now that you understand the importance of meeting required standards, visit your university, school or department website/VLE or contact your tutor to find out about standards required at your university. Do this now, while it is fresh in your mind. This will help to reinforce your learning and increase your understanding of the standards required at your university.

Ask your tutor whether your proposed work will meet the required standards. And *please* listen to, and take note of, their feedback. **Sociology tutor**

Get hold of your school/department dissertation assessment criteria. They should be on your university website or ask your tutor. Read them carefully. Consider whether you will be able to address all the points with your proposed research. Then refer back to them as you write up your dissertation. **Geography lecturer**

Read your dissertation format regulations. Universities have strict rules about the format of dissertations and if you don't follow these your dissertation could be rejected or your marking could be delayed. **Physics tutor**

I want to see originality in ideas. I want to see that you know what you're talking about and are able to apply your knowledge and understanding. I want to see critical awareness of potential problems and I want to see that you are able to critically evaluate current evidence. **Politics supervisor**

Find out what the standards are, then you can work towards meeting them. **Maths tutor**

There are a variety of standards you need to meet so start planning early. Ethical standards are really important and you will need to consider these to get ethical approval. Standards of professionalism and integrity are also important. How are you going to conduct ethical, open, honest and transparent research? Then there are the standards required to pass. By your third year you should have a good idea of these, but speak to your supervisor if you're unsure. **Anthropology supervisor**

Figure 6.4   Tutor tips: meeting required standards

HOW IS RESEARCH ASSESSED?

One of the tutors in the tips provided in Figure 6.4 suggests getting hold of your university assessment criteria. This is a very useful piece of advice. It is important to consider how your work will be assessed during the planning stages as, again, it will help you to make sure that your work is pitched at the right level and meets the required standards. Most assessment criteria are available from your university, school or department website/VLE. If you can't locate them, ask your tutor.

Figure 6.5 gives an example of assessment criteria in both undergraduate and postgraduate research. However, it is important that you find out the assessment criteria specific to your university, school or department as they might differ from the list given.

Figure 6.5   General assessment criteria

Now that you understand more about the practicalities involved in planning your research, we can move on to the next topic. Before we do, let's test your understanding of what you have learnt so far, with a short quiz.

Activity 6.10: Multiple-choice quiz

Read each question and choose the correct answer. The topics in all three of these questions have been covered in this chapter, so if you can't answer any of the questions, return to some of the activities to refresh your memory. Answers can be found at the end of the chapter.

1   What should a research question focus on?

    a   Multiple concepts or topics.
    b   Three concepts or topics.
    c   One concept or topic.

2   Which of the following is an 'aim' in research?

    a   A simple and broad statement of intent that describes exactly what you want to achieve from your research.
    b   A specific and actionable question around which the research is centred.
    c   A detailed and more specific statement that describes specifically how you are going to address your research question.

3   Which of the following group of words describes a good research question?

    a   Broad, universal, eclectic.
    b   Defendable, credible, feasible.
    c   Enticing, dramatic, astounding.

ACTIVITY ANSWERS: CHAPTER 6
Activity 6.1: Reflection

The following list summarizes the answers that have been given by students when we have undertaken this activity in the past. Some of them might stimulate your thoughts and help you to see that you have also developed these skills through your experiences over the years. Keep a copy of the list of skills and evidence you have developed and add to it as you progress with your research and studies. These are transferable skills that will be useful if you intend to obtain employment after you have finished your studies (and all employers want to see that you are able to provide evidence for the development of your skills). We return to transferable skills in Chapter 13.

Skills	Evidence
Social skills	Dealing politely with customers
Written communication skills	Successful written assignments
Verbal communication skills	Training a team member
Listening skills	Working together on a student project
Empathy	Helping a friend through a crisis
Negotiation skills	Negotiating access on a field trip
Adaptability	Working with a difficult team member
Flexibility	Choosing and changing modules

Organization skills	Planning long assignments
Time-management skills	Juggling work and study commitments
Meeting deadlines	Handing assignments in on time
Working under pressure	Bar work on a Saturday evening
Crisis management	Overcoming disruption at an event
Working independently	Successful completion of an assignment
Problem-solving skills	Completing problems in coursework
Finding sources	Navigating the internet and library
Evaluating sources	Assessing credibility of online sources
Reviewing	Judging the value of an article
Critiquing	Evaluating and commenting on a paper
Editing/proofreading skills	For all assignments
IT skills	Learning a new system at work
Numerical skills	Interpreting mathematical information
Thinking analytically	Success in online logic games
Reading skills	Reading academic texts successfully
Presentation skills	Successful seminar presentation
Team-working skills	Winning a team-player award at work

Activity 6.2: Application

The following list summarizes the answers that have been given by students when we have undertaken this activity in the past. They help to stimulate your thoughts and might encourage you to amend or add to your own list.

Skills	**Relevance**
Social skills	Working with research participants
Written communication skills	Describing the purpose of my research
Verbal communication skills	Discussing my research with others
Listening skills	Interviewing participants
Empathy	Establishing rapport and building trust
Negotiation skills	Negotiating access for fieldwork
Adaptability	Changing direction if required

Flexibility	Dealing with unexpected situations
Organizational skills	Planning my research project
Time-management skills	Producing my dissertation on time
Meeting deadlines	Working to my research timetable
Working under pressure	Coping with research demands
Crisis management	Overcoming disruptions in my research
Working independently	Completing research successfully
Problem-solving skills	Addressing and overcoming problems
Finding sources	Undertaking a literature search
Evaluating sources	Assessing the relevance to my research
Reviewing	Judging the value for my research
Critiquing	Evaluating a paper for my research
Editing/proofreading skills	Producing a well-written dissertation
IT skills	Using software for coding and analysing
Numerical skills	Analysing and interpreting my data
Thinking analytically	Processing complex data
Reading skills	Reading around my topic
Presentation skills	Undertaking a viva voce, if required
Team-working skills	Working with tutors or collaborators

Activity 6.4: Application

How to produce a research proposal:

- Read Chapter 8
- Consult your university guidelines
- Denscombe, M. (2019) *Research Proposals: A Practical Guide*, 2nd edition. London: Open University Press
- Punch, K. (2016) *Developing Effective Research Proposals*, 3rd edition. London: Sage

Whether I need to obtain ethical approval:

- Read Chapter 4
- Consult your university guidelines
- Ask your tutor/supervisor

How to obtain ethical approval:

- Read Chapter 4
- Consult your university guidelines
- Ask your tutor/supervisor

Materials and resources I need for my research:

- Read Chapter 8
- Ask your tutor/supervisor

The costs involved in my research:

- Read Chapter 8
- Ask your tutor/supervisor

How long my research will take:

- Read Chapter 8
- Ask your tutor/supervisor

How to find sources for my literature review:

- Read Chapter 8
- Greetham, B. (2021) *How to Write Your Literature Review*. London: Bloomsbury Academic
- Ridley, D. (2012) *The Literature Review: A Step-By-Step Guide for Students,* 2nd edition. London: Sage

How to engage critically with the literature:

- Read Chapter 8
- Greetham, B. (2021) *How to Write Your Literature Review*. London: Bloomsbury Academic
- Ridley, D. (2012) *The Literature Review: A Step-by-Step Guide for Students,* 2nd edition. London: Sage

The software and hardware required for my research:

- Ask your tutor/supervisor
- Consult with university IT services (or equivalent)
- Consider what others have used

Where to source software and hardware:

- Ask your tutor/supervisor
- Consult with university IT services (or equivalent)

The data collection methods I intend to use:

- Consult Chapters 7 and 9
- Dawson, C. (2019) *Introduction to Research Methods: A Practical Guide for Anyone Undertaking a Research Project*, 5th edition. London: Robinson

The data analysis methods I intend to use:

- Consult Chapter 10
- Dawson, C. (2019) *Introduction to Research Methods: A Practical Guide for Anyone Undertaking a Research Project*, 5th edition. London: Robinson

How to manage my research data:

- Consult Chapters 4 and 11
- www.dcc.ac.uk/resources/data-management-plans
- https://ardc.edu.au/resource/data-management-plans
- Corti, L., Van den Eynden, V., Bishop, L. and Woollard, M. (2019) *Managing and Sharing Research Data: A Guide to Good Practice*. London: Sage

How to keep research data safe and secure:

- Consult Chapters 4 and 11
- www.dcc.ac.uk/resources/data-management-plans
- https://ardc.edu.au/resource/data-management-plans
- Corti, L., Van den Eynden, V., Bishop, L. and Woollard, M. (2019) *Managing and Sharing Research Data: A Guide to Good Practice*. London: Sage

How to structure my dissertation/thesis:

- Consult Chapter 12
- Dawson, C. (2019) *Introduction to Research Methods: A Practical Guide for Anyone Undertaking a Research Project*, 5th edition. London: Robinson

How to structure my argument:

- Consult Chapter 12
- Seek advice from your tutor
- www.sheffield.ac.uk/academic-skills/study-skills-online/academic-argument

The standards required for an undergraduate dissertation or postgraduate thesis:

- Continue to the end of this chapter
- Ask your tutor/supervisor
- Consult your university guidelines

My university assessment/marking criteria for undergraduate dissertations (or post-graduate theses):

- Continue to the end of this chapter
- Ask your tutor/supervisor
- Consult your university guidelines

Activity 6.7: Word search

Activity 6.8: Checklist (right and wrong answers)

Question 1. No. This is an example of a bad research question. It is too general, unfocused and can be answered with a simple 'yes' or 'no'.

Question 2. Yes. This is an example of a good research question. It is specific and focused on one topic; it identifies the target group, target programmes and the country in which the research will take place; and it is testable and workable.

Question 3. No. This is an example of a bad research question. It is too general, unfocused and uses the vague term 'social media'. If you want to conduct research into social media, it is better to mention specific types of social media in your research question. This question could be narrowed to make it more focused, by adding an age group and specific types of social media, for example.

Question 4. Yes. This is an example of a good research question. It cannot be answered with a simple yes or no. It is focused on a specific topic, is relevant and interesting and is testable and workable.

Question 5. Yes. This is an example of a good research question. It is simple, refined, polished and focused. It is significant and relevant, and cannot be answered with a simple yes or no.

Activity 6.10: Multiple-choice quiz

1   What should a research question focus on?

    a   Multiple concepts or topics.
    b   Three concepts or topics.
    c   One concept or topic (correct answer).

2   Which of the following is an 'aim' in research?

    a   A simple and broad statement of intent that describes exactly what you want to achieve from your research (correct answer).
    b   A specific and actionable question around which the research is centred.
    c   A detailed and more specific statement that describes specifically how you are going to address your research question.

3   Which of the following group of words describes a good research question?

    a   Broad, universal, eclectic.
    b   Defendable, credible, feasible (correct answer).
    c   Enticing, dramatic, astounding.

7

SELECTION – LET'S CHOOSE OUR METHODOLOGY AND METHODS ...

CHAPTER CONTENTS

CHAPTER ACTIVITIES

CHAPTER OBJECTIVES

By the end of this chapter, you will be able to:

- Define what is meant by qualitative, quantitative and mixed approaches
- Assess the advantages and disadvantages of qualitative, quantitative and mixed approaches
- Define methodology and method and explain how the two differ
- List and discuss a number of methodologies and methods
- Summarize the factors that influence choice of methodology
- Begin to choose your methodology and methods
- Assess whether your choices are suitable
- Justify and defend your choices

Choosing how to go about conducting your research can be both exciting and nerve-racking. Some students find it easy to make their choices, whereas others struggle. Whichever it is for you, the main point to note is don't rush into your decisions. Take time to think about how your research should proceed. If you make the right choices at the start of your project, time will be saved in the long run by reducing, or even eliminating, problems further down the line.

The key to making the right choice is knowledge and understanding. By increasing your knowledge and understanding of research approaches, methodologies and methods you will begin to understand more about which are suitable for your proposed topic. You will also be able to reject those that are unsuitable. This chapter introduces you to different research approaches. It goes on to explain what is meant by research methodology and method and introduces you to some of the more popular methodologies and methods. It will also help you to assess whether your choices are suitable for your tutor, course and assessment. The intention is that once you have worked your way through the activities in this chapter, you will have developed your knowledge and understanding enough to feel confident in moving forward with your choices.

You might have skipped straight to this chapter because you are keen to start your research. This book has been written in a way that enables you to do this. However, as mentioned in the previous chapter, once you have completed these activities and digested the information provided, you might find it useful to work your way through earlier chapters as they help you to understand more about the research process.

WHAT ARE QUANTITATIVE AND QUALITATIVE RESEARCH?

There are different types of research that you can undertake. Broadly speaking, they are split into two: quantitative research and qualitative research. It is also possible to combine the two types with a hybrid or mixed approach. Activity 7.1 encourages you to think about the definition of each of these types of research.

Activity 7.1: Matching

Match the definition with the type of research it refers to. Read and digest the definitions carefully as it is important that you get a good understanding of the different types of research that you could conduct. Answers can be found at the end of this chapter.

Types of research	Definition (See below: 1, 2 or 3)
Quantitative research	
Qualitative research	
Hybrid/mixed research	

Definitions

1   The observation, collection, description, exploration, creation and/or interpretation of perceptions, opinions, worldviews, objects or artefacts. It uses multiple systems of inquiry to gain an understanding, or explain, human phenomena (e.g. attitudes, beliefs and motivation).
2   The merging or blending of data collection, creation, exploration and/or analysis methods. Numerical and non-numerical data can be collected and analysed at the same time, or the different types of research can be used sequentially, perhaps using one to deepen understanding of the findings of the other, for example.
3   The collection, organization, analysis, examination and/or measurement of numerical data, which can include mathematical, statistical or computational data. It uses logical and statistical procedures to test causal relationships, find patterns and make generalizations.

WHAT ARE THE ADVANTAGES AND DISADVANTAGES OF QUANTITATIVE AND QUALITATIVE RESEARCH?

This is a good question to ask as it will help you to weigh up the pros and cons of different approaches and home in on the most suitable choices for your research.

Activity 7.2 will help you to consider the advantages and disadvantages of each of these approaches. However, it is important to note that researchers have different thoughts and beliefs about these advantages and disadvantages. Do you remember in Chapter 2 where we considered whether finding the truth is the primary goal of your research? We also looked at the different definitions of truth, and how people's opinions about this have an influence on the way they conduct their research. These issues are very relevant here. People tend to consider advantages and disadvantages in relation to their current attitudes and beliefs about knowledge and truth. Therefore, there is a tendency to think that their approaches (those that fit with their attitudes and beliefs) have more advantages than disadvantages. Also, what one researcher considers a disadvantage, another might consider an advantage. Later, Activity 7.3 presents a dialogue between two researchers that makes this clearer. Meanwhile, try to keep these issues in mind when you undertake Activity 7.2.

Activity 7.2: Classification

Consider each of the advantages and disadvantages contained within the list below. Classify them according to whether you think the item should be placed in the qualitative or quantitative columns. You might need to refer back to the definitions in Activity 7.1 to help you to do this. I am not going to give any right or wrong answers to this activity for the reasons outlined above. However, this activity will help you to think more about what is involved in each approach and about the potential pros and cons. It will also help you to think more about your own beliefs concerning the value of different approaches.

Quantitative research   **Qualitative research**

Human behaviour can be studied in natural settings

Discovers facts about social phenomena

Reality is measured

Methods are flexible and adaptive

Methods follow set procedures

Data collection and analysis are subjective

Data collection and analysis are objective

Results are valid, reliable and generalizable

A series of standardized steps helps to reduce bias

Greater understanding can be gained through prolonged contact

Results cannot be generalized to the whole research population

Studies cannot be replicated

Bias can influence data collection and analysis

Discussion encourages a search for shared meaning

Some of you might have found Activity 7.2 easy and quick to complete, whereas others might have found it difficult. Perhaps you couldn't classify all the items because some are contestable, or don't fit neatly into either category. This is all good: you are thinking more about what is meant by qualitative and quantitative approaches. Activity 7.3 helps to clarify these points.

Activity 7.3: Dialogue

Read through the following piece of dialogue between two students. Consider whether any of the points they make have relevance to your own research.

Asha:	We follow the scientific method in my discipline. So, for my research I'll make an observation, form a hypothesis, conduct my experiment, make conclusions and write up my research. It's what I've done over my three years at university. Easy!
Izan:	It sounds rather inflexible to me. I'm studying human behaviour so I need to be flexible and adaptable. Something unexpected might come up. I want to be able to deal with that.
Asha:	That seems wrong to me. Surely that'll add bias? You're changing your methods to suit what people say. I'll get rid of bias by following set procedures.
Izan [laughs]:	But you're a human being. You're full of bias, especially unconscious bias: the clue's in the name, you don't even know about it! And don't get me started on structural bias within science. You can't get rid of that just by following set procedures. Anyway, I'm not changing my methods. I'm using methods that'll let me deal with unexpected situations. People do and say all sorts of things that are unexpected. If they were expected I wouldn't need to do the research!
Asha:	But you need to be able to control your conditions so that you can test and measure properly. It's important so other people can see what you've done and they can conduct similar experiments. In science, research has to be valid and reliable.

Izan: I don't think it's just about science, it's about quantitative research. I know in quantitative research validity and reliability are really important. I've talked about this with my tutor. Because people [laughs] probably like you think qualitative research is less scientific we've got to be really careful. So, we talked about making sure my research is accurate, authentic, dependable, trustworthy and transparent. Really, I've got to work harder on this than you because I don't hide behind set procedures. I've got to think really hard about what these words mean and try to make sure my research fits the description.

Asha: But those set procedures make my research useful. What I find will be of benefit to all humankind.

Izan: Well, to me that's not important and I think it'd be really very difficult to do anyway. My research will be useful, but in a different way. There's no way I can make generalizations. Why would I do that? The things I'm researching are very specific to the people I'm working with. My research will provide useful insights in similar contexts and it'll be useful to the people I'm researching. That's what's important to me.

Asha: That sounds highly subjective to me.

Izan: And, your point being...?

Asha: Research has to be objective.

Izan: Does it?

Asha: Yes.

Izan: Well, I disagree. As I said before, we're all human. We're subjective creatures. And our research is subjective, from the topic we choose to the way we decide to publish.

Asha: I think we might have to agree to disagree on quite a lot of this.

Izan: Yes, but good luck with your research.

Asha: Luck is far too subjective for me! Thanks anyway.

CAN QUANTITATIVE AND QUALITATIVE RESEARCH BE COMBINED?

Yes, quantitative and qualitative research can be combined into a mixed or hybrid approach (a definition of this approach is provided in Activity 7.1). If you choose to do this there are real benefits to be gained. The disadvantages of single approaches (highlighted in Activity 7.2) can be overcome by combining approaches; the strengths of particular approaches can be utilized; and you can gain a better understanding than that gained through using a single approach, for example.

Activity 7.3 demonstrated that people can have very different ideas about the strengths and values of different approaches. If you choose a mixed or hybrid approach, those with opposing views will at least agree with part of your approach. However, when making your choices, you must take your audience into account. It can include funding bodies, examiners and stakeholders. These people may view your research with their own biases and preferences. Therefore, become familiar with your mixed or hybrid approach so that you are able to persuade others that this approach is the best and most appropriate for your research. Figure 7.1 summarizes the issues you need to consider if you are contemplating a mixed or hybrid approach and Activity 7.4 will help you to consider them in more depth.

Mixed or hybrid approaches	Will the mixed approach help you to answer your research question?
	Are the approaches you intend to use compatible?
	What type of mixed approach will you use (e.g. parallel, exploratory or embedded)?
	Can you justify your use of a mixed approach?
	Do you need extra time and resources to adopt a mixed approach?
	Do you have the required level of knowledge and understanding to use different approaches?
	What are the pros and cons of adopting a mixed approach?
	Do the approaches complement each other?
	Is your tutor happy with your choice of a mixed approach?

Figure 7.1 Mixed or hybrid approaches: issues to consider

Activity 7.4: Reflection

If you are contemplating a mixed or hybrid approach, reflect on each of the questions posed in in Figure 7.1. Doing this now will help you to consider whether a mixed or hybrid approach might be suitable. It also enables you to anticipate any problems you might encounter if you adopt this approach.

WHAT IS METHODOLOGY?

Do you remember in Chapter 2 you were presented with a drawing of a house? The foundations represented epistemology, the walls represented theoretical perspective and the roof represented methodology. You were told we would return to methodology later in the book and here we are! Activity 7.5 encourages you to think more deeply about what is meant by methodology.

Activity 7.5: Application

Read and digest the following quotation, which describes research methodology. Once you have done this, think about how the information contained within the quotation applies to your own research.

'Research methodology' is a guideline system or framework that is used for solving a problem. It includes practices, procedures and rules used by those involved in inquiry and covers issues such as constraints, dilemmas and ethical choices within research. Methodology also includes the theoretical analysis of these systems or frameworks, a critique of other frameworks and a careful analysis of the interrelationship between epistemological standpoint, theoretical perspective and methodology.

Dawson, C. (2016) *100 Activities for Teaching Research Methods*. London: Sage, p. 53.

WHAT'S THE DIFFERENCE BETWEEN METHODOLOGY AND METHOD?

Sometimes the word 'methodology' is misused. It sounds impressive, which can on occasions lead people to use it even when they are not really talking about methodology.

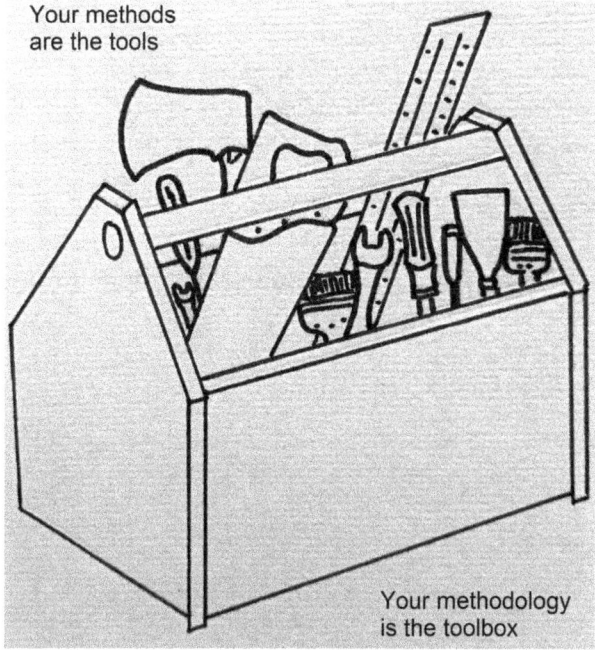

Figure 7.2 Toolbox image

In most cases, they are actually talking about methods, but this word doesn't sound quite so impressive. So, what is the difference between the two? Figure 7.2 explains the difference in a simple and clear way.

A toolbox is strong and robust. It is able to hold all the tools you require. A good methodology does the same: it supports your methods and frames and guides your research. You might have a full toolbox, with lots of different tools that are used for different purposes. Or you might only have one or two tools for specialist jobs. This is the same with your methods: you might choose only one or two methods for the whole data collection and analysis process, or you might choose multiple methods for different parts of the research process. As every handyperson will tell you, the trick is choosing the right toolbox to hold your tools and choosing the right tools for the job.

HOW DO I CHOOSE MY METHODOLOGY?

One of the first steps in choosing a methodology is to understand more about the different types of methodology. Activity 7.6 introduces you to some of the more popular methodologies that tend to be used by students. This is a useful list to refer to when you begin to choose your own methodology.

Activity 7.6: Matching

Match the definition with the methodology it refers to. Clues can be found in the definitions: start with the easiest first and the others will fall into place. Read and digest the definitions carefully as it is important that you get a good understanding of the different types of methodology that are used in research. Answers can be found at the end of the chapter.

Types of methodology	Definitions (See the following page: 1–12)
Action research	
Computer modelling and simulation	
Discourse analysis	
Ethnography	
Experimental research	
Grounded theory	
Historical method	

Narrative inquiry

Phenomenological research

Practice-based research

Survey research

Visual semiotics

Definitions

1   A framework, guidelines and techniques for researching, writing and presenting histories
2   A framework that enables researchers to incorporate creative practices and/or focus on the study of practices, processes, objects or artefacts
3   A range of approaches used to study psyche, events or society through written and spoken language
4   A framework for studying how visual images communicate a message through signs
5   A process of systematic and diligent inquiry that involves controlled testing to understand causal processes
6   A process of creating and manipulating computer-aided representations of natural or artificial phenomena or systems
7   A framework for the collection of thoughts, opinions and attitudes from a sample of individuals through questioning
8   A framework for collaborative study to investigate issues, solve problems, improve practice and develop strategies
9   A range of approaches for the observation and systematic recording of experiences, culture and society
10   A framework for study of the nature and meanings of phenomena
11   A framework for qualitative inquiry that uses systematic techniques to generate theory that is grounded in the data
12   A framework for gathering, analysing and telling stories or narrating experience

Do you remember in Chapter 2 that we talked about epistemology and theoretical perspective? They have an influence on your choice of methodology. Now that you have been introduced to a variety of methodologies, you might find it useful to return to Chapter 2 as this helps to make your choices clearer. Your choice of methodology is also influenced by your research topic and your research question. Activity 7.7 will help you to think about all these points in more detail.

Activity 7.7: Reflective questions

Work through each of the following questions, taking time to reflect on each. This will help you to home in on your methodological choices. Then go to the end of the chapter for some guidance and information about where to find out more.

1   Where does knowledge come from? How is it generated? How might your thoughts on this influence your choice of methodology?
2   Have you considered your theoretical position? This will help you to organize and explain observations and evidence. If you have, do you understand how this relates to your methodological choices?
3   Have you chosen a research topic? If yes, does it suggest a particular methodology would be best? Why is this the case? Why are others not appropriate?
4   Have you developed a research question? If yes, does it suggest that a particular methodology might be appropriate? Why is this the case? Why are others not appropriate?

HOW DO I CHOOSE MY METHODS?

As we have seen previously, your methods are the tools you use to gather and analyse your data. There are a wide variety of research methods that can be used for different research projects and you will already know about some of them, even if you think you don't. For example, you might have completed an online questionnaire, or a questionnaire that fell through your letterbox; or you might have been interviewed by a market researcher asking about a particular product, or an interviewer asking about how you have voted. Before you can choose your methods, you need to know more about the wide variety of methods that are available. Activity 7.8 will help you to do this.

Activity 7.8: Quiz

This quiz can be played individually or with some of your peers. Work through the questions and then go to the end of the chapter to find out the answers. The quiz answers provide useful definitions of the various research methods mentioned.

1   What is the name given to a method of gathering data through noticing, watching or perceiving?
2   In research, what do you call a collection of people brought together to discuss a particular topic, where the discussion is led by a moderator?

3 What is the name given to a method of interviewing that records an individual's biography in their own words?

4 What is the name given to the study of signs and sign-using behaviour?

5 In research, what do you call a scientific test in which one element remains unchanged or unaffected by other variables?

6 What is the name given to a method of recruiting people for a study, where one participant recommends another and so on?

7 In research, what do you call a detailed study or examination of a person, place, event, phenomenon or organization?

8 What do you call a research method that is used to ask all participants the same predetermined questions, verbally?

9 What do we call the close study, interpretation and evaluation of text (such as plays, stories or poems)?

10 What is the name given to a written data collection tool, that can be administered online or in-person, used to collect qualitative and/or quantitative data?

Your choice of methods is framed and guided by your choice of methodology, which, as we have seen previously, is framed and guided by your epistemology, theoretical perspective, research topic and research question. Figure 7.3 provides a simple illustration of what should influence your choice of methods (the dark colour grey) and what might influence your choice of methods (the light colour grey).

CAN I USE A MIX OF METHODS?

Yes, you can use a mix of methods. Some examples of the different ways you can mix methods are provided in Figure 7.4.

If you decide to use a mix of methods, make sure that they are compatible, support each other and enable you to answer your research question. They should also help to increase the validity and dependability of your research. All choices must be justifiable and defendable. Finally, make sure that you have the time available to mix your methods.

ARE MY CHOICES CONSTRAINED BY DISCIPLINE?

It is true that some methodologies (and methods) are more popular in certain disciplines. Let's return to the list of methodologies that were presented in Activity 7.6 so that we can think more about how they might be popular in different disciplines. Activity 7.9 will help you to do this.

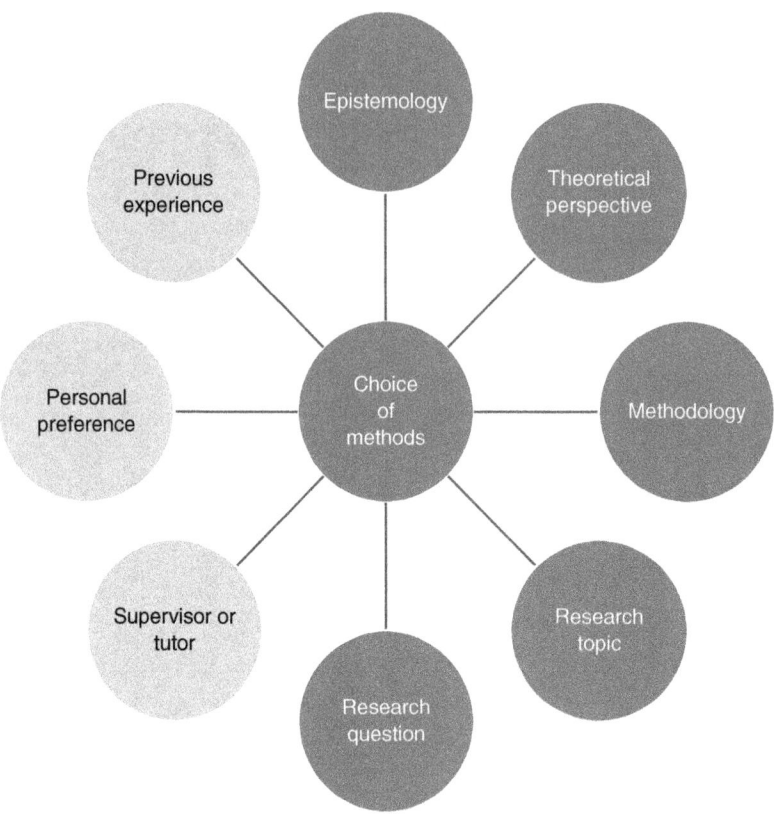

Figure 7.3 Influences on research method choice

Activity 7.9: Classification

Consider each of the items contained within the list (below and continued on the following page). Classify them according to whether you think the methodology is most popular in the arts and humanities, sciences or social sciences. Then go to the end of the chapter to find out more.

Arts and humanities	Sciences	Social sciences
Action research	Discourse analysis	Grounded theory
Computer modelling and simulation	Ethnography	Historical method
	Experimental research	Narrative inquiry

(List continued)

Selection – methodology and methods ...

Phenomenological research

Practice-based research

Survey research

Visual semiotics

I used open and closed questions on my questionnaire. I wanted to get some answers to set questions so I could compare numbers, but I also wanted to find out what people thought, rather than have answers imposed on them. I had to use two different ways of analysing them as well: statistical software for my numbers and thematic analysis where I found patterns, ideas and themes in the answers given for the open questions. I think this mix worked really well. **Bel, undergraduate student**

I spent some time in my community researching Indigenous medical practice. When I moved to my university town to compare medical practice, my methods involved statistics rather than observation. Western medical practice places great faith in statistics. **Taworri, postgraduate student**

I ran an online questionnaire, but some of the results needed expansion and further explanation. I decided to run three focus groups to discuss the findings and get deeper insight. **Janice, undergraduate student**

For my research I analysed, in parallel, Twitter comments and statistics concerning gender inequality and gender disparity. This gave a fuller picture, a more complete understanding and provided a better way to answer my research question. **Panca, postgraduate student**

Being an engineer, I followed a design process to design, develop, build and test my product. Within that I used different methods, including experiments and product testing interviews. **Mick, undergraduate student**

My field research involved observing and photographing wild birds in a particular area. I spent several months observing but also counting. I needed numbers as well as observations and photographs. **Petra, undergraduate student**

Figure 7.4 Student experiences: mixing methods

WILL MY TUTOR LIKE MY CHOICES?

This is an interesting question that I often get asked. It is true that some people have methodological preferences, and this might be the case with your tutor, supervisor or examiner. However, their preferences (or your perception about their preferences) should not influence your choices. Instead, ensure that your choices are based on sound judgement. As we have seen previously, your choices are influenced by epistemology, theoretical perspective, your research topic, your research question and your personal preferences and experiences – this is not about what your tutor likes, it is about your ability to make the right choices. However, your tutor is experienced and has good advice to offer about appropriate methods, this is why they are also included as an influence in Figure 7.3. Listen to your tutor and take note of their advice, if given.

Once you have made your choices you need to be able to justify and defend them. Your methodology and methods become more robust if you are able to produce a detailed justification and defence. They also enable you to anticipate and overcome potential criticism.

Activity 7.10: Application

Once you have chosen your methods and methodology, produce a defence (or justification). The following questions will help you to do this.

1 Why have you chosen your methodology?
2 Why have you chosen your methods?
3 Did you consider any other methodologies? If yes, why were they rejected in favour of the one you have chosen?
4 Did you consider any other methods? If yes, why were they rejected in favour of the one(s) you have chosen?
5 Are your methods appropriate for your methodology? Why?
6 Are your methods and methodology suitable for your research topic? In what way?
7 How will your chosen methodology and methods help you to answer your research question?
8 How does your chosen methodology fit with your epistemological standpoint and theoretical perspective?
9 Are you able to refine, combine or alter your methodology if you need to, yet still retain a coherent epistemological position?
10 Do you have any doubts about your choices? What do you intend to do to overcome these doubts?

ARE MY CHOICES ACCEPTABLE FOR ASSESSMENT?

Once you have made your choices, speak to your tutor or supervisor as they will be able to offer advice about whether your choices are acceptable for assessment. You might also find it useful to consult your university assessment guidelines as they provide helpful pointers concerning the standards your research needs to meet. Activity 7.11 encourages you to do this.

Activity 7.11: Action

Visit your university website/VLE to find out about dissertation or thesis assessment procedures at your university. This helps to increase your knowledge and understanding of the standards and procedures at your university and encourages you to plan accordingly.

Now that you have thought more about your methodology and methods, we can move on. However, before we continue to the next chapter, let's test your understanding of what has been covered in this chapter with a short multiple-choice quiz.

Activity 7.12: Multiple-choice quiz

Read each question and choose the correct answer. The topics in all three of these questions have been covered in this chapter, so if you can't answer any of the questions, return to some of the activities to refresh your memory. Answers can be found at the end of the chapter.

1   What is qualitative research?

   a   The collection, organization, analysis, examination and/or measurement of numerical data, which can include mathematical, statistical or computational data.

   b   The observation, collection, description, exploration, creation and/or interpretation of perceptions, opinions, worldviews, objects or artefacts.

   c   The merging or blending of data collection, creation, exploration and/or analysis methods.

2 What is survey research?

    a   A framework for the collection of thoughts, opinions and attitudes from a sample of individuals through questioning.

    b   A framework for study of the nature and meanings of phenomena.

    c   A framework for qualitative inquiry that uses systematic techniques to generate theory that is grounded in the data.

3 What is action research?

    a   A process of creating and manipulating computer-aided representations of natural or artificial phenomena or systems.

    b   A process of systematic and diligent inquiry that involves controlled testing to understand causal processes.

    c   A framework for collaborative study to investigate issues, solve problems, improve practice and develop strategies.

ACTIVITY ANSWERS: CHAPTER 7
Activity 7.1: Matching

Types of research	Definition (1, 2 or 3)
Quantitative research	3
Qualitative research	1
Hybrid/mixed research	2

Activity 7.6: Matching

Types of methodology	Definitions (1–12)
Action research	8
Computer modelling and simulation	6
Discourse analysis	3
Ethnography	9
Experimental research	5
Grounded theory	11
Historical method	1
Narrative inquiry	12

Phenomenological research	10
Practice-based research	2
Survey research	7
Visual semiotics	4

Activity 7.7: Reflective questions

Question 1. This question relates to epistemology, which we covered in Chapter 2. This is the study of the nature of human knowledge and how it is acquired. Epistemology has an influence on the way your research is designed and the methodology that you choose. Return to Chapter 2 if you need to clarify any of these points.

Question 2. Theoretical positions were covered in Chapter 2. This is your belief system that guides and frames your research. It will also help you to organize your thoughts and communicate them to others. Return to Chapter 2 if you need to clarify any of these points.

Question 3. Chapter 6 offered advice about choosing a suitable research topic. If you are struggling to find a topic, return to Chapter 6 and seek advice from your tutor. If you have chosen a topic, you might find that the topic suggests a particular methodology, as the following examples illustrate:

Topic	Possible methodology
Controlling noise in a small room	Computer modelling and simulation
Learning choices of adult returners	Grounded theory
Public perception of immigration	Survey research
Artefacts of slavery	Historical method
Change in early childhood stories	Narrative inquiry
Recovering metals from water treatment sludge	Experimental research

Question 4. Developing a research question is covered in Chapter 6. If you are struggling to develop your question, return to Chapter 6 and seek advice from your tutor. If you have developed a question, you might find that the type of question, or the wording used, suggests a leaning toward a particular methodology, as the following examples illustrate:

Question wording	Possible methodologies
Discover, describe, explore, understand	Ethnography, grounded theory, historical method, phenomenological research
Compare, cause, relate, influence	Experimental research, computer modelling and simulation
Lived experiences and worldviews	Narrative inquiry, discourse analysis, visual semiotics, phenomenological research

Activity 7.8: Quiz

1 Observation is the name given to a method of gathering data through noticing, watching or perceiving.
2 A focus group is a collection of people brought together to discuss a particular topic, where the discussion is led by a moderator.
3 A life history is the name given to a method of interviewing that records an individual's biography in their own words.
4 Semiotics is the name given to the study of signs and sign-using behaviour.
5 A controlled experiment is a scientific test in which one element remains unchanged or unaffected by other variables.
6 Snowball sampling is the name given to a method of recruiting people for a study, where one participant recommends another and so on.
7 A case study is a detailed study or examination of a person, place, event, phenomenon or organization.
8 A structured interview is used to ask all participants the same predetermined questions, verbally.
9 Literary analysis is the close study, interpretation and evaluation of texts (such as plays, stories or poems).
10 A questionnaire is a written data collection tool that can be administered online or in person, used to collect qualitative and/or quantitative data.

Activity 7.9: Classification

When students have been asked to complete this activity, the following classification is the usual outcome. However, it is important to note that there are no right or wrong answers to this. As you begin to understand more about the different methodologies, and as you begin to take notice of them in research papers and reports, you will notice that methodologies are not necessarily constrained by discipline. A social scientist might choose discourse analysis or visual semiotics, whereas someone from the arts and humanities might choose to conduct a large-scale survey, for example. Or perhaps someone from the social sciences might decide that experiments or computer modelling are the way forward.

However, it is important to note that, although your choices are not constrained by discipline, some methodologies might be favoured in certain disciplines. Therefore, always discuss your choices with your tutor or supervisor to check that they are suitable.

Arts and humanities	Sciences	Social sciences
Discourse analysis	Computer modelling	Action research
Historical method	Experimental research	Ethnography
Narrative inquiry		Grounded theory
Practice-based research	Phenomenological research	
Visual semiotics		Survey research

Activity 7.12: Multiple-choice quiz

1   What is qualitative research?

   a   The collection, organization, analysis, examination and/or measurement of numerical data, which can include mathematical, statistical or computational data.
   b   The observation, collection, description, exploration, creation and/or interpretation of perceptions, opinions, worldviews, objects or artefacts (correct answer).
   c   The merging or blending of data collection, creation, exploration and/or analytical methods.

2   What is survey research?

   a   A framework for the collection of thoughts, opinions and attitudes from a sample of individuals through questioning (correct answer).
   b   A framework for study of the nature and meanings of phenomena.
   c   A framework for qualitative inquiry that uses systematic techniques to generate theory that is grounded in the data.

3   What is action research?

    a   A process of creating and manipulating computer-aided representations of natural or artificial phenomena or systems.

    b   A process of systematic and diligent inquiry that involves controlled testing to understand causal processes.

    c   A framework for collaborative study to investigate issues, solve problems, improve practice and develop strategies (correct answer).

8

PREPARATION – LET'S GET READY TO START ...

CHAPTER CONTENTS

CHAPTER ACTIVITIES

CHAPTER OBJECTIVES

By the end of this chapter, you will be able to:

- Discuss the purpose of a research proposal, explain why it is important and describe its structure and content
- Explain what is meant by a literature review, outline the steps required to produce your review and summarize assessment criteria
- Describe what is meant by a pilot study, discuss the benefits and outline the steps required to undertake a pilot study
- Assess how much your research will cost and find potential sources of funding
- Produce a timetable for your research

Detailed preparation is the key to successful research. Some students are impatient to start: perhaps they are running out of time, or maybe they don't understand the importance of careful preparation. Perhaps they believe they know everything there is to know and all will be well if they start straightaway.

However, if you take time to prepare for your research you will save considerable time later: your research design can be honed and strengthened by producing a detailed research proposal; your understanding and knowledge can be enhanced and heightened with a detailed literature review; and problems with your design and data collection instruments can be discovered, highlighted and avoided by conducting a pilot study. You can also ensure that your research is conducted on time and to schedule by producing a detailed timetable and working out the costs associated with your research so that you are not left out of pocket. This chapter provides advice and guidance on these issues, enabling you to prepare thoroughly and get started with your research.

DO I NEED TO PRODUCE A RESEARCH PROPOSAL?

Whether or not you need to produce a research proposal depends on your university requirements, the level at which you are studying and whether you intend to apply for funding. Even if you are not required to produce a research proposal, you might find it beneficial to do so as it will help you to get all your thoughts together, design a workable project and discuss the feasibility of your proposal with your tutor or supervisor before you move to the main body of your research.

Activity 8.1 will help you to think more about what a research proposal is and why it is important.

Activity 8.1: Missing-word puzzle

Complete this missing-word puzzle by filling in the blanks from the list of words provided. This will help you to understand more about research proposals. Answers can be found at the end of the chapter.

Your research proposal provides a detailed [_____] of your intended research project. It illustrates that you have the background understanding and required knowledge of your topic and relevant research [_____], and that you are able to carry out research that is [_____] and/or offers new insight or development. It shows that you have the ability to [_____] and implement a project and produce a detailed and workable [_____] with all eventualities covered. It also provides a [_____] for your research, illustrating why it is important and worthwhile.

description

design

justification

techniques

timetable

unique

There are various sections required in a research proposal. Figure 8.1 provides an illustration of a general structure, but you should check with your tutor or supervisor to find out whether your university has any specific requirements. Don't be daunted by the different sections in Figure 8.1 as information and guidance for all this content can be found throughout this book.

WHAT IS A LITERATURE REVIEW?

Most undergraduate and postgraduate students are required to produce a literature review as part of their research for their dissertation or thesis. Activity 8.2 will help you to find out more about literature reviews.

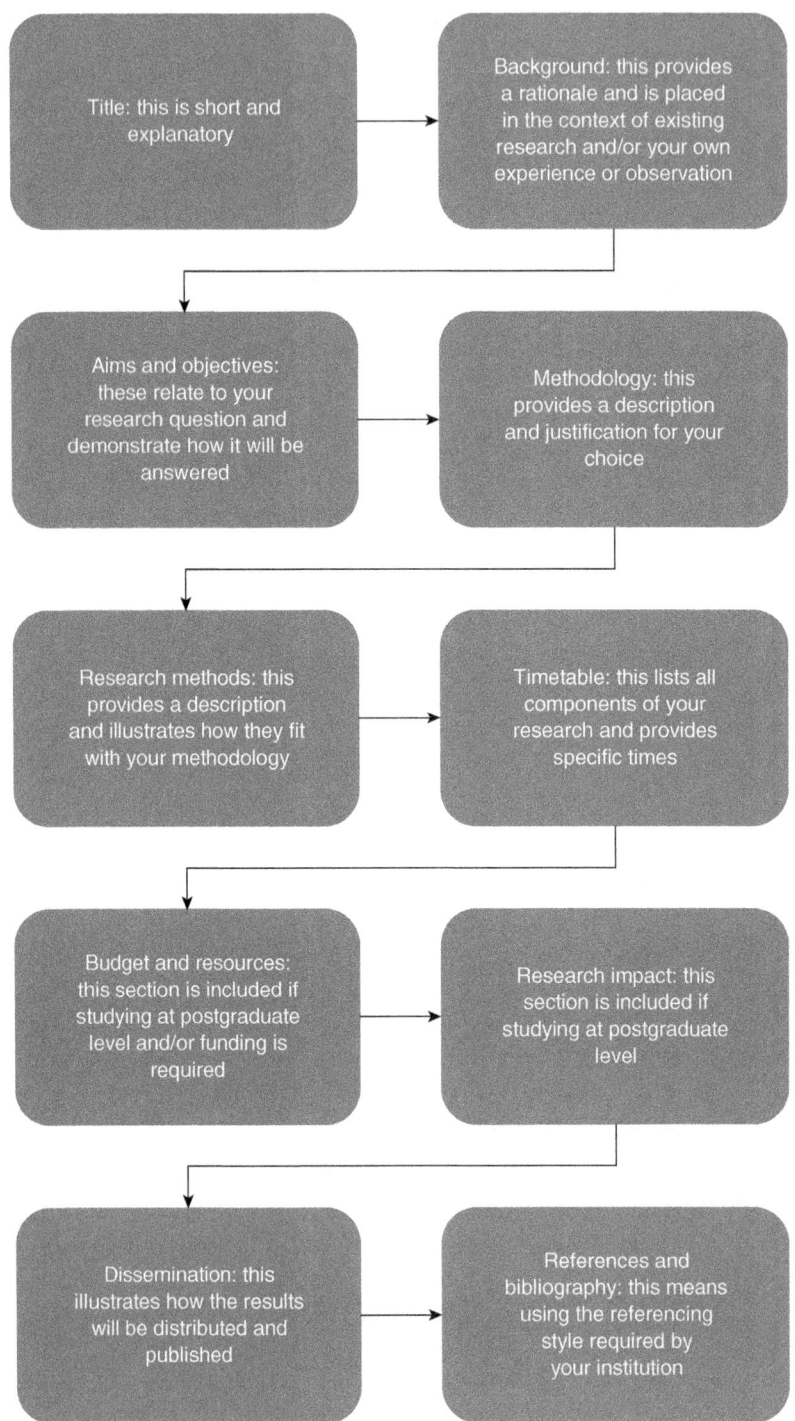

Figure 8.1 Components of a research proposal

Activity 8.2: Missing-word puzzle

Complete this missing-word puzzle by filling in the blanks from the list of words provided. It summarizes what is meant by a literature review and describes its purpose. Answers can be found at the end of the chapter.

A literature review is a detailed [_____] of previous research on your topic. It is not purely a [_____] account, but instead describes, summarizes, synthesizes, analyses and [_____] work relevant to your area of research. It demonstrates links and relationships between existing research and your research.

The purpose of a literature review is to help you become more familiar with your research area and demonstrate how your research fits into the wider body of [_____] knowledge. It provides a useful [_____] for your research and enables you to home in on the important aspects of your topic.

Your literature review demonstrates to tutors and examiners that you are familiar with and have [_____] pertinent issues. It establishes your [_____] and enables you to display deeper [_____] and understanding of your subject area.

assimilated

credibility

critiques

descriptive

established

foundation

knowledge

summary

DO I HAVE TO DO A LITERATURE REVIEW?

Most students embarking on their undergraduate dissertation or postgraduate thesis need to undertake a literature review. The review is included in your final written work and is assessed alongside your research. This section of your report might be called a 'literature review', 'background reading' or 'narrative review', for example. Activity 8.3 will help you to find out more about literature reviews.

Activity 8.3: Action

Access your university library catalogue or dissertation/thesis repository. Here you can search for previous dissertations and theses produced by students at your university. Select some that are in your discipline or subject area and read their literature reviews. This gives you a better idea of what is required and will help you to think more about the content and structure of your own literature review.

TIP 8.1

Don't view your literature review as a chore that has to be done to pass your course. See it as something that is vital to your research. It will help you to develop your knowledge and understanding of your topic. You will be able to work out whether your research is important and worthwhile or establish whether there is already a great deal of knowledge on your topic and, therefore, necessitates a refocus or rethink.

HOW DO I PRODUCE A LITERATURE REVIEW?

There are a number of simple steps to take when producing a literature review. Activity 8.4 will help you to think more about these different steps and assess the order in which to work through them.

Activity 8.4: Step sequencing

Read through the following list of steps to be taken when producing a literature review. Order the steps into a logical sequence. A suggested answer, along with a deeper explanation for each step, can be found at the end of the chapter. This provides a useful guide that will help you to produce your literature review.

Steps for sequencing

Edit and proofread your literature review

Read relevant sources and make notes

Identify and define your research topic

Write your literature review

Organize your thoughts and notes

Identify relevant sources

Record bibliographic information for each source

Your university might have additional requirements about producing a literature review. Therefore, seek advice from your tutor and undertake Activity 8.5 to ensure that your review meets your university requirements.

Activity 8.5: Action

Visit your university website/VLE to find out about producing a literature review for your dissertation or thesis. View documents and templates, and make sure that you become familiar with rules and guidelines. This will help you to understand what is required and enables you to start to think about the structure and content of your literature review.

HOW IS A LITERATURE REVIEW ASSESSED?

Although assessment criteria vary, in general, your literature review is assessed using the criteria illustrated in Figure 8:2. Your tutor or supervisor can give you more information specific to your university.

WHAT IS A PILOT STUDY?

A pilot study is something that both undergraduate and postgraduate students need to consider producing. To find out what a pilot study is, work your way through Activity 8.6.

Activity 8.6: Checklist (right and wrong answers)

Work through the list provided at the top of the following page, putting a 'yes' next to the statements you think are correct and a 'no' next to those you think are wrong. This will help you to understand what is meant by a pilot study. Answers and explanations can be found at the end of the chapter.

173

Statement (yes or no)

1   A pilot study is carried out before the main piece of research.
2   A pilot study can also be called a pilot experiment or a feasibility study.
3   A pilot study assesses your suitability for flying an aircraft.
4   A pilot study is a small-scale, preliminary study.
5   A pilot study helps the researcher to identify research design difficulties.
6   A pilot study is an annual survey of pilots and navigators.
7   A pilot study can help to improve the design of a research project.
8   A pilot study can replace the main body of research.

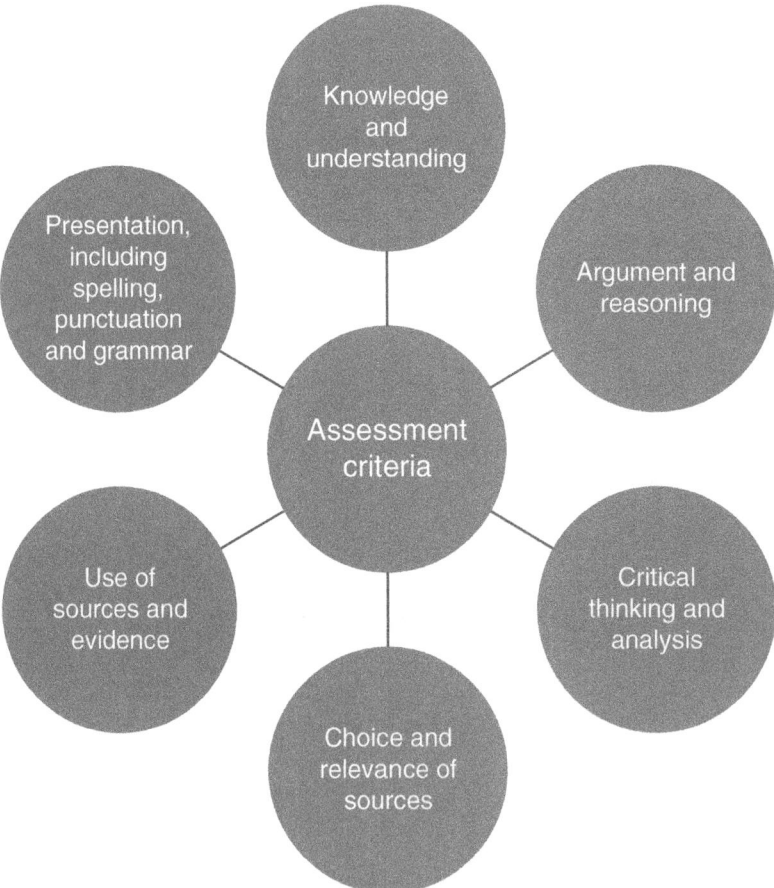

Figure 8.2   Literature review assessment criteria

DO I HAVE TO DO A PILOT STUDY?

Although it might not be compulsory for you to undertake a pilot study, it is highly
recommended that you do so. Consider the case studies in Activity 8.7, which illustrate

the importance of undertaking a pilot study. Other reasons for undertaking a pilot study are provided in the answers for Activity 8.6.

Activity 8.7: Case studies

Case study 1: Karl

Karl's research was looking into alcohol consumption among first year students. He decided that he would interview students to find out how much they drank and ascertain their reasons for drinking alcohol. He developed some questions, chose five first year students and held an interview with each one, which he recorded. When he came to analyse the interviews, he realized that there was a problem with his research design and that he was not getting the type of information he required.

He was interested in finding out how much students drank. However, in the interviews, students were unable, or found it difficult, to say exactly how much they drank. Students responded in quite different ways: some gave estimates, some did not know, others were reluctant to say. Karl could not gather reliable figures on alcohol consumption using the interview method alone.

He decided that a much better way to find out this information was to ask students to keep an alcohol consumption diary, perhaps over a fortnight or a month. Once the diary had been completed, he would interview each student, with the diary providing useful points for discussion (e.g. when, why and where a student had consumed the alcohol that had been reported in the diary). This insight into how to improve his methods came only as a result of his pilot study.

Case study 2: Sun Hee

Sun Hee studied for a PhD on food security among Indigenous peoples of South Korea. Her aim was to optimize the resilience of food systems to biological, environmental, social and economic instability, breakdown or collapse. Her research began during the Covid-19 pandemic, which necessitated online communication, rather than face-to-face interaction. She ran a pilot study that involved contacting Indigenous communities, practitioners, farmers, producers, policy makers and other stakeholders. She also tried to access relevant food security data.

However, she soon discovered that access to technology was unequal: some of the people she needed to make contact with didn't have the required technology, others were unable, or reluctant, to use it. She also realized that there were problems with weak, restricted, non-existent or invisible data systems, which disadvantaged local communities and were leading to skewed results.

The pilot study illustrated that she had to rethink. She realized that some of her data collection would have to wait until she was able to meet people in person.

She also realized that unequal access to both technology and data had to be factored into her research design, and that she needed to consider their influence not only on her research design but also on food security.

HOW DO I CARRY OUT A PILOT STUDY?

The way that you carry out a pilot study depends on a number of factors, including your research topic, methodology, methods and the level at which you are studying. Figure 8.3 gives some general guidance about producing a pilot study: if you need guidance specific to your project, contact your tutor or supervisor. Remember, don't be daunted about these different steps as advice and guidance for each appears throughout this book.

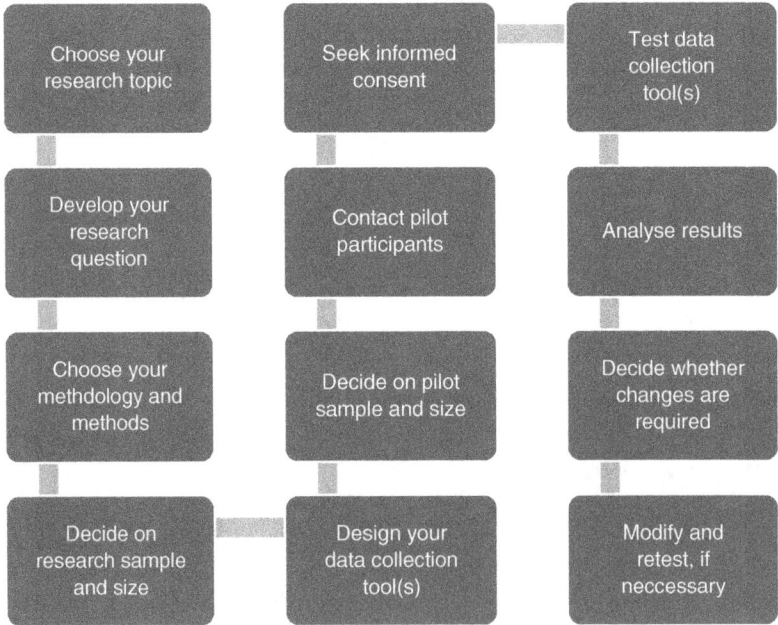

Figure 8.3 Producing a pilot study

(which is discussed in Chapter 5) you must tell your participants that they will be part of a pilot study. You also need to provide a description of your pilot study and explain its purpose in a way that they can understand. Participants can then decide whether or not to take part and provide their consent.

HOW MUCH WILL MY RESEARCH COST?

The cost of your research depends on a number of factors, including your research topic, methods, resources required and length of project. Some undergraduate dissertations can be produced for very little cost (e.g. those that use online data collection tools; see Example 1 in Activity 8.8), whereas some postgraduate theses can accrue considerable costs (e.g. those that involve international travel or the use of expensive scientific equipment). It is important that you understand the costs involved in your research: if you have to meet all costs yourself make sure that you can do so, and if you are hoping to apply for funding you need a detailed list of all costs associated with your research. Activity 8.8 provides two examples, one from an undergraduate project, the other from a postgraduate project.

Activity 8.8: Practical examples

Sally, undergraduate student

All my research was done online. I sent out a questionnaire via email and then sent reminder emails to people who hadn't returned the questionnaire. There was no cost to me or to the people filling in the questionnaires. I used university software to analyse my results, so there was no cost there. The only thing I had to pay for was getting my dissertation printed and bound. My department needed two copies and I decided to get one for myself. My university print services did a deal on three copies, which cost me £31.99 altogether. So that's all I had to pay for in my research.

Pierre, postgraduate student

My budget was as follows:

Interlibrary loan costs	£32.00
Digital voice recorder	£59.99
Travel	£698.00
Printing costs	£80.00

Postage costs	£170.00
Thesis printing and binding	£83.30
Total	£1123.29

I was able to apply for a university small research grant to cover all these costs, apart from my thesis printing and binding, which I had to pay for myself.

CAN I GET FUNDING FOR MY RESEARCH?

In Activity 8.8, the second example illustrates that it is possible to get funding for your research. Some universities provide small research grants to enable students to pay for parts of their research. Others provide bursaries or scholarships that cover some or all of the costs (see Figure 8.4). Contact your university student funding office (or equivalent) and consult the Go further 8.1 box for information about sources of funding that might be available to you.

GO FURTHER 8.1

British Academy/Leverhulme Small Research Grants: https://www.thebritishacademy.ac.uk/funding/?order=-last_published_at [accessed 17 November 2023]

European Funding Guide: www.european-funding-guide.eu [accessed 17 November 2023]

Open Education Database, 100 places to find funding for your research: https://oedb.org/ilibrarian/100_places_to_find_funding_your_research [accessed 17 November 2023]

The Scholarship Hub: www.thescholarshiphub.org.uk [accessed 17 November 2023]

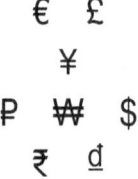

If you are applying for funding, ensure that all your costs are reasonable, realistic, justifiable, allowable and allocable (necessary for the success of your research project).

Figure 8.4 Currency signs

HOW LONG WILL MY RESEARCH TAKE?

The answer to this question is that it almost always takes longer than you think. It can be difficult for students who have not conducted research before to understand how long different components of the project will take. This is another reason why a pilot study is important: it enables you to test out your data collection tools to see how long it takes to collect data, analyse your findings and modify your tools. It also enables you to understand other issues, such as how long it takes to make contact with participants or how many times you need to remind someone to return a questionnaire. Activity 8.9 provides some reflective notes from the field that illustrate some of the issues you may face when working out how long your research will take.

Activity 8.9: Notes from the field

Read the following notes from the field and think about the takeaway points that might be relevant to your own research.

Week 4

I expected my fieldwork to take five weeks. I'm now in week 4 and I still haven't gathered all the samples I need. There were problems I hadn't thought about. The weather for one. I can't collect samples from the peat bogs when there is lightning. It's just too dangerous. I hadn't anticipated that type of weather, especially at this time of year. Then there were the midges. My goodness, I've never encountered anything like that before. I think I was bitten 32 times in the first half hour of being there. I had to stop and seek advice. I was told to avoid dawn and dusk, avoid breeding areas (which is a bit hard as they like marshes, ponds and boggy areas), wear protective clothing (I had to go shopping) and use a good repellent (more shopping). Then the weather again. It rained and rained and rained. Again, it was just too dangerous. So, I will have to extend my fieldwork, which will put my analysis back. I should have factored in more time at the start. Hopefully, I will be able to get some time back when I'm writing up the results if I put in some extra hours. I have a deadline for my completion that I've got to meet.

DO I NEED TO PRODUCE A TIMETABLE?

Although you might not be required to produce a timetable, it is helpful to do so. A timetable (or research schedule) will help you to think about each component of your research and consider how long each of the components takes to complete. It provides structure to your work and helps to ensure that your research remains on track. Your tutor wants to see that you understand how long each component of your research takes and that you can complete all components in the time you have available (see Figure 8.5). Activity 8.10 will help you to think more about producing a timetable.

Activity 8.10: Develop your own checklist

Produce a checklist of all the research activities you need to schedule into your timetable. For each activity listed, provide a suggested timescale. This can be in weeks or by specified dates. Once you have done this, go to the end of the chapter for some suggestions.

Keep an eye on the time. Your deadline will be easier to achieve if you stick to your schedule.

Figure 8.5 Clock image

Now that you understand more about preparing for, and getting started with, your research, we can move on to the next topic. Before we do, let's test your understanding of what you have learnt so far, with a short quiz.

Activity 8.11: Multiple-choice quiz

Read each question and choose the correct answer. The topics in all three of these questions have been covered in this chapter, so if you can't answer any of the questions, return to some of the activities to refresh your memory. Answers can be found at the end of the chapter.

1   What is a research proposal?

    a   A document giving details of a university-wide programme of research.

    b   A document that sets out what you intend to research, why it is important and how you propose to conduct the research.

    c   A document that provides an analysis of your pilot study.

2   What is a literature review?

    a   A detailed list of all the monographs, papers and online sources used in your research.

    b   A detailed summary of your methodology and methods, along with research methods books to which you have referred.

    c   A detailed description, summary, synthesis, analysis and evaluation of existing research relevant to your area of research.

3   What is a pilot study?

    a   A small-scale, preliminary study used to test your research design and instruments.

    b   A large-scale study undertaken after the main body of research to test your research design and instruments.

    c   A small-scale study carried out in its own right.

ACTIVITY ANSWERS: CHAPTER 8

Activity 8.1: Missing-word puzzle

Your research proposal provides a detailed *description* of your intended research project. It illustrates that you have the background understanding and required knowledge of your topic and relevant research *techniques*, and that you are able to carry out research that is *unique* and/or offers new insight or development. It shows that you have the ability to *design* and implement a project and produce a detailed and workable *timetable* with all eventualities covered. It also provides a *justification* for your research, illustrating why it is important and worthwhile.

Activity 8.2: Missing-word puzzle

A literature review is a detailed *summary* of previous research on your topic. It is not purely a *descriptive* account, but instead describes, summarizes, synthesizes, analyses and *critiques* work relevant to your area of research. It demonstrates links and relationships between existing work and your work.

The purpose of a literature review is to help you become more familiar with your research area and demonstrate how your research fits into the wider body of *established* knowledge. It provides a useful *foundation* for your research and enables you to home in on the important aspects of your topic.

Your literature review demonstrates to tutors and examiners that you are familiar with, and have *assimilated*, pertinent issues. It establishes your *credibility* and enables you to display deeper *knowledge* and understanding of your subject area.

Activity 8.4: Step sequencing

Step 1: Identify and define your research topic. This step is a crucial first step. You can't find relevant literature unless you have identified and defined your research topic. Return to Chapter 6 if you are having difficulty doing this.

Step 2: Identify relevant sources. Make sure that your search is both thorough and efficient. Discard irrelevant information and don't get sidetracked. Use reliable sources and evaluate, analyse and critique all sources carefully, even if you believe them to be valid and reliable. Check that information is accurate and cross-check where possible. Ascertain the quality, validity and reliability of the information presented.

Step 3: Read relevant sources and make notes. Once relevant sources have been identified, read through them, making written or verbal notes as you do so. Your reading should not be passive but should be active: ensure that you are engaged actively and critically with the material. Remain observant, perceptive, focused and interested.

Step 4: Record bibliographic information for each source. You need to cite any material used and this is easier to do if you collect bibliographic details of all sources when you use them. Use the correct referencing procedures from the outset so that you do not have to return to source material later.

Step 5: Organize your thoughts and notes. Begin to think about structure: chronological or a chain of reasoning that provides a logical and/or convincing argument, for example. Produce an outline for your literature review and organize your notes accordingly.

Step 6: Write your literature review. Present, analyse and discuss facts and evidence. Use quotations, summaries, data and references where required. Avoid generalizations. Illustrate the importance and relevance of what you are writing and demonstrate the overall significance of the issues that have been covered. Ensure that what you write is relevant to your research topic and research question.

Step 7: Edit and proofread your literature review. Read through your review, checking and refining the presentation of ideas and information. Scrutinize content, overall structure, paragraph length and structure, coherence, style, citations, argument and evidence. Look for errors in spelling, grammar, syntax, punctuation and formatting.

Activity 8.6: Checklist (right and wrong answers)

Statement 1. Yes, this statement is correct. A pilot study is set up before the main research starts. It enables you to improve the design of your research before you undertake the main body of your work. A pilot study will help you to test and modify your data collection methods (e.g. interviews, focus groups, experiments or questionnaires); consider how long research activities will take; analyse your proposed sampling methods; anticipate adverse events; and plan for other issues such as cost and resources.

Statement 2. Yes, this statement is correct. You might also hear a pilot study called a pilot test or a pilot project.

Statement 3. No, this statement is incorrect for obvious reasons! Pilot competencies are used to assess the skills and abilities of those flying aircraft.

Statement 4. Yes, this statement is correct. A pilot study takes place before the main study and is on a much smaller scale. The research population for the main study (a well-defined collection of people or objects with similar characteristics) is also used for the pilot study. This gives insight into your chosen sample (a subset of your research population), recruitment methods and the numbers you might require to obtain useful and meaningful results. More information about these issues is provided in Chapter 9.

Statement 5. Yes, this statement is correct and is a very important reason for undertaking a pilot study. You might think that you have designed a good project but, until you test it, you cannot be sure. Highlighting difficulties early in the preparation stages saves a lot of trouble later in your project.

Statement 6. No, this statement is incorrect. Although there are different types of survey that consider issues such as pilot wages and hours, they are not referred to as a pilot study.

Statement 7. Yes, this statement is correct and, again, is an important reason for undertaking a pilot study. You want to produce a good piece of research and pass your course. Taking time to conduct a pilot study will help you to assess whether your project is feasible, realistic and workable.

Statement 8. No, this statement is incorrect. A pilot study is a mini version of the large piece of research but should not be viewed as a piece of research in its own right. It helps to inform the larger project. Despite this, you might find research papers reporting on a pilot study. In these cases, the pilot study has found something that is worth reporting or, in other cases, it might be that the researcher has conducted the pilot study, found something interesting, but decided that it was not worth continuing with the main study (or, for example, funding was not granted for the main study).

Activity 8.10: Develop your own checklist

Your checklist is unique to you and to your research topic, methods and methodology. It also depends on whether you are studying at undergraduate or postgraduate level. Here are some examples from students studying in the UK (term or semester lengths and dates might differ, depending on your country of study).

Example 1

Suggestions for an undergraduate dissertation in the social sciences (some of these actions take place concurrently):

Planning and deciding on my topic/methods	2–4 weeks
Background reading	4–6 weeks
Producing and testing my questionnaire	3–5 weeks
Modifying and administering my questionnaire	4–6 weeks
Chasing up questionnaires	1–2 weeks
Analysing results	2–4 weeks
Writing my dissertation	8–12 weeks

Example 2

Suggestions for a PhD thesis in the humanities (some of these actions take place concurrently):

Year 1

Decide on my topic	Sept./Oct.
Read around the topic	Sept.–ongoing
Identify and meet with experts in the field	Oct./Nov.
Choose and meet with my supervisory team	Oct./Nov.
Produce a research question	Oct./Nov.
Decide on methods and methodology	Oct./Dec.
Produce a research proposal	Dec.–Feb.
Submit for ethical review	Feb.
Develop and pilot data-gathering tools	Mar.– July

Year 2

Modify and refine data-gathering tools	Sept.
Gather data	Oct.–Feb.
Keep abreast of developments in field	Oct.– ongoing
Monitor data gathering and undertake preliminary analysis	Oct.–Apr.
Decide on additional methods/data required and develop	Apr.–June
Continue with data collection and analysis	June–Sept.

Year 3

Begin to draft literature review and first chapters	Sept.–Dec.
Fill in any gaps in data	Sept.– Dec.
Receive feedback on drafts and continue writing	Dec.–May
Submit draft to supervisory team	May
Alter, change or modify, depending on feedback	May–July
Submit	Sept.

Example 3

Suggestions for an undergraduate thesis in the sciences (in paragraph format, rather than checklist, which some students prefer):

I intend to start to think about my research in the summer vacation of my second year. This will give me time to get my ideas together and work out what I want to research while I haven't got other assignments to complete. Then I will continue refining my ideas through more reading and speaking to my tutor. I will make sure that I put my research proposal together before the end of the first semester in my final year.

My experiments will start in the second semester of my final year. They will be complete by April. Then I will write up the results and produce a draft report by June. This will give me time to check that it is all okay with my tutor and make any changes if needed. It will also give me time to produce the dissertation in the required format and submit before my deadline.

Activity 8.11: Multiple-choice quiz

1   What is a research proposal?

    a   A document giving details of a university-wide programme of research.

    b   A document that sets out what you intend to research, why it is important and how you propose to conduct the research (correct answer).

    c   A document that provides an analysis of your pilot study.

2   What is a literature review?

    a   A detailed list of all the monographs, papers and online sources used in your research.

    b   A detailed summary of your methodology and methods, along with research methods books to which you have referred.

    c   A detailed description, summary, synthesis, analyses and evaluation of existing research relevant to your area of research (correct answer).

3   What is a pilot study?

    a   A small-scale, preliminary study used to test your research design and instruments (correct answer).

    b   A large-scale study undertaken after the main body of research to test your research design and instruments.

    c   A small-scale study carried out in its own right.

9

ACTION – LET'S BEGIN OUR RESEARCH …

CHAPTER CONTENTS

CHAPTER ACTIVITIES

CHAPTER OBJECTIVES

By the end of this chapter, you will be able to:

- Discuss and justify a number of participant selection and recruitment methods
- Summarize the steps involved in designing paper and online questionnaires
- Give examples of the different types of online interview, explain how and why they are used in research and list a number of ways to undertake successful interviews
- Define focus groups, discuss how they are used in research and summarize the steps involved in conducting focus groups
- Describe the different types of observation and explain how they are used in research
- Summarize the stages involved in conducting experiments
- Provide practical examples of projects that combine digital and in-person methods
- Explain what is meant by rapport and describe how to get people to trust you
- List a number of methods used to record data and summarize the factors that should be considered when choosing recording methods

---

Now that your planning and preparation are over you can begin your research. For many students this is the most exciting part of the project. If you have taken time over your planning and preparation, applied for and received ethical approval, and worked out which rules and legislation are relevant to your research, you are ready to go.

This chapter offers advice about choosing and recruiting people (or objects, groups or organizations) who are going to take part in your research. It goes on to cover a variety of data collection methods, including designing face-to-face and online questionnaires, conducting interviews and focus groups, using observation methods, combining in-person and online methods, conducting experiments and methods of recording. It also offers guidance on establishing rapport and getting people to trust you.

Starting your project is an exciting time. However, if you are a little daunted, don't worry. This chapter offers advice that guides you through each step, while providing useful tips and reassurance.

HOW DO I CHOOSE PARTICIPANTS?

The way that you choose your participants depends on the focus and purpose of your research, and on your chosen methodology. A definition of methodology is provided in Chapter 7, and Activity 9.1 will help you to understand how focus, purpose and methodology affect your choice of participants.

Activity 9.1: Matching

Read through the list of research projects, which describes focus, purpose and/or methodology of different types of research. Then read the list of ways to choose participants. Once you have done this, match the research project with the most appropriate method of choosing participants. Answers and further explanation can be found at the end of this chapter.

Research projects

1   This research project considers the prevalence of school anxiety and refusal among children aged 11–16 in Wales. The research will provide quantitative data: figures and statistics that can be analysed on a national basis, and qualitative data that provides insight into children's experiences.
2   This research project has been set up to improve the effectiveness and efficiency of a charity that trains local people in India to run their own sustainable food-related businesses. The focus is on improving working practices of staff and volunteers within the charity.
3   This research project considers the risk factors associated with inherited cardiac conditions, with the aim of identifying high- and low-risk patients and producing appropriate treatment systems.
4   This research seeks to provide deep, narrative accounts of the October Crisis of 1962 (also known as the Cuban Missile Crisis), given by Cubans who lived through the events.

METHODS FOR CHOOSING PARTICIPANTS

a   Participants are selected for the study based on an examination of their medical records. Using random assignment, participants are assigned to treatment or control groups.
b   Using both offline and online methods, researchers let people know about their research and wait for participants to contact them. Once a participant comes forward, researchers decide whether or not to select the participant, and also ask whether the person who has come forward knows of anyone else who might be interested in participating.
c   The researchers hold a meeting with all members of staff and volunteers. Every member of staff and every volunteer can take part in this research, if

they are interested. They can all work together with the researchers to improve working practices.

d   Six regions are selected. A list of all secondary schools within those regions is obtained and five schools from each are chosen using a random number generator. Figures for non-attendance are gathered from each of these schools. Requests are put forward by the researchers to hold interviews with children who display school anxiety and refusal behaviour (following correct procedures and protocols).

The answers for Activity 9.1 mention different types of 'sampling'. In research, a sample is a subset of the research population (the definition of 'research population' is a collection of individuals, groups or objects with similar characteristics, which is the focus of the research). Sampling in research is illustrated in Figure 9.1.

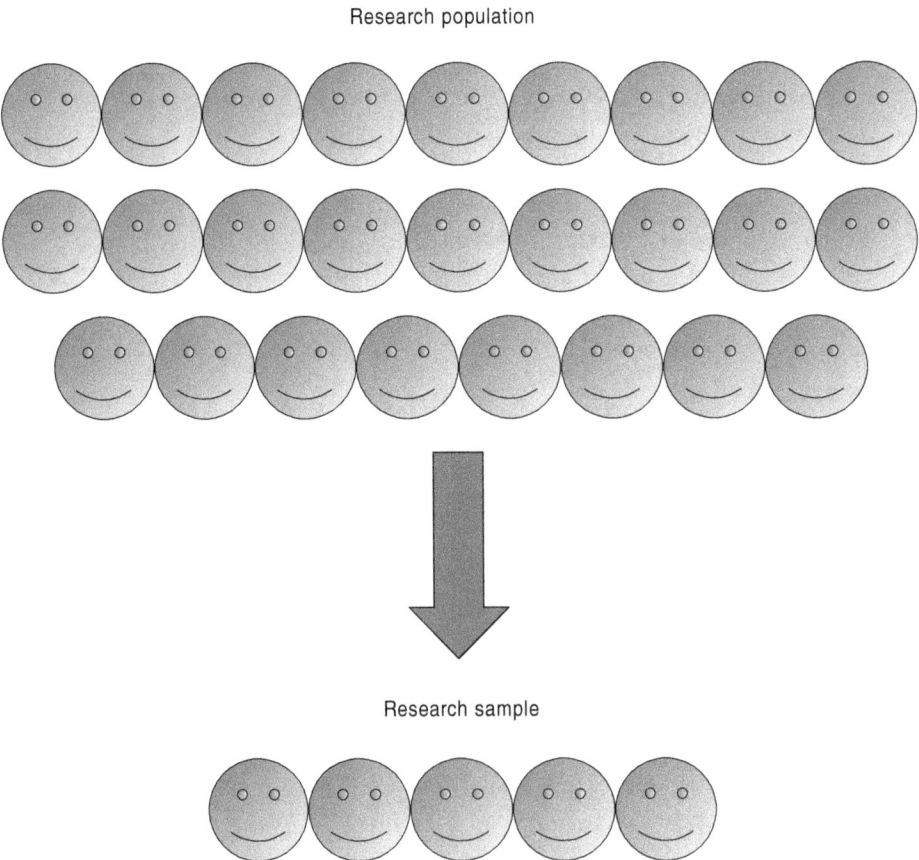

Figure 9.1   Sampling in research

HOW MANY PEOPLE, GROUPS OR ORGANIZATIONS DO I NEED TO INCLUDE IN MY STUDY?

The number of people, groups or organizations included in your study again depends on the focus and purpose of your research and on your chosen methodology. Activity 9.2 helps to illustrate this.

Activity 9.2: Matching and justification

Read through the list of research projects that were introduced in Activity 9.1. Match the research project with the appropriate number of participants, groups or organizations from the list given below, then provide a justification for the answers you have given. Answers and justifications can be found at the end of this chapter.

Research projects

1   This research project considers the prevalence of school anxiety and refusal among children aged 11–16 in Wales. The research will provide quantitative data: figures and statistics that can be analysed on a national basis, and qualitative data that provides insight into children's experiences.

2   This research project has been set up to improve the effectiveness and efficiency of a charity that trains local people in India to run their own sustainable food-related businesses. The focus is on improving working practices of staff and volunteers within the charity.

3   This research project considers the risk factors associated with inherited cardiac conditions, with the aim of identifying high- and low-risk patients and producing appropriate treatment systems.

4   This research seeks to provide deep, narrative accounts of the October Crisis of 1962 (also known as the Cuban Missile Crisis), given by Cubans who lived through the events.

Number of participants, groups or organizations

a   14 people
b   4 people
c   30 organizations
d   2,686 people

HOW DO I RECRUIT PEOPLE INTO MY STUDY?

There are a variety of ways in which you can recruit people into your study depending on your research topic, methodology and methods. Activity 9.3 encourages you to consider what they might be.

Activity 9.3: Brainstorm

Take a few minutes to brainstorm a list of the ways that researchers can recruit participants. Try to list as many items as possible, as soon as they come into your mind, and write them down (or record a voice note) without analysis or judgement. Once you have spent a few minutes brainstorming, go to the end of the chapter for some examples given by other students. This list provides useful ideas for your own project.

THINK ETHICS 9.1

When recruiting research participants, ensure that all communication is done in line with your university ethical policy. Although this policy may vary from university to university, in general you need to include your name, affiliation, university logo, university contact number (or university email address), name and contact of your supervisor (for postgraduate research) and a statement that your project has received ethical approval. All communications must demonstrate that participation is voluntary: your language must not be coercive or overly persuasive. Potential participants must be given enough information to know what is involved. Visit your university website/VLE to find out about your university policy.

HOW DO I DESIGN A QUESTIONNAIRE?

There is no one correct way to go about designing and administering a questionnaire as your approach depends on the discipline and subject, epistemological and methodological standpoint, research question, aims and objectives, research population, available resources, time and budget. However, there are various stages involved in designing a questionnaire that are general to all approaches: they are illustrated in Figure 9.2.

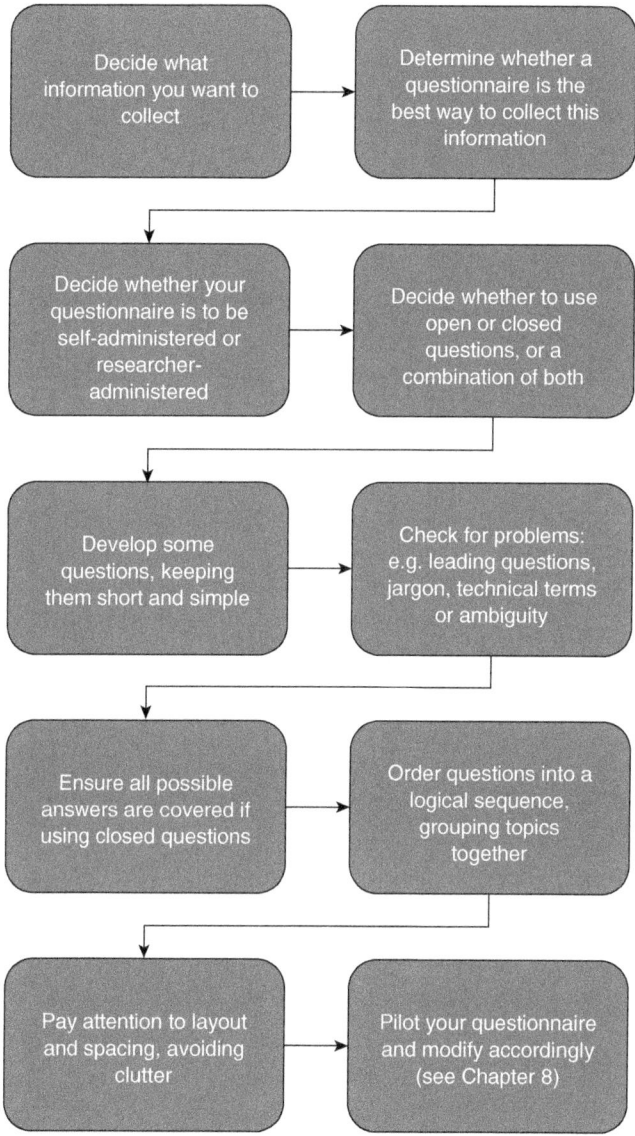

Figure 9.2 Designing a questionnaire

Ensure that your questionnaire is well designed, free of mistakes and robust: it needs to be well constructed and analysed correctly so that the data are reliable and can lead to valid conclusions. We will consider data analysis and drawing conclusions later in the book. At this stage, it is important to get your design right: useful sources of information can be found in Go further box 9.1.

GO FURTHER 9.1

These books provide comprehensive information about choosing, using and designing questionnaires:

Arundel, A. (2023) *How to Design, Implement, and Analyse a Survey*. Cheltenham: Edward Elgar Publishing.

Gillham, B. (2007) *Developing a Questionnaire*, 2nd edition. London: Continuum.

Leonard, K.F. and Robinson, S.B. (2019) *Designing Quality Survey Questions*. Thousand Oaks, CA: Sage.

For a shorter, practical guide on constructing questionnaires, see Chapter 9: How to construct a questionnaire, in:

Dawson, C. (2019) *Introduction to Research Methods*, 5th edition. London: Robinson.

You can also search 'designing a questionnaire' on YouTube to view some interesting and useful videos.

HOW DO I PRODUCE AN ONLINE QUESTIONNAIRE?

The information provided in Figure 9.2 is relevant to those of you who are thinking about producing an online questionnaire. Revisit Figure 9.2 so that you are familiar with the steps involved. However, there are additional issues you need to consider if you intend to produce and administer a questionnaire online. Activity 9.4 will help you to consider them.

Activity 9.4: Step Sequencing

Read through the following list of steps to be taken when producing, administering and testing an online questionnaire. Order the steps into a logical sequence. A suggested sequence (there is no specific right or wrong answer) is given at the end of the chapter, which provides useful guidance if you decide to use online questionnaires in your research.

Steps for sequencing

Pilot the questionnaire with a few of your respondents and modify it accordingly.

Decide on question content.

Choose design tools, templates, software packages and hosting platform.

Check that third-party providers adhere to relevant legislation and data protection rules.

Develop questions and order them into a logical sequence.

Check that your questionnaire is well constructed and works as intended.

Ensure your questionnaire is adaptive (layout and size change to suit the size of the screen).

Choose respondents.

Choose software that enables you to produce charts and graphs, and export and share data.

Produce straightforward instructions and be realistic about the time it will take to complete.

Inform respondents about the purpose of your research and let them know what will happen to the results.

Assure respondents that you understand and will comply with relevant data protection legislation.

Check that respondents have the required technology and know how to use the technology.

HOW DO I CONDUCT ONLINE INTERVIEWS?

There are different types of online interview, which are illustrated in Figure 9.3. Activity 9.5 goes on to help you think about online interviewing in more depth.

Activity 9.5: Dialogue

Read through the following dialogue between a student and his supervisor. It will help you to give more thought to a decision to conduct online interviews and give you some ideas about how you might proceed.

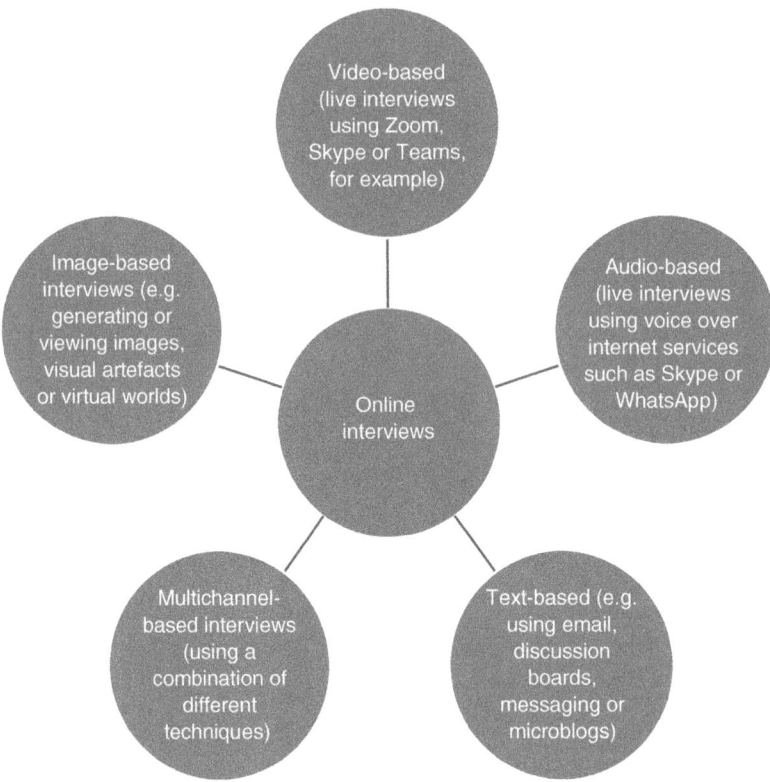

Figure 9.3 Types of online interview

Research into eating disorders among male Asian students

Prof. Huangdi:	You say that you intend to use online interviews for your research? Why?
Rakesh:	I won't have to pay for travel, it will take less time and I can reach people I wouldn't be able to reach otherwise.
Prof. Huangdi:	Are you familiar with the technology?
Rakesh:	Yes.
Prof. Huangdi:	What about the people you intend to interview?
Rakesh:	I'm pretty sure they will be as they are students and use the technology all the time.
Prof. Huangdi:	Okay, what type of online interview are you going to use?
Rakesh:	I've decided on video-based, probably Zoom meetings because a lot of people use Zoom and it's free to download.
Prof. Huangdi:	That sounds logical, but you should check first. When you carry out your pilot study find out whether Zoom is the best tool to use. Do you need to stick to one tool? Perhaps Microsoft

Rakesh:	Teams or Google Chat might also work? Have you thought about advantages and disadvantages when using this approach? I'll be able to hear what people say and also see them, so I can consider body language, you know, signs that they are uncomfortable talking about something or smiles or the level of eye contact, things like that. I guess a disadvantage might be that people with eating disorders might feel uncomfortable appearing, and talking, on video.
Prof. Huangdi:	There are lots of reasons why someone might feel uncomfortable on video. Have you thought of using other types of online interview if people are uncomfortable with video? Perhaps a text-based method might work better for some people? Interviews can be in real-time or over a period of time. It's useful if people want to add information later, something they didn't think of at first.
Rakesh:	Okay, I'll think about that.
Prof. Huangdi:	Read other research that's used these different methods. It'll help you make decisions. Also, try different approaches in your pilot study to see which works best, or whether a hybrid approach works best.
Rakesh:	Okay.
Prof. Huangdi:	Let's talk a bit more about the type of interview you're going to use. Is it a structured approach where you ask the same questions to all participants and answers can be quantified? Or an unstructured approach, where participants are free to discuss what is important to them, with you helping to move the interview forward? Or perhaps a semi-structured approach, which is a combination of both?
Rakesh:	I was thinking I want numbers I can report in my dissertation, but I also want people to talk about things important to them and raise issues I'd not thought of. So, I want to ask the same questions to all of them first and then ask some much more open questions later, when they feel more comfortable and we've both relaxed.
Prof. Huangdi:	Excellent. That sounds well thought out.
Rakesh:	Should I write down all the questions I'm going to ask?
Prof. Huangdi:	Yes, that's a good idea. You need to ask the same questions to all participants if you're to quantify your results, so produce some well-structured questions. Again, do some more background reading so you know how to produce questions and avoid pitfalls. With the open questions you might want to write down a list of topics to discuss or some specific questions to get the conversation moving. It's important to learn how to probe for more information. Things like 'You were saying...' or repeat the last thing they have said and wait for a response. Don't be afraid of silences. Your interviewee will fill the silence

	with more information. Practise your questions with a friend. It'll help you feel more confident.
Rakesh:	Okay.
Prof. Huangdi:	Also, practise with your technology. Make sure you're very familiar with whichever tool you choose. Come across as competent and confident. Check you have a reliable connection, good sound quality and clear video. Next week we'll talk about privacy issues, keeping your videos safe and secure and disposing of them when you finish your research.
Rakesh:	Thank you. It's a lot to think about but I'm excited to start!

WHAT TECHNIQUES WILL HELP ME TO INTERVIEW PEOPLE SUCCESSFULLY?

To answer this question, let's undertake another brainstorm. You might also find it useful to follow up some of the resources listed in the Go further 9.2 box.

Activity 9.6: Brainstorm

Take a few minutes to brainstorm a list of techniques that will help you to interview people successfully. Try to list as many items as possible, as soon as they come into your mind, and write them down (or record a voice note) without analysis or judgement. Once you have spent a few minutes brainstorming, go to the end of the chapter for some examples given by other students. This provides a useful checklist for those of you who intend to conduct interviews for your research.

GO FURTHER 9.2

These books provide comprehensive information about conducting interviews:

Brinkmann, S. and Kvale, S. (2018) *Doing Interviews*, 2nd edition. Thousand Oaks, CA: Sage.
King, N., Horrocks, C. and Brooks, J. (2019) *Interviews in Qualitative Research*, 2nd edition. London: Sage.

For a shorter, practical guide on conducting interviews, see Chapter 7: How to conduct interviews, in:

Dawson, C. (2019) *Introduction to Research Methods*, 5th edition. London: Robinson.

You can also search 'conducting interviews for research' on YouTube to view some interesting and useful videos.

HOW DO I CONDUCT FOCUS GROUPS?

Before we answer this question, let's think a little more about what focus groups are, and when and why they are used. Activity 9.7 will help you to do this.

Activity 9.7: Missing-word puzzle

Complete this missing-word puzzle by filling in the blanks from the list of words provided. It will help you to understand more about what focus groups are and how they are used in research. Answers can be found at the end of the chapter.

Focus groups are a [_____] of interacting individuals, with common characteristics or interests, holding a [_____] on a particular topic that is introduced and led by a [_____]. They can be in person or online (e.g. using video interaction, live chat rooms, web cams, instant messaging, text-based forums or bulletin boards).

Focus groups are used as a research method within a variety of qualitative methodologies. They can also be used in mixed methods approaches, perhaps to help explain [_____] that have been gathered in survey research, for example. They can be used in the [_____] stages of a research project, perhaps to help inform and develop a questionnaire, or they can be used as the [_____] data collection method in a research project.

The aim of a focus group is not to reach [_____]: instead, it is to gain a greater understanding of opinions, attitudes, beliefs, perceptions, behaviour and/or reactions to stimuli.

collection

consensus

discussion

moderator

planning

sole

statistics

Now that you understand more about focus groups, let's consider how you might go about conducting one. The various stages involved are illustrated in Figure 9.4, which provides a brief summary. If you are interested in using focus groups in your research, consult some of the resources listed in the Go further 9.3 box.

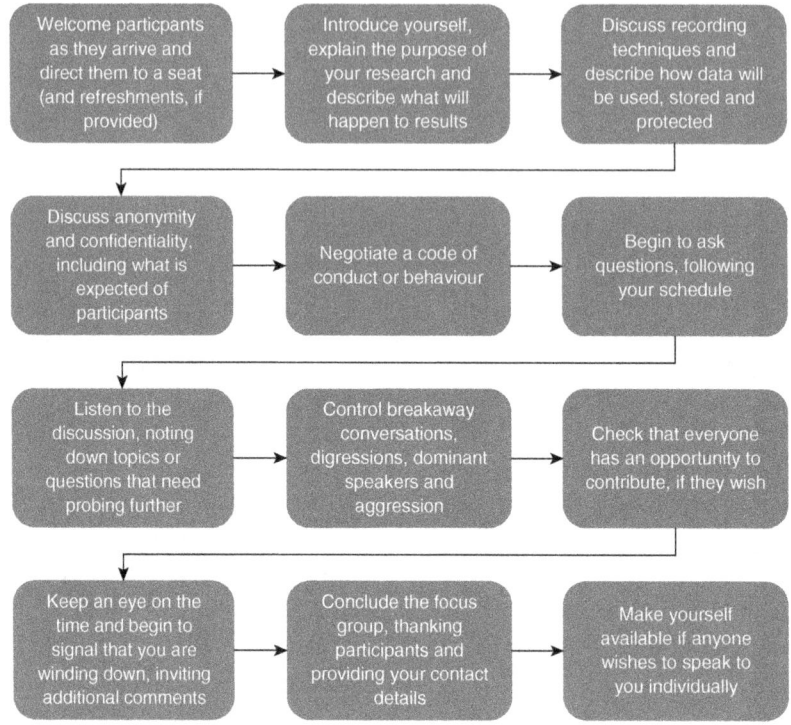

Figure 9.4 Conducting a focus group

GO FURTHER 9.3

These books provide comprehensive information about focus groups in research:

Barbour, R. (2018) *Doing Focus Groups*, 2nd edition. London: Sage.

Kruegar, R. and Casey, M. (2015) *Focus Groups: A Practical Guide for Applied Research*, 5th edition, Thousand Oaks, CA: Sage.

Morgan, D.L. (2018) *Basic and Advanced Focus Groups*. Thousand Oaks, CA: Sage.

For a shorter, practical guide on conducting focus groups, see Chapter 8: How to conduct focus groups, in:

Dawson, C. (2019) *Introduction to Research Methods*, 5th edition. London: Robinson.

You can also search 'running a focus group' on YouTube to view some interesting and useful videos.

WHAT ARE THE DIFFERENT TYPES OF OBSERVATION?

There are a number of different types of observation that can be used in research. Activity 9.8 will help you to understand what they are and how they are used. If you are interested in using observation in research, useful sources can be found in the Go further 9.4 box.

Activity 9.8: Missing-word puzzle

Complete this missing-word puzzle by filling in the blanks from the list of words provided. It will help you to understand more about the different types of observation and how they are used in research. Answers can be found at the end of the chapter.

Observation involves close [_____] or monitoring of a phenomenon, event or person and can include noticing facts, taking measurements, gathering evidence and recording judgements and inferences. It can take place in natural settings or in a [_____]. The different types of observation include [_____] observation, naturalistic observation, structured observation, case studies and archival research.

The way that observation is used in research depends, in part, on discipline, theoretical perspective and methodology. For example, ethnographers undertaking qualitative research might use observation to interpret, describe and record everyday [_____]; scientists who are positivists might use observation to formulate and test [_____]; and archivists studying historical documents might use unobtrusive observation of records and data to look for interesting [_____] and relationships in human activity.

hypotheses

laboratory

lives

participant

patterns

watching

─── **GO FURTHER 9.4** ───

These books provide comprehensive information about observation methods:

DeWalt, K. and DeWalt, B. (2011) *Participant Observation: A Guide for Fieldworkers*, 2nd edition, Lanham, MD: AltaMira Press.

Smart, B., Peggs K. and Burridge, J. (eds) (2013) *Observation Methods* (four volume set). London: Sage.

For a shorter, practical guide on participant observation, see Chapter 7: How to carry out participant observation, in:

Dawson, C. (2019) *Introduction to Research Methods*, 5th edition. London: Robinson.

You can also search 'observation in research' on YouTube to view some interesting and useful videos.

HOW DO I CONDUCT EXPERIMENTS?

There are three main types of experiment used in research: controlled experiments, field experiments and natural experiments. Experiments involve systematic and controlled testing, scientific observation and logical analysis. They move through a series of stages to explain emerging ideas and significant findings. These stages are illustrated in Figure 9.5. If you are interested in conducting experiments in your research, useful resources can be found in the Go further box 9.5.

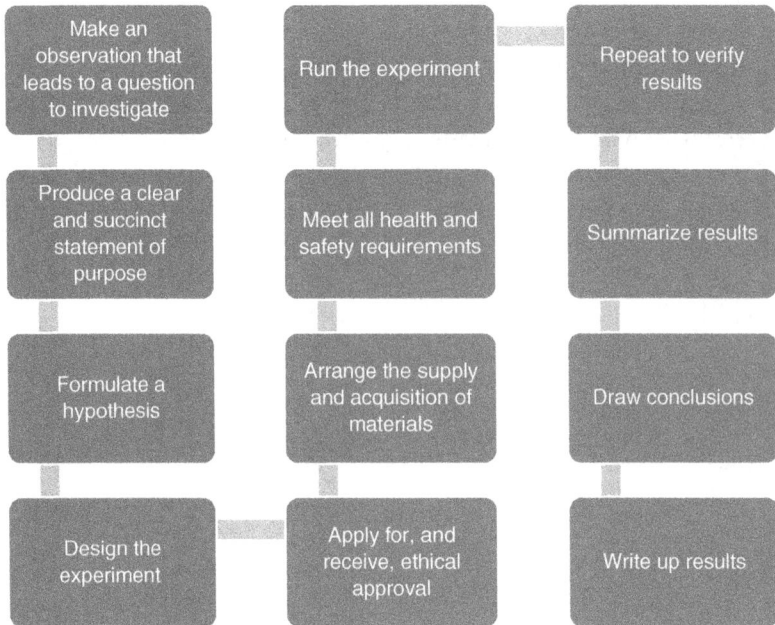

Figure 9.5 Conducting experiments

GO FURTHER 9.5

These books provide comprehensive information about experiments in research:

Duflo, E. and Banerjee, A. (eds) (2017) *Handbook of Field Experiments*, volumes 1 and 2. Amsterdam: North-Holland.

Field, A. and Hole, G. (2003) *How to Design and Report Experiments*. London: Sage.

Harris, P., Easterbrook, M. and Horst, J. (2021) *Designing and Reporting Experiments in Psychology*, 4th edition. Maidenhead: Open University Press.

Veltri, G. (2023) *Designing Online Experiments for the Social Sciences*. London: Sage.

For a shorter, practical guide on conducting experiments, see Chapter 11: How to conduct experiments, in:

Dawson, C. (2019) *Introduction to Research Methods*, 5th edition. London: Robinson.

You can also search 'experiments in research' on YouTube to view some interesting and useful videos.

CAN I COMBINE DIGITAL AND FACE-TO-FACE METHODS?

Yes, you can combine digital and face-to-face (or in-person) methods. A useful way to illustrate this is by providing examples of research projects in which students have combined methods. You can see in these examples that one student chose to combine methods from the start, whereas the other had to react to potential bias in her research.

Activity 9.9: Practical examples

Read through the examples given by students who have chosen to combine digital and face-to-face methods. Consider whether any of the points raised have relevance to your own research.

Example 1: David, human geography

In my city there are three dog-walking parks. I decided to research how people travel to the parks to walk their dogs. I spent some time meeting dog walkers in the park, telling them about my research and asking whether they would like to take part. When they agreed I asked them where they had travelled from, the route they had taken and their mode of transport. I thought it was important that I understood their journey. Instead of physically repeating each of the separate journeys, I decided to use Google Maps and Street View. I could see the route they had taken and follow their journey step-by-step without physically having to do so. This type of technology was extremely useful in my research. I could also find out mileage without having to measure it out.

Example 2: Anastasia, business studies

I was interested in finding out what customers thought about a new shop that had opened in my local town. It was part of my business course and gave me a chance to work with a local business owner. He contacted his customers to ask whether they were happy to be contacted by me. Those who agreed were asked to join a consumer panel. I wanted to ask them a series of questions over a period of time and I intended to do this online, using questionnaires and text-based interviews. However, I found that some of the customers weren't online, others didn't want to use the technology and others couldn't. I hadn't anticipated this. I realized that I would have to also meet face to face with some panel members so that my research wasn't biased against those people not using the technology.

HOW DO I GET PEOPLE TO TRUST ME?

In research we talk about establishing 'rapport'. This refers to a balanced and amicable relationship in which trust and empathy are established so that everyone can communicate effectively and freely (see Figure 9.6). Activity 9.10 provides an interesting way for you to think more about the intricacies of establishing rapport.

Activity 9.10: Play excerpt

Read the following (fictional) excerpt from a play. Once you have done this, consider how the university student should have acted differently to stop Lady Montague being so worried. How should he have introduced himself? How could he have established a rapport with her? Clues are provided in the play excerpt and some suggestions can be found at the end of this chapter.

Scene 1

A mother and daughter are sitting in a country house library, sipping tea from English Rose cups and saucers. The mother is wearing a smart two-piece suit with a pearl necklace. The daughter is casually dressed in sweatshirt and jeans.

Lady Montague:	It's so lovely to see you, dear. It's been too long.
Theresa:	I know. I'm sorry. Work commitments and all that.
Lady Montague:	I do understand, dear. But I was a little worried and simply had to see you.
Theresa:	Why, what's the matter?
Lady Montague:	I think there is someone staking out the estate.

Theresa puts down her cup and leans forward.

Theresa:	What?
Lady Montague:	Yes, a young man came to the door yesterday. He was scruffily dressed. Asking all sorts of questions. Abrupt, you know, even a little rude. Had a clipboard.
Theresa:	Did you ask who he was?
Lady Montague:	Yes, he said he was from the local university. He waved some badge in front of me. I hadn't got my glasses on. I'm forever losing them.
Theresa:	He might be legitimate.
Lady Montague:	But I just couldn't understand what he was talking about. And he asked some strange questions. All about who I am and how long I've lived here. I am a little concerned, dear. Your grandmother's jewels and your father's silver…
Theresa:	Did he leave any information about himself?
	Lady Montague passes a sheet of paper to her daughter.
Lady Montague:	He gave me this, but I can't read it without my glasses. He wouldn't look at me. He just kept looking down at his clipboard and asking all sorts without even listening to what I was saying.
Theresa:	There's a phone number here. At the university. I'll give it a ring and find out what's going on. Don't worry mum. I'm sure it's all fine.

Theresa stands up, walks towards the phone and lifts the receiver.

WHAT ARE THE DIFFERENT WAYS TO RECORD DATA?

There are a variety of ways to record data and some examples are provided in Figure 9.7. Can you think of any others that are not included in the diagram?

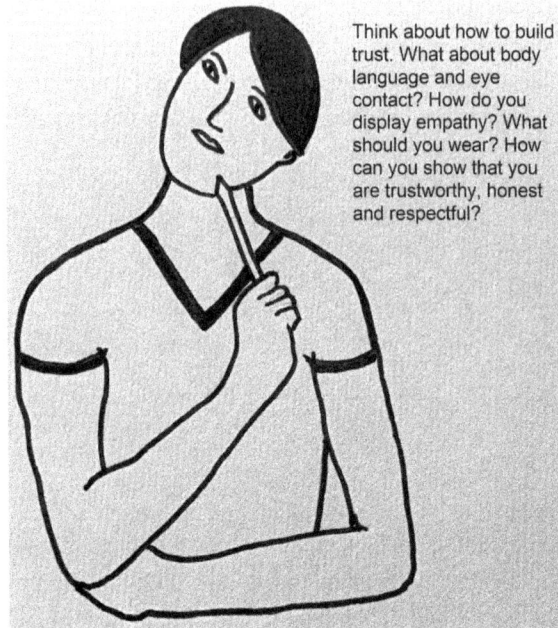

Figure 9.6 Thinking about building trust image

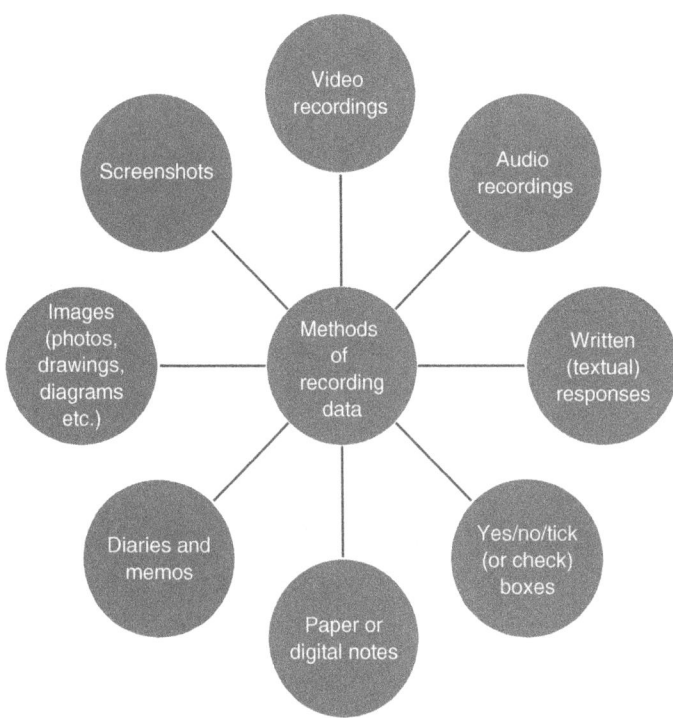

Figure 9.7 Methods of recording data

When choosing recording methods and equipment, consider the ethical implications (see Think ethics 9.2), cost, strengths and weaknesses, compatibility with research methods, user-friendliness and sourcing (your tutor can offer advice about equipment that is available for student use). Also, think about how your participants might react to a particular recording method and develop a contingency plan to put in place if they don't want to be recorded in the way that you have chosen.

THINK ETHICS 9.2

Ethical issues associated with recording include gaining the necessary permissions, data protection, anonymity, confidentiality, informed consent, storage, preservation and disposal. These issues are covered later in the book.

Now that you understand how to begin your research, we can move on. However, before we continue to the next chapter, let's test your understanding of what has been covered in this chapter with a short multiple-choice quiz.

Activity 9.11: Multiple-choice quiz

Read each question and choose the correct answer. The topics in all three of these questions have been covered in this chapter, so if you can't answer any of the questions, return to some of the activities to refresh your memory. Answers can be found at the end of the chapter.

1   What is the name given to a sampling technique where one participant recommends another and so on?

    a   Cluster sampling.
    b   Snowball sampling.
    c   Simple random sampling.

2   What do you call a person who leads a focus group?

    a   A mediator.
    b   An intermediary.
    c   A moderator.

3   What might an ethnographer use observation methods for?

    a   To describe, interpret and record everyday lives, relationships and interaction.
    b   To formulate and test hypotheses.
    c   To track eye movements and record body language.

ACTIVITY ANSWERS: CHAPTER 9

Activity 9.1: Matching

The answers are as follows:

1   *Research project 1 is matched with answer d.* This is cluster sampling. It is used when it is not possible, or it is impractical, to include all elements within the research population which, in this case, is all schools in Wales (e.g. due to the amount of travel required or the costs involved). Using geographic clusters makes the project more manageable. Once the specific clusters have been selected, a simple random sample is used to choose the schools within each cluster. Non-attendance figures from these schools provide quantitative data for analysis. Qualitative data is obtained by holding interviews with children whose names have been put forward. This is judgement sampling, with participants chosen because they are relevant or of interest to the research topic, based on the knowledge and expertise of the teachers in the schools.

2   *Research project 2 is matched with answer c.* In this research it is possible to select everyone (all members of staff and all volunteers) as numbers are small. This research project is action research where researchers, members of staff and volunteers all work together to meet the aims of the project which, in this case, is to improve the effectiveness and efficiency of the organization.

3   *Research project 3 is matched with answer a.* This research is a randomized control trial. Participants are first selected based on their medical records: only those with inherited cardiac conditions are chosen. Once patients have been chosen, randomization is used to assign participants to treatment or control groups. This helps to control validity issues by taking account of potential confounding variables (e.g. outside factors that could influence the results).

4   *Research project 4 is matched with answer b.* This is a self-selecting sample in which participants put themselves forward and the researchers decide whether or not to include them. It is also snowball sampling, where one participant (or potential participant) recommends another and so on. This type of research involves life history interviewing: only a small number of participants are interviewed, but interviews are very detailed and can take a few hours to complete. Researchers might also return to participants at a later date for further information.

Activity 9.2: Matching and justification

1   *Research project 1 is matched with answer c.* You were given a clue to this answer in Activity 9.1: six geographic regions were chosen and five schools from each selected. Therefore, 30 is the answer. This type of cluster sampling

can lead to over- or under-representation of certain characteristics in the different clusters. Therefore, the larger the sample size the better. For this project 30 was large enough (at the time of the project there was a total of 182 secondary schools in Wales) and the researcher also intended collecting qualitative data to help explain, or expand upon, the quantitative data.

2   *Research project 2 is matched with answer a.* Although you don't know how many members of staff and volunteers work for this organization, you can make a reasoned judgement that the answer is 14. It is a reasonable number of people to become involved in an action research project, and it seems a likely number of staff members and volunteers. Also, you will be able to eliminate the other answers given in the list. Fourteen is a manageable number for an action research project.

3   *Research project 3 is matched with answer d.* In this type of randomized control trial, a larger sample size enables researchers to detect smaller differences and draw more precise and accurate conclusions. This large sample size works for a clinical trial because funding and resources are available for a large research team. As a student you need to consider the resources you have available when you make decisions about sample size.

4   *Research project 4 is matched with answer b.* This research project intends to produce deep, narrative accounts of personal experiences. The goal is to provide rich, descriptive accounts, not to make generalizations. Research of this type selects only a small number of participants: sometimes there may only be one participant.

THINK ETHICS 9.3

If you intend to make inferences (or generalize) to the whole population, the larger the sample size the better. However, this is not the case if your research involves animals. Ethical principles require you to use the minimum number of animals possible to obtain scientifically valid data. The National Centre for the Replacement, Refinement & Reduction of Animals in Research provides guidance on sample size if you work with animals: https://eda.nc3rs.org.uk/experimental-design-group#poweranalysis [accessed 17 November 2023]

Activity 9.3: Brainstorm

Methods that can be used to recruit participants, given by students when this activity has been undertaken in class, include:

- Personal recommendation (from peers, relatives, colleagues or others)
- Using a gatekeeper (someone who controls access to research and potential participants)
- Producing posters, flyers or adverts (offline or online)

- Meeting people at conferences, seminars or webinars
- Approaching people in a particular area (indoors or outdoors)
- Joining an online community
- Using social networks (offline or online)
- Using social media
- Cold-calling (unsolicited contact via phone, email or in person)
- Using mailing lists (offline or online)
- Using a research recruitment agency
- Contacting professional bodies or organizations
- Asking one participant to introduce you to another

Activity 9.4: Step sequencing

Below is a suggested sequence for producing, administering and testing an online questionnaire. However, you might choose to undertake one or two steps at a different time, or some might be undertaken concurrently, for example.

Step 1. Choose design tools, templates, software packages and hosting platform.

Step 2. Choose software that enables you to produce charts and graphs, and export and share data.

Step 3. Check that all third-party providers adhere to all relevant legislation and data protection rules.

Step 4. Decide on question content.

Step 5. Develop questions and order them into a logical sequence.

Step 6. Produce straightforward instructions and be realistic about the time it will take to complete.

Step 7. Check that your questionnaire is well-constructed and works as intended.

Step 8. Ensure your questionnaire is adaptive (layout and size changes to suit size of screen).

Step 9. Choose respondents.

Step 10. Inform respondents about the purpose of your research and let them know what will happen to the results.

Step 11. Assure respondents that you understand and will comply with relevant data protection legislation.

Step 12. Check that respondents have the required technology and know how to use the technology.

Step 13. Pilot the questionnaire with a few of your respondents and modify accordingly.

Activity 9.6: Brainstorm

Techniques to help you interview people successfully suggested in brainstorms with other students include the following (they have been edited, amalgamated and expanded where required):

- Prepare carefully
- Produce a good interview schedule
- Keep questions short and to the point
- Move from general topics to specific ones
- Leave sensitive or controversial issues until later
- Develop a list of probe questions
- Practise, practise, practise (with technology, interview schedule and interview style)
- Dress appropriately
- Arrive in good time
- Take time to establish rapport (e.g. talk about the venue, photographs, weather or accept a cup of tea)
- Build trust
- Be courteous and polite
- Make good eye contact
- Listen carefully (and demonstrate that you are listening carefully)
- Monitor body language (of participant, and react accordingly)
- Be respectful of time (finish interview on time, unless the participant is happy to continue)
- Provide contact details

Activity 9.7: Missing-word puzzle

Focus groups are a *collection* of interacting individuals, with common characteristics or interests, holding a *discussion* on a particular topic that is introduced and led by a *moderator*. They can be in-person or online (e.g. using video interaction, live chat rooms, web cams, instant messaging, text-based forums or bulletin boards).

Focus groups are used as a research method within a variety of qualitative methodologies. They can also be used in mixed methods approaches, perhaps to help explain *statistics* that have been gathered in survey research, for example. They can be used in the *planning* stages of a research project, perhaps to help inform and develop a questionnaire, or they can be used as the *sole* data collection method in a research project.

The aim of a focus group is not to reach *consensus*: instead, it is to gain a greater understanding of opinions, attitudes, beliefs, perceptions, behaviour and/or reactions to stimuli.

Activity 9.8: Missing-word puzzle

Observation involves close *watching* or monitoring of a phenomenon, event or person and can include noticing facts, taking measurements, gathering evidence and recording judgements and inferences. It can take place in natural settings or in a *laboratory*. The different types of observation include *participant* observation, naturalistic observation, structured observation, case studies and archival research.

The way that observation is used in research depends, in part, on discipline, theoretical perspective and methodology. For example, ethnographers undertaking qualitative research might use observation to interpret, describe and record everyday *lives*; scientists who are positivists might use observation to formulate and test *hypotheses*; and archivists studying historical documents might use unobtrusive observation of records and data to look for interesting *patterns* and relationships in human activity.

Activity 9.10: Play excerpt

The student should have:

- Sent a letter to Lady Montague before he approached her in person. This should have followed his university protocols and included information about himself, his university and his research. It should also have included an informed consent form for Lady Montague to sign and return
- Arranged a time and date for the interview, so that Lady Montague would have known when to expect him
- Produced all written information in a way that could be read and understood by Lady Montague. He should have checked that she was able to read and understand what he had given her
- Been empathetic and understood that someone living on their own might have been nervous, even if they live in a large country house

- Dressed appropriately – in this case, smartly as that is what Lady Montague would have expected
- Been courteous and polite, making good eye contact and listening to everything that Lady Montague said
- Assessed her body language: it might have provided clues to her being worried

Activity 9.13: Multiple-choice quiz

1   What is the name given to a sampling technique where one participant recommends another and so on?

   a   Cluster sampling.

   b   Snowball sampling (correct answer).

   c   Simple random sampling.

2   What do you call a person who leads a focus group?

   a   A mediator.

   b   An intermediary.

   c   A moderator (correct answer).

3   What might an ethnographer use observation methods for?

   a   To describe, interpret and record everyday lives, relationships and interaction (correct answer).

   b   To formulate and test hypotheses.

   c   To track eye movements and record body language.

10

INVESTIGATION – LET'S THINK ABOUT ANALYSING RESEARCH DATA ...

CHAPTER CONTENTS

CHAPTER ACTIVITIES

─────── **CHAPTER OBJECTIVES** ───────

By the end of this chapter, you will be able to:

- Define what is meant by data analysis and discuss the difference between qualitative and quantitative data analysis
- Assess when and how to analyse data
- Produce a data analysis plan
- List and define a number of data analysis methods
- Illustrate how to assess the neutrality of raw data
- Discuss how to recognize, reduce or eliminate bias when analysing and interpreting data
- Explain how to recognize false, fabricated or misleading analyses
- Discuss how to avoid coming to the wrong conclusions when analysing and interpreting data

Data analysis is one part of the research process that can create very different emotions. Some students are very excited about beginning their analysis. They are eager to find out what their data are telling them and what they can tell others about their findings. Others are daunted: they worry about the statistical tests required, or their ability to undertake their analysis at the level required to pass their course. If you fall into this latter group, don't worry. This chapter walks you through the various stages required, highlighting different analysis methods and helping to raise awareness of problems that might arise.

Try to view your analysis as an important and exciting part of your research. It might take place at the end of your data collection, or you might analyse as you collect your data. This depends on your methodology: if you need refreshing on what is meant by methodology and how this influences the methods that you choose, return to Chapter 7. There is a great deal of help at hand: tools and software, university departments, workshops, courses, and tutors or supervisors. Read through this chapter, build your understanding, plan your data analysis, think about your interpretations and become excited about sharing your findings with others.

WHAT IS DATA ANALYSIS?

Put simply, data analysis is the process that gives structure to collected data. It can organize and summarize, search for patterns and/or develop themes. Activity 10.1 will help you to understand more about what this means in practice.

Activity 10.1: Story

Read the following story and produce a list of issues you believe are relevant to data analysis. Some suggestions can be found at the end of this chapter.

Inspector Smythe and the case of the missing octopuses

Octopuses are notoriously slippery creatures. I should know. I've spent the last three months investigating their disappearance. One after the other. Gone. No trace. I, the diligent Inspector Smythe, have to admit that I'm baffled. This is not like the case of the missing cat: it is a whole new kettle of fish.

So, what's happening? Let's consider the facts. Eighteen octopuses have disappeared from the aquarium over a total of 92 days. Each disappeared at night. They were there when the doors were closed at 9pm, then they were gone when the doors opened at 8am. There appears to be nothing out of the ordinary: similar weather conditions, similar visitor numbers and the same opening hours for each disappearance.

I've checked all other aquariums and nothing like this has happened elsewhere. I've also checked the historical records and have found no similar case anywhere in the country.

I've spent weeks talking to people. Now, I've gathered together all my evidence: statements from staff members; interviews with activists who think there is no place for octopuses in captivity; owners of local seafood restaurants (I know, that is a long shot, but I have to explore all avenues). I've organized my evidence into themes: empathy with octopuses; loathing of captivity; dissatisfaction at work; financial problems; taste for grilled seafood. Now patterns are beginning to emerge and I can begin to look a little closer.

Not a disgruntled employee, but a new volunteer. I think, my friend, you are on borrowed time. But before I make my case I must check and check again. False accusations or jumping to wrong conclusions are not the practice of the diligent Inspector Smythe. Now to build my case …

This story raises a variety of issues that are relevant to data analysis. Think about what they might be, then go to the end of the chapter for some suggestions. This will help you to think more fully about what we mean by data analysis and what it involves.

WHAT ARE THE DIFFERENCES BETWEEN QUALITATIVE AND QUANTITATIVE DATA ANALYSIS?

There are different ways to analyse data, depending on whether they are qualitative or quantitative data. Qualitative data are non-numerical data: they include perceptions, opinions, worldviews, objects or artefacts. Quantitative data are numerical: they include mathematical, statistical or computational data. Activity 10.2 will help you to think about how different methods of analysis are used for different types of data.

Activity 10.2: Classification

Classify the following data analysis methods according to whether you think they should be used with qualitative or quantitative data. At this stage, don't worry if the terms are new to you: all will become clear as you work your way through this chapter. Answers, with definitions of each data analysis term, can be found at the end of this chapter.

Data analysis method	Qualitative data	Quantitative data
1 Inferential statistics		
2 Data analytics		
3 Thematic analysis		
4 Content analysis		
5 Descriptive statistics		
6 Comparative analysis		

HOW LONG SHOULD I PLAN FOR MY DATA ANALYSIS?

In Chapter 8 it was suggested that you produce a timetable for your research project and you were given some examples of timetables produced by other students. In that timetable you will have factored in time for your data analysis. Now that you are beginning to think more about how to analyse your data, it is useful to produce a more detailed data analysis plan. This is a map, or illustration, of your data analysis action. It provides a step-by-step account of activities you need to work through, which will help you to think more specifically about how long your data analysis will take. Although your data analysis plan is unique to you and your research, there are certain components that should be included. They are listed below. Read through this list before embarking on Activity 10.3.

Components of a data analysis plan:

- *Your research question.* This is important as you can refer back to it at each stage of your analysis to ensure that your research remains on topic. See Chapter 6 for information about developing a research question.
- *The aim and objectives of your study.* This helps to ensure that your analysis enables you to meet your aims and objectives. See Chapter 6 for more information on producing aims and objectives.
- *A description of your data.* This can be textual, in the form of transcripts, or numerical data gathered from online questionnaires, for example.
- *A step-by-step outline of what you intend to do with your data.* This includes methods of analysis and the tools you intend to use, such as data analysis software, visualization tools or statistical tests.
- *Output and interpretations.* More information about interpreting your data is provided later in this chapter.

The amount of detail required depends on your research and level of study. Undergraduate plans may only need to be simple, whereas postgraduate plans will be more complex. Find out whether data analysis templates are available from your university.

Activity 10.3: Action

Produce a data analysis plan. Once you have completed your plan, return to the timetable that you produced when you read Chapter 8. Consider how much time you have allocated to data analysis. If you think that you have not given yourself enough time for data analysis, modify your timetable accordingly. It is important to note that data analysis often takes longer than you think.

WHEN DO I ANALYSE MY DATA?

When you analyse your data depends on your methodology and methods. Activity 10.4 will help to increase your understanding of this.

Activity 10.4: Classification

Consider each of the research projects listed below. Classify them according to whether you think data analysis takes place at the end of the data collection stage or concurrently with data collection. Answers and further explanation can be found at the end of the chapter.

After data collection   **Concurrently with data collection**

Project 1. This is a grounded theory study of student nurses embarking on their first year of training.

Project 2. This study seeks to test whether playing online games promotes relaxation.

Project 3. This is an ethnographic study of a multi-client call centre.

Project 4. This study investigates mistakes made in undergraduate chemistry experiments.

HOW DO I ANALYSE MY DATA?

There is a vast array of data analysis techniques and six of them were introduced in Activity 10.2. Some other types of data analysis are included in Activity 10.5. There is also a vast array of tools available to help you to analyse your data, and they are discussed in the next section of this chapter.

Activity 10.5: Matching

Match the definition with the type of data analysis it refers to. Don't be daunted by these terms if you have never come across them: clues can be found in the definitions. Read and digest the definitions carefully as it is important that you get a good understanding of different types of data analysis methods. Answers can be found at the end of this chapter.

Types of data analysis   **Definition (See following page: 1–11)**

Acoustic analysis

Cluster analysis

Conversation analysis

Data mining

Discourse analysis

Experimental analysis

Geospatial analysis

Regression analysis

Text analytics

Thematic analysis

Visual semiotics

Definitions

1 A range of approaches used to analyse the context or situation of written or spoken communication, and relations between those communicating
2 A framework for studying how visual images communicate a message through signs, the relationships between signs, and patterns of symbolism
3 Applies algorithms to the extraction of hidden information with the aim of building an effective predictive or descriptive model of data
4 The collection, analysis and visualization of data containing explicit geographic positioning information or reference to a specific location or place
5 A variety of methods used to record and analyse sound or voice, including intensity, waveform and phonetic analysis
6 Reading through sets of data (e.g. transcripts or text) to identify themes. It can involve counting, coding, analysing and modifying
7 The study of social interaction within a conversation, including verbal and non-verbal communication
8 The application of statistical and linguistic methods to extract, sort and classify unstructured text, and identify patterns, sentiment and relationships
9 A set of statistical procedures used to test cause-and-effect relationships between two or more variables
10 A method for grouping, sorting, classifying and exploring data to uncover or identify groups or structures within the data
11 Statistical tests are conducted on data collected under controlled conditions

WHAT TOOLS ARE AVAILABLE?

There is a vast array of tools available to help with your data analysis, and the type of tool that you choose depends on the type of data you have collected, how you wish to analyse your data and the way that you intend to present your data. It is important to note that tools used in data analysis are not discipline-specific, although certain tools have been developed for, and tend to be used by, researchers in certain disciplines (e.g. SPSS: Statistical Package for the Social Sciences, which is an all-purpose quantitative analysis tool). It is also important to note that you do not have to use only one tool: sometimes it might be beneficial to use a mix of tools or data analysis methods to gain a more complete understanding of your data. Figure 10.1 encourages you to think about some of the issues you need to consider when deciding on appropriate data analysis tools and Figure 10.2 highlights the importance of choosing the right tools for the job.

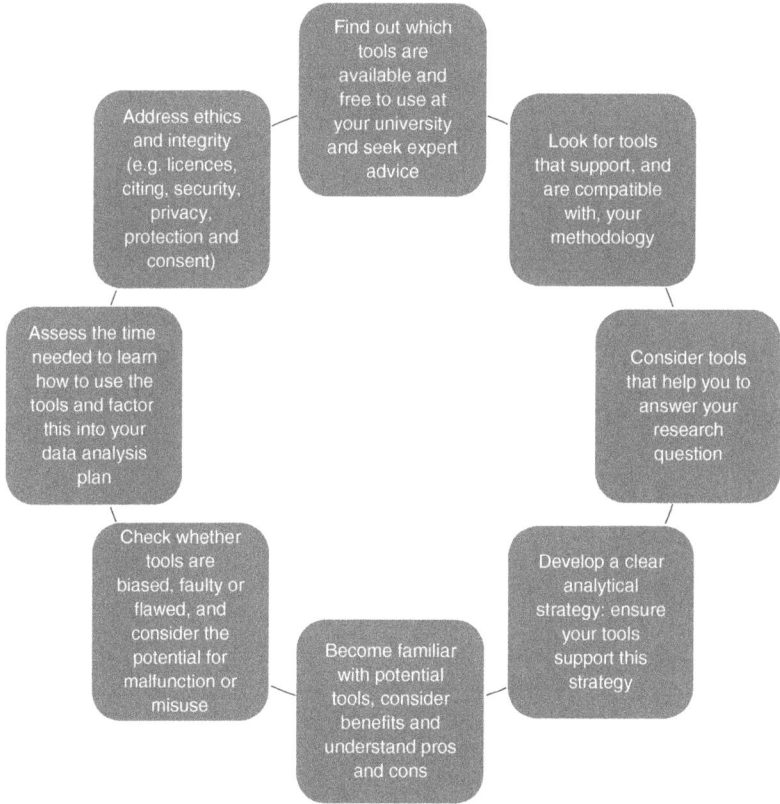

Figure 10.1 Choosing data analysis tools

It can be difficult eating soup with a fork. Choosing the right tool is important and will help you to complete the job successfully.

Figure 10.2   Choosing the right tool

HOW DO I ASSESS THE NEUTRALITY OF RAW DATA?

Raw data, or primary data, are data that have been collected by the researcher that have not been processed in any way. They can include data that are collected by researchers through the use of instruments such as experiments, questionnaires or interviews, and they can include data that are gathered through activities, interactions and digital technology (e.g. smartphones, wearables or purchases made through apps or cash registers). It should not be assumed that any raw data are neutral, even if they are collected by what is considered 'reliable technology'. Therefore, it is important that you understand how to assess the neutrality of raw data that are to be used in your research, whether collected by you or by others. Activity 10.6 will help you to do this.

Activity 10.6: Develop your own checklist

Produce a checklist of questions that you can ask to assess the neutrality of raw data. Once you have done this, go to the end of the chapter for some suggestions that have been given by other students when this activity has been undertaken in class.

HOW DO I RECOGNIZE AND ADDRESS BIAS WHEN ANALYSING DATA?

Before we answer this question, let's think a little more about what is meant by bias. Activity 10.7 will help you to do this and the Go further 10.1 box provides links to a useful resource that lists and discusses different types of bias in research.

Activity 10.7: Missing-word puzzle

Complete this missing-word puzzle by filling in the blanks from the list of words provided. It will help you to understand more about what is meant by bias and how it is viewed by different researchers. Answers can be found at the end of the chapter.

'Bias' is the term used to describe a [_____], inclination or tendency for a particular line of thought, idea, perspective or result. In research, bias can have an influence on how the research topic has been chosen, the methods that are used, the way data are analysed and/or the way that the research is reported or [_____].

The extent to which bias is seen to be introduced into the research process depends, in part, on [_____] and theoretical perspective. Researchers undertaking quantitative research, who pay close attention to [_____], adopt the correct statistical procedures or tests and keep meticulous records in an attempt to reduce, avoid and [_____] bias.

Researchers undertaking qualitative research, or a more [_____] approach, tend to believe that it is impossible to eliminate bias completely. Instead, they take time to consider biases, including their own, which can influence all stages of the research process. To them, it is important that the different types of bias are recognized, discussed and [_____] as they cannot be eliminated.

acknowledged

eliminate

methodology

objectivity

preference

published

subjective

GO FURTHER 10.1

The Catalogue of Bias describes a wide range of biases, providing definitions and discussing the possible impact on research studies. It is a useful resource that will help you to understand more about the various types of bias that can affect research: https://catalogofbias.org [accessed 13 July, 2023].

Now that you have worked your way through the missing-word puzzle and you understand a little more about what is meant by bias, let's think about how we can recognize and address bias when analysing data. Activity 10.8 will help you to do this.

Activity 10.8: Application

Figure 10.3 gives examples of different types of action you can take to recognize, reduce and/or eliminate bias. Work your way through them, thinking about those that apply to your research. The action that is relevant to your research might depend on your theoretical perspective and methodology, as we have seen in Activity 10.7, or you might decide that all types of action listed are relevant to your research. This activity provides a useful list of action that you can refer to when you begin to analyse your data.

HOW CAN I RECOGNIZE FALSE, FABRICATED OR MISLEADING ANALYSES?

In Figure 10.3 you were presented with examples of action that can be taken to recognize, reduce and/or eliminate bias. Some of them will also enable you to recognize false, fabricated or misleading analyses when completing Activity 10.9.

Reflect and/or self-evaluate with reference to equality, diversity and inclusion

Verify with more or different data sources

Use alternative and varied data sources to validate your results

Handle missing data

Ask participants to check analyses and conclusions

Look at ways to disprove your model

Consider alternative explanations or interpretations

Ask other researchers/coders to undertake analysis/coding

Identify and handle outliers

Check all data analysis software and tools for bias in design

Choose the right statistical procedures or tests

Become familiar with your data

Look for mistakes

Identify flaws in analyses and/or arguments

Keep meticulous records of all analyses, interpretations and justifications

Recognize false assumptions

Check that data have not been added or omitted without clear justification

View and interpret data from several different perspectives

Figure 10.3   Recognizing, reducing and/or eliminating bias

Activity 10.9: Develop your own checklist

Produce a checklist of action steps you can take to recognize false, fabricated or misleading analyses. Once you have done this, go to the end of the chapter for some suggestions that have been given by other students when this activity has been undertaken in class.

HOW DO I INTERPRET MY FINDINGS?

Interpreting your findings involves making sense of what you have found. You delve deeper into your data, considering what they mean or what they represent. Your interpretation provides a description of your findings and then goes on to speculate on their meaning. This is done with reference to previous research, for comparison and/or in support of your interpretation. There are a number of issues that you should be aware of when interpreting your data. The tutor tips offered in Figure 10.4 will help you to think about them.

> Make sure your interpretations are appropriate to your theoretical perspective and epistemological and methodological stance. **Psychology supervisor**

> When making interpretations, think about the social context and structures, setting and frameworks that you make your interpretations in. How might these influence your interpretations and how might they influence how others view your interpretations? **Sociology tutor**

> You have gained knowledge and built expertise over your studies: use these to interpret your data. What does your data mean? Construct a logical argument to explain your data. Remember, your data is not an absolute truth, nor is it subjective opinion. It is logical, uses analytical methods and is based on what you know. **Clinical tutor**

> You've got to be rigorous. Your interpretations must be rigorous and accurate. **Ergonomics tutor**

> Think about the story your data is telling and think about how this story is relevant to your reader (this will probably be your examiner). **Anthropology supervisor**

> Don't confuse data analysis with data interpretation. Analysis brings structure whereas interpretation is about producing meaningful insight. Think about the significance of your data and the implications of your findings. **Geography tutor**

Figure 10.4 Tutor tips: interpreting findings

HOW DO I AVOID COMING TO THE WRONG CONCLUSIONS?

This is a very important question that is often overlooked. We all make mistakes: it is part of life. However, in research you need to do everything you possibly can to make sure that you don't make mistakes and come to the wrong conclusions. Activity 10.10 will help you to do this.

Activity 10.10: Checklist (right and wrong answers)

Read through the following checklist. If you are able to answer 'yes' to all the relevant questions, you will be able to avoid coming to the wrong conclusions in your research. (Note that some of the questions might not be relevant, given your chosen methodology and methods.) Refer back to this checklist as you analyse, interpret and report your data.

Yes, no, n/a

Have you evaluated and addressed personal bias?

Have you complied with all regulatory, legal and disciplinary obligations?

Are your analysis and interpretation robust, accurate and credible?

Have you taken all evidence into account?

Have you avoided false, fabricated or misleading analyses and interpretation?

Have you checked for, identified and rectified mistakes?

Have you checked that you have not confused correlation (a pattern or relationship between two values or variables) with causation (one value or variable directly affects another)?

Have you provided a justification (and evidence) for all conclusions?

Have you provided a description of how all conclusions have been reached?

Have you made all data, codes and analyses available for others to use/view?

Is all material provided so that your research can be reproduced and replicated?

Have you been honest, open and accountable?

Have you done the best you can?

Have you taken care to avoid plagiarism? Have you acknowledged and cited all sources?

WHO CAN HELP ME IF I STRUGGLE WITH MY ANALYSIS?

There are various people and departments that can help if you find yourself struggling with analysis. Figure 10.5 gives some examples of sources of help, and Activity 10.11 provides an example of how a student sought help when she undertook her data analysis.

Figure 10.5   Sources of help with data analysis

Activity 10.11: Diary entry

Read the following diary entry from an undergraduate student and think about the takeaway points that might be relevant to your own struggles with data analysis.

21 March

Only two more months to go and I've got over my block. My tutor told me to read up on approaches to quantitative data analysis and I did, but it was all so confusing. I've never done statistics and it all went over my head. The tool I'd chosen for my questionnaire produced graphs and charts so I didn't think I needed to actually understand what was happening and how the charts were generated. But I did. You can't look at them in isolation without understanding what they mean and what they show. And I knew that meant I needed to understand more about how the statistics work.

Reading the help sections in the questionnaire tool didn't work. I guess they're trying to sell their product so they make it all sound so easy. But I still wasn't understanding the statistics. Staff in our IT department were quite useful: they talked me through the graphs and charts and explained what was happening. I understood more, but I still felt I was lacking basic knowledge.

Then I got talking to a mate who knew someone who was doing a statistics degree. We got introduced and she was absolutely brilliant. Apparently, she's thinking about doing a master's and maybe even going into teaching. She has the gift. She talked me through some things like measures of central tendency and measures of variability, sampling distribution and p-values and chi-square tests. She's recommended some introductory books: I think my tutor thought I knew more than I did, so his recommendations were beyond me.

So, block over. I'm not saying I understand it all, but I think I know enough about what else I need to find out to make sure my analysis is right.

Now that you understand more about analysing your data, we can move on to the next topic. Before we do, let's test your understanding of what you have learnt so far, with a short quiz.

Activity 10.12: Multiple-choice quiz

Read each question and choose the correct answer. The topics in all three of these questions have been covered in this chapter, so if you can't answer any of the questions, return to some of the activities to refresh your memory. Answers can be found at the end of the chapter.

1   What is the name given to non-numerical data that includes perceptions, opinions, worldviews, objects or artefacts?

    a   Quantitative data.
    b   Qualitative data.
    c   Hybrid data.

2   What is the name given to a range of approaches used to analyse the context or situation of written or spoken communication, and relations between those communicating?

    a   Content analysis.
    b   Discourse analysis.
    c   Text analytics.

3   What is the name given to a variety of methods used to record and analyse sound or voice, including intensity, waveform and phonetic analysis?

    a   Acoustic analysis.
    b   Cluster analysis.
    c   Regression.

ACTIVITY ANSWERS: CHAPTER 10
Activity 10.1: Story

Inspector Smythe, through his story, raises a number of issues that are relevant to data analysis. They include:

- Collecting and organizing evidence
- Developing themes
- Searching for patterns
- Comparing cases
- Considering the variables
- Exploring different approaches
- Considering the wider picture
- Examining evidence
- Interpreting the evidence
- Drawing conclusions
- Checking analysis and conclusions
- Presenting evidence

Activity 10.2: Classification

The answers are as follows:

Data analysis method	Qualitative data	Quantitative data
Inferential statistics		Yes
Data analytics		Yes

Thematic analysis	Yes	
Content analysis	Yes	
Descriptive statistics		Yes
Comparative analysis	Yes	

Definitions of qualitative data analysis methods:

- *Thematic analysis.* Themes and patterns in textual (or visual) data are identified, analysed and interpreted
- *Content analysis.* Words, themes or concepts are identified and counted in textual (or visual) data to provide an objective, systematic and quantified description of qualitative data. You might have struggled as to where to place this: remember, however, that it starts with qualitative data before going on to quantify
- *Comparative analysis.* Similarities and differences between groups, cultures, societies or objects are identified, analysed and explained

Definitions of quantitative data analysis methods:

- *Descriptive statistics.* Summary statistics used to describe basic features of the data; they do not generalize
- *Inferential statistics.* Samples are analysed and conclusions drawn. Deductions can be made from the data collected and the researcher can test hypotheses and relate findings to the sample or population
- *Data analytics.* Inferences and conclusions are drawn from close examination of data sets or raw data

Activity 10.4: Classification

Concurrently with data collection

Projects 1 and 3 are examples of projects in which data analysis takes place concurrently with data collection. These two projects are examples of different types of qualitative research. In both of these examples, researchers choose to collect data and undertake a preliminary analysis as the research moves forward. They might do this because what they begin to find out helps to inform further data collection, or their analysis might raise new themes that have not previously been considered and need to be followed, for example. Although both of these examples are types of qualitative research, it is important to note that not all qualitative research collects and analyses data concurrently. In other projects data analysis takes place after data collection (e.g. an analysis of transcripts from open-ended interviews or responses to open-ended questions on a questionnaire).

After data collection

Projects 2 and 4 are examples of projects in which data analysis takes place after data collection. Research that seeks to test a hypothesis, conduct an experiment or analyse quantitative data is included in this category. Projects 2 and 4 seek to do this. These projects follow the scientific method where data analysis takes place after data collection. However, as was noted in the previous answer, data analysis can take place after data collection in other types of research, including qualitative research.

ACTIVITY 10.5: MATCHING

Types of data analysis	Definition (1–11)
Acoustic analysis	5
Cluster analysis	10
Conversation analysis	7
Data mining	3
Discourse analysis	1
Experimental analysis	11
Geospatial analysis	4
Regression analysis	9
Text analytics	8
Thematic analysis	6
Visual semiotics	2

Activity 10.6: Develop your own checklist

The following are examples of questions produced by other students when this activity has been undertaken in class, and have been edited and amalgamated for brevity and clarity. This is a useful list for you to reference when assessing the neutrality of raw data.

- What exactly do we mean by 'raw data'?
- How are they collected or generated?
- Are there any design defects in the collection tools, methods and technology?
- Is there any bias in the design of the collection tools, methods and technology?

- What are the historical, political, cultural and social contexts in which data are collected?
- Who collects or generates them and why?
- How has human and machine-based reasoning been used to produce data?
- How might bias and inequality be embedded in data?
- Is it possible to trace the life of the data or know and understand the data journey?
- What influence do capital-driven data collection and generation have on neutrality?
- How are data made available?
- Why are they made available?
- How are they used by others?
- Why are they used by others?

Activity 10.7: Missing-word puzzle

'Bias' is the term used to describe a *preference*, inclination or tendency for a particular line of thought, idea, perspective or result. In research, bias can have an influence on how the research topic has been chosen, the methods that are used, the way data are analysed and/or the way that the research is reported or *published*.

The extent to which bias is seen to be introduced into the research process depends, in part, on *methodology* and theoretical perspective. Researchers undertaking quantitative research, who pay close attention to *objectivity*, adopt the correct statistical procedures or tests and keep meticulous records in an attempt to reduce, avoid and *eliminate* bias.

Researchers undertaking qualitative research, or a more *subjective* approach, tend to believe that it impossible to eliminate bias completely. Instead, they take time to consider biases, including their own, which can influence all stages of the research process. To them, it is important that the different types of bias are recognized, discussed and *acknowledged*, as they cannot be eliminated.

Activity 10.9: Develop your own checklist

The following are examples produced by other students when this activity has been undertaken in class. Here they have been edited and amalgamated for brevity and clarity. This list will help you to recognize false, fabricated or misleading analyses:

- Think about why someone might falsify, fabricate or mislead (e.g. consider motivations such as a desire to succeed or get published, lack of understanding or laziness)
- Check researcher credentials

- Assess whether the researcher displays honesty, sincerity and truthfulness
- Check that the correct procedures have been followed (if information about methods is missing, find out why)
- Assess whether data have been interpreted correctly
- Identify flaws in the analysis
- Check that figures have not been manipulated to fit the argument
- Look for false assumptions (assess whether all assumptions and conclusions have been backed up with evidence)
- Check that all data have been reported (even those that weaken or contradict those presented)
- Use additional sources to check and verify results
- Check whether there has been any repetition or retest by the same researcher or by others
- Find out whether the results can be, or have been, replicated
- Check whether the published work has been peer reviewed
- Assess whether results are credible and believable from the perspective of participants and other researchers

Activity 10.12: Multiple-choice quiz

1   What is the name given to non-numerical data that includes perceptions, opinions, worldviews, objects or artefacts?

    a   Quantitative data.
    b   Qualitative data (correct answer).
    c   Hybrid data.

2   What is the name given to a range of approaches used to analyse the context or situation of written or spoken communication, and relations between those communicating?

    a   Content analysis.
    b   Discourse analysis (correct answer).
    c   Text analytics.

3   What is the name given to a variety of methods used to record and analyse sound or voice, including intensity, waveform and phonetic analysis?

    a   Acoustic analysis (correct answer).
    b   Cluster analysis.
    c   Regression.

11

PROTECTION – LET'S ENSURE WE PROTECT OUR RESEARCH DATA …

CHAPTER CONTENTS

CHAPTER ACTIVITIES

CHAPTER OBJECTIVES

By the end of this chapter, you will be able to:

- Discuss why it is important to protect your research data
- Describe potential threats to your research data and list possible solutions
- Define confidentiality, anonymity and privacy and discuss how they differ
- Discuss the ethics, integrity and practice of anonymization
- Explain how to anonymize research data
- Describe how to store, preserve and share research data safely
- Discuss the ethical implications of data sharing

Knowing how to protect your research data and keep it safe and secure is an extremely important part of your research. There is legislation in place to ensure that personal data are protected and you were encouraged to consider this in Chapter 4. You were also introduced to the ethical approval process: issues of data protection need to be considered when you apply for ethical approval. If you need to refresh your memory on relevant legislation and the ethical approval process, return to Chapter 4.

There are a number of potential threats to research data and it is important that you are aware of them and understand how to combat, reduce and/or remove them. When doing this, consider all research data, including digital and non-digital data. Part of this protection is understanding how to store and preserve data, and knowing what to do with data once your research has finished.

Some students are worried about these issues, in particular, their ability to understand and make the most of relevant technology. However, there is a great deal of help available from your tutor, specialist members of staff and your university website/VLE, so try not to feel daunted. This chapter introduces you to the relevant issues. It provides practical information and step-by-step guidance that will enable you to protect your research data and keep them safe and secure.

WHY IS IT IMPORTANT TO PROTECT MY RESEARCH DATA?

There are a number of reasons why it is important to protect your research data: Activity 11.1 introduces you to some of these reasons.

Activity 11.1: Missing-word puzzle

Complete this missing-word puzzle by filling in the blanks from the list of words provided. This will help you to understand more about why it is important to protect your research data. Answers can be found at the end of the chapter.

Research data are [_____]: a great deal of time, effort and finance have been used to gather them. They are valuable to the researcher, participants, stakeholders and society and must, therefore, be protected so that the investment remains worthwhile and benefits can be lasting. If data are protected, researchers can confirm [_____], re-analyse and/or share data.

Researchers rely on the [_____] of participants. They take part in research only if they trust researchers to protect them from [_____]. Keeping personal data safe and secure is important in harm prevention: if data are lost, stolen or disclosed to [_____] third parties, it can lead to participant stress, trauma, anxiety, prosecution, identification, redundancy or demotion, for example.

If data are not protected there could be legal, social, financial or [_____] implications for researchers and their universities; future generations will be unable to benefit from excellent research; and [_____] in research will be lost.

cooperation

findings

harm

reputational

trust

unauthorized

valuable

WHAT ARE THE THREATS TO MY RESEARCH DATA?

There are a variety of threats to your research data, including theft, hacking, loss, insertion of rogue data and unauthorized access and disclosure. Activity 11.2 will help you to understand more about the different types of threat and how they can affect research.

Activity 11.2: Practical examples

Read through the following examples given by students who have experienced threats to their research data. Consider whether any of these examples have relevance to your own research.

Example 1: Shona, sociology

My research involved in-depth interviews with survivors of domestic abuse. I was coming home on the bus one day. It was raining, I was tired and I was late for an evening engagement. Well, I left my laptop on the bus. I was horrified when I realized. I'd just finished transcribing two of my interviews and the documents were on my laptop. I hadn't even gone through them removing all personal information. I was going to do that the next day. If those transcripts got into the hands of abusers … I just couldn't imagine the harm it would do the survivors who trusted me to keep their information safe. Anyway, I rang the bus company straightaway. The driver found it where I'd left it and I went to pick it up. I told my tutor and he said I had to report it to the Head of Information Governance at my university as soon as possible. We discussed taking appropriate measures, containing damage and minimizing harm. Then I was told to visit IT services to find out about password protection and encryption of files. And the worst thing was I'd got all this in my data protection plan, I'd just been too rushed to do it all. It was all a real wake-up call for me.

Example 2: Lisha, international business and management

I was part of a research team collaborating with universities in other countries. Someone accidentally sent an email containing details of companies that had taken part in our research and it was copied to outside organizations, although I wasn't told which they were. It was commercially sensitive information that shouldn't have been sent to the recipients. I think there were also details about CEO salaries and personal information. The breach had to be reported and some of the companies withdrew from the project. They didn't trust us any more and that was understandable even though it was an accident.

Example 3: Eduardo, biomedical science

Our research data is kept on our secure university server which we access remotely so we don't keep data on our laptops or other devices. Then we were told of a hacking attempt from outside the university. There was some 'attempted unauthorized entry to secure areas' apparently. They didn't get in though. Even so, the incident had to be reported and there was a lot of work undertaken to make the systems more secure. My research data is sensitive and needs additional protection. Imagine if I'd not got all the protection offered by the university systems. Even then, someone tried to access the information. Luckily, they didn't succeed.

Example 4: Min-Ji, economics

We were given an attic room to share, all the postgraduate students. There were three filing cabinets. I put my paper research information in my drawer. Then one day I came in to find someone rifling through them. I asked what they were doing and they said 'nothing' and went out the room. I realized I had to get a key and lock the filing cabinet. We also discussed it with our supervisors and they arranged for us to have a key to the door to the attic. We were all told to make sure that filing cabinets and doors were locked (see Figure 11.1).

HOW CAN I PROTECT MY RESEARCH DATA?

There are a wide variety of tools and methods available to help you protect your research data. There is also help available at your university. Activity 11.3 will help you to think more about the tools, methods and people that help you to protect your research data.

Activity 11.3: Brainstorm

Take a few minutes to brainstorm a list of the tools, methods, people and/or resources that can be used or consulted to help you keep your research data safe and secure. Try to list as many items as possible, as soon as they come into your mind, and write them down (or record a voice note) without analysis or judgement. Once you have spent a few minutes brainstorming, go to the end of the chapter for some examples given by other students. This list is useful to reference when assessing how to protect your research data.

Hard copies of identifiable information should be kept in a locked filing cabinet, a locked office and/or locked storage facilities. Keep all keys safe and secure.

Figure 11.1 Key image

WHAT'S THE DIFFERENCE BETWEEN CONFIDENTIALITY, ANONYMITY AND PRIVACY?

Some students struggle to understand the difference between confidentiality, anonymity and privacy, often using the terms interchangeably. However, it is important that you understand what is meant by these terms and know how to distinguish between them as this will help you to protect your research participants and the information they provide. You also need to demonstrate how you will pay attention to confidentiality, anonymity and privacy when you make your application for ethical approval (see Chapter 4). Activity 11.4 will help you to understand the differences.

Activity 11.4: Matching

Match the definition with the appropriate term. Answers can be found at the end of this chapter.

Term	Definition (See below: 1, 2 or 3)
Confidentiality	
Anonymity	
Privacy	

Definitions

1   The identity of individual participants is hidden. There is no personally identifying information collected or personally identifying information is removed. This includes direct and indirect information such as names, addresses, photographs, email addresses, fingerprints, birthdates and IP addresses. If video or telephone interviews take place, or if photographs are important to the research design, researchers need to consider whether it is realistic to guarantee this particular form of protection.

2   This relates to a person's body or mind (e.g. a person's personal, sensitive or intimate data or where they are located). The participant has control over how, when and where they take part in research and they maintain control over their decisions once taking part in a study. They also decide what can be made public and what should remain private. The researcher must consider how to access information about potential participants (when contacting and recruiting) so that this is maintained.

3   Personal or sensitive information is not disclosed to third parties without prior consent. If a participant supposes that information is given in confidence, it must be treated as such. Researchers must obtain written consent if they wish to share data with other researchers (under strict terms and conditions). The researcher takes a number of steps to ensure that a participant's personal information is not revealed. This includes using password protected files, encryption, ID numbers or pseudonyms, and reporting and sharing only aggregate findings (e.g. reporting on groups rather than individuals).

WHAT IS ANONYMIZATION?

Anonymization is the process of removing personally identifying information so that participants cannot be identified. As we have seen previously, this information can be direct, such as names, telephone numbers and photographs, or indirect, such as salaries, place of work or postcodes. There are various steps involved in anonymization, which are summarized in Figure 11.2.

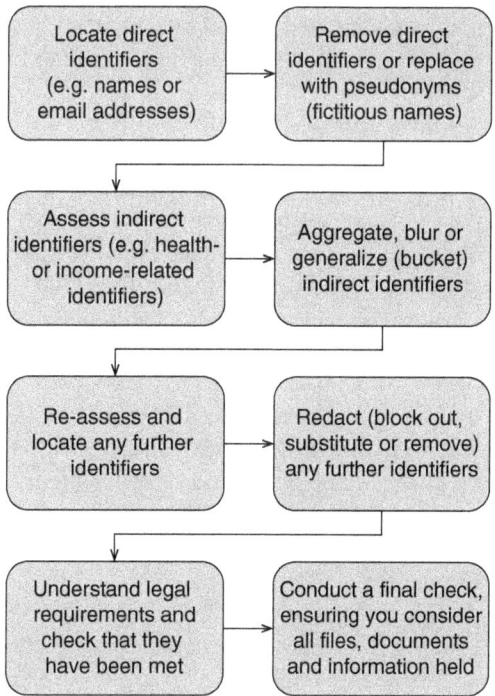

Figure 11.2 Anonymizing data

WHAT DO I NEED TO KNOW ABOUT THE ETHICS, INTEGRITY AND PRACTICE OF ANONYMIZATION?

That is a good question! Some students follow set procedures for anonymizing data without really thinking about what they are doing, why they are doing it and the potential consequences. Activity 11.5 will help you to think a little more about the ethics, integrity and practice of anonymization.

Activity 11.5: Dialogue

Read through the following dialogue from participants in a seminar on the ethics of anonymization. Consider how some of the points raised might have relevance to your own research.

Seminar leader:	Who does anonymization protect?
Participant 1:	Well, I guess it's there to protect the people who take part in research.
Participant 2:	It could also protect the researcher. If they don't do it properly, they could be sued. Or maybe they could lose their job.
Participant 3:	But what if people who take part want to be identified? Like celebrities?
Participant 4:	Or politicians. They like to be heard.
Participant 5:	What do we do then?
Participant 1:	I don't think you can identify them, even if they want to be.
Participant 2:	But what about those of us who work with First Nations or Indigenous knowledge? What right do we have to anonymize their voices? Is this a Western-centric view?
Participant 4:	What do you mean?
Participant 2:	Some communities expect to be identified. They value reciprocity. And it devalues our research. I had to blur images in a video. Families had taken them and wanted them used but I had to blur them so people couldn't be identified. Important gestures and body language were lost and couldn't be analysed again.
Seminar leader:	Perhaps we should be asking whether anonymization is culturally neutral?
Participant 1:	I think that's irrelevant.
Participant 2:	But surely it's not? In the Western world we impose our values on others and think we're right and everyone else should agree. I don't think we should silence the voice of others through anonymization.

Participant 1:	But their voices are still there, you just don't know whose voice, which protects them in case others disagree with what they say.
Participant 5:	I wonder if it's even possible to guarantee anonymity, like with your research, if you're taking videos. Is it immoral to talk about anonymity when it really can't be guaranteed?
Participant 3:	And of course, we might be really careful about anonymizing data, but what about others, like software companies or those we share our research data with? Are they as careful?
Participant 1:	The thing is there are rules and regulations we've got to follow. Even if we do disagree with some of this, we've still got to adhere to university policy and relevant legislation.
Seminar leader:	Thank you so much for all your input. That's given us a lot to think about.

HOW DO I STORE AND PRESERVE DATA SAFELY?

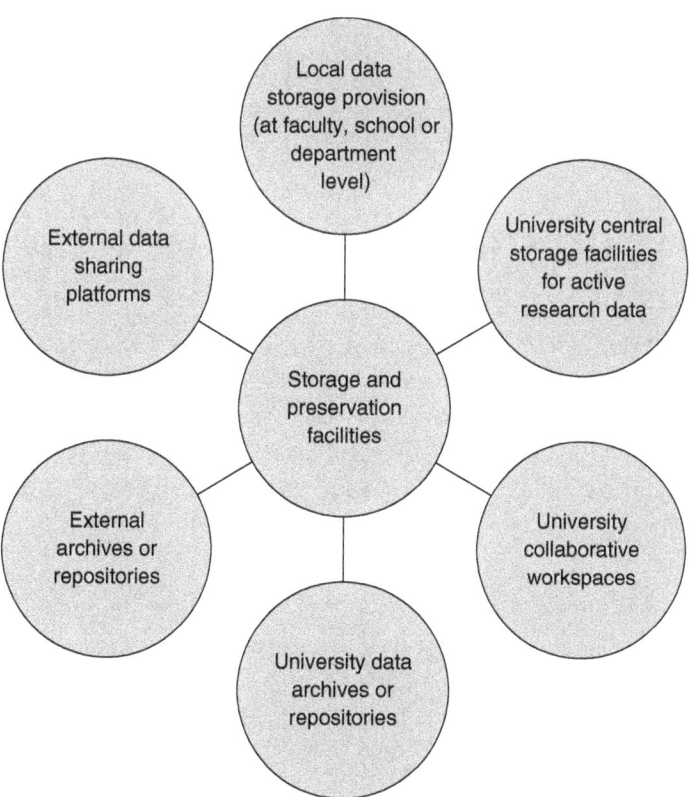

Figure 11.3 Storing and preserving data safely

In Chapter 4 you were introduced to data management plans. A checklist activity asked you to consider all the components required and check whether or not they had been included in your plan. One of the areas you were asked to consider was data storage. You might find it helpful if we consider this in a little more depth. Have a look at Figure 11.3 on the previous page, which provides some examples of methods you can use to store or preserve your data safely. Then undertake Activity 11.6.

Activity 11.6: Action

Find an example of a specific type of storage facility mentioned in each cell in Figure 11.3. You could consult your school, faculty or departmental website to find out whether they have safe and secure storage provision, and your university website/VLE to find out about university facilities for active research data, repositories, archives and collaborative workspaces, for example. Or speak to your tutor or contact your university Research Data Services (or equivalent) to find out about both internal and external safe and secure provision. Members of staff can offer advice about safe storage facilities and those to avoid (e.g. commercial cloud storage facilities that do not meet university requirements).

HOW LONG SHOULD I STORE MY DATA FOR?

There is no specific answer to this question as it depends on your research, your university and the type of data you intend to store. If you have received funding for your research (e.g. some postgraduate projects) find out whether your funding body has specific requirements about how long data are kept. The Digital Curation Centre (DCC) in the UK has produced a useful guide that will help you to appraise your research data and decide what to keep and for how long (see the Go further 11.1 box).

GO FURTHER 11.1

DCC (2014) *Five Steps to Decide What Data to Keep: A Checklist for Appraising Research Data*, v.1. Edinburgh: Digital Curation Centre. Available online: www.dcc.ac.uk/guidance/how-guides/five-steps-decide-what-data-keep [accessed 01 September 2023].

WHAT ARE THE ETHICAL IMPLICATIONS OF DATA SHARING?

There are a variety of ethical implications to consider when you are assessing whether or not to share your research data. The tutor tips provided in Figure 11.4 will help you to think about what they might be and Activity 11.7 encourages you to assess how they might relate to your own research.

> Consider the benefits of sharing your data: for example, it builds science, capacity, fairness and respect; increases transparency; enables others to replicate your research and helps to reduce research burden. **Hydrology tutor**

> There are different spectrums of access to data such as partial, open or controlled. Look into them and assess what is most suitable for your data. **Lecturer in botany**

> Remember that data can be misused and abused. Think about whether this could happen to your data. If it could, should you share your data? **Economics tutor**

> Become familiar with, and make sure you follow, institutional, national and international guidelines on data sharing. **History tutor**

> If you are considering sharing data always speak to your tutor first. They will be able to provide advice on anonymization, informed consent and university guidelines. **Lecturer in criminal law**

> Check whether you own the data. If you don't you mustn't share without the permission of the owner. **Sociology tutor**

> Your data sharing must be consistent with the informed consent you obtained from participants. They must understand, and agree to, data sharing. **Library science tutor**

Figure 11.4   Tutor tips: assessing the ethical implications of sharing data

Activity 11.7: Action

Read the tutor tips provided in Figure 11.4. Think about each tip in relation to your own research data. Consider whether the tip is relevant and, if so, assess the action you need to take to address the issues raised. Some of the information provided in the next two sections of this chapter might be useful when you assess the action required.

HOW DO I SHARE RESEARCH DATA SAFELY?

Once you have assessed the ethical implications of sharing your research data, you can decide whether or not to go ahead. If you decide that you do want to share your research data you must understand how to do this safely. Activity 11.8 will help you to do this.

Activity 11.8: Develop your own checklist

Produce a checklist of action you should take that will enable you to share your research data safely. Then go to the end of the chapter to find some suggestions. This list provides a useful checklist that you can refer to if you decide to share your research data.

WHAT IS A DATA ACCESS (OR AVAILABILITY) STATEMENT?

A data access (or availability) statement accompanies an academic publication. It explains where and how research data that support the publication can be accessed. It also gives information about who can access the data. This statement can be found in a dedicated section of a research paper or in the acknowledgement section of an article, paper or other publication. It is useful if you want to delve deeper into the research data, which can include transcripts, survey data, fieldwork notes, lab work, digital images, video, readings and measurements, for example. If you are in your final year of study, you might already have referred to data access statements to find out more about the research data accompanying relevant publications.

If you are a postgraduate student your funding body may have guidelines about sharing your research data, and part of this includes producing a data access statement. You should also speak to your supervisor and consult your university guidelines about producing a statement. If you are an undergraduate student, and you decide to publish your research, speak to your tutor and consult your university guidelines. Figure 11.5 will help you to think about some of the points you need to consider when you produce a data access statement and share your data.

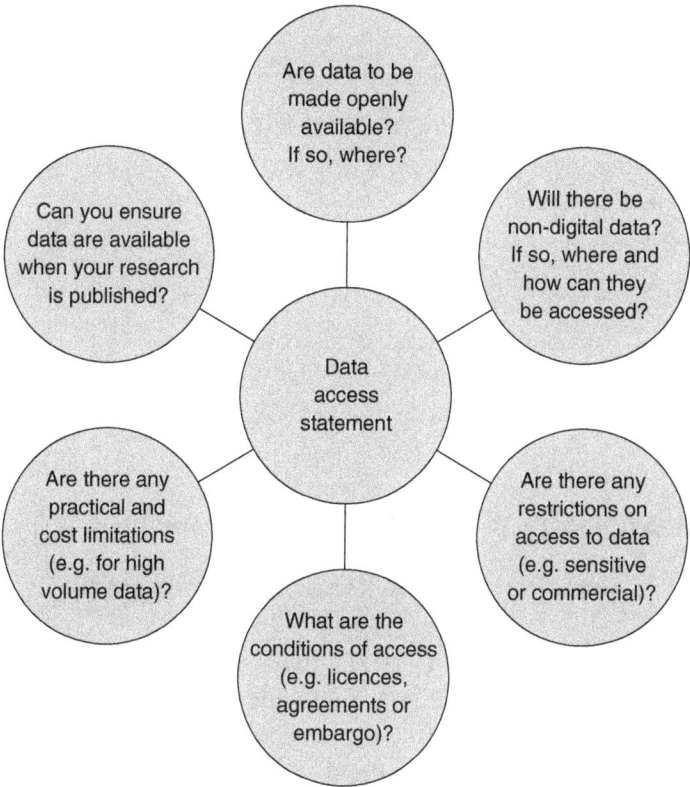

Figure 11.5 Data access statement: points to consider

Now that you understand more about protecting your data, we can move on to the next topic. Before we do, let's test your understanding of what you have learnt so far, with a short quiz.

Activity 11.9: Multiple-choice quiz

Read each question and choose the correct answer. The topics in all three of these questions have been covered in this chapter, so if you can't answer any of the questions, return to some of the activities to refresh your memory. Answers can be found at the end of the chapter.

1   If a researcher knows who a participant is, but does not reveal their identity or what they have said to others, to which of the following terms does this refer?

   a   Confidentiality.
   b   Anonymity.
   c   Privacy.

2   What is the purpose of a data access statement?

   a   It provides information about how to use a particular dataset.
   b   It provides information about where and how to access data supporting a research publication.
   c   It provides information about other publications that have used the data.

3   What does the acronym FAIR stand for, in relation to research data?

   a   Factual, Accurate, Identifiable and Recoverable.
   b   Findable, Accessible, Interoperable and Reusable.
   c   Fair, Assessable, Investigable and Replicable.

ACTIVITY ANSWERS: CHAPTER 11
Activity 11.1: Missing-word puzzle

Research data are *valuable*: a great deal of time, effort and finance have been used to gather them. They are valuable to the researcher, participants, stakeholders and society and must, therefore, be protected so that the investment remains worthwhile and benefits can be lasting. If data are protected, researchers can confirm *findings*, re-analyse and/or share data.

Researchers rely on the *cooperation* of participants. They take part in research only if they trust researchers to protect them from *harm*. Keeping personal data safe and secure is important in harm prevention: if data are lost, stolen or disclosed to *unauthorized* third parties, it can lead to participant stress, trauma, anxiety, prosecution, identification, redundancy or demotion, for example.

If data are not protected there could be legal, social, financial or *reputational* implications for researchers and their universities; future generations will be unable to benefit from excellent research; and *trust* in research will be lost.

Activity 11.3: Brainstorm

There are a variety of tools, methods, people and/or resources that can be used or consulted to help you keep your research data safe and secure. The following are examples of answers given by students previously, when they have been asked to undertake this activity (they have been arranged alphabetically):

- Access restrictions
- Antivirus software
- Approved storage
- Back-ups
- Checksums
- Controlled access to buildings
- Data protection officer advice and approval
- Encryption
- Firewalls
- Integrity checks
- IT technicians/computer services
- Locked filing cabinets
- Passwords
- Permissions
- Personal tutors/supervisors
- Power surge protection
- Research ethics committee advice and approval
- Safe disposal
- Secure buildings
- Secure servers
- Trustworthy repositories
- University data protection handbook
- University policy
- University research/governance office
- Up-to-date software
- Verification checks

Activity 11.4: Matching

Term	Definition (1, 2 or 3)
Confidentiality	3
Anonymity	1
Privacy	2

Activity 11.8: Develop your own checklist

Examples of action you can take to share research data safely include the following (you might find that some of them are not relevant to your research or level of study):

- Seek advice from your tutor or supervisor
- Consult your university guidelines and/or policy
- Consult your funding body guidelines and/or policy (if relevant)
- Consider the ethics of data sharing (e.g. the dignity and rights of participants; informed consent and consent to share; potential misuse and abuse of data)
- Think about why you should share your data and assess benefits
- Think about what data to share
- Assess potential costs
- Undertake a potential misuse of data risk assessment (following your funding body/university guidelines, if available)
- Consider the FAIR principles and try to meet them (this means making your data findable, accessible, interoperable and reusable)
- Find an appropriate data repository and ensure that it is trustworthy (a useful resource on how to do this is provided in Go further box 11.2)
- Include a data access statement with your publication

GO FURTHER 11.2

You can discover how to find a trustworthy repository for your data by visiting www.openaire.eu/find-trustworthy-data-repository [accessed 14 September 2023].

Activity 11.9: Multiple-choice quiz

1   If a researcher knows who a participant is, but does not reveal their identity to others, to which of the following terms does this refer?

   a   Confidentiality (correct answer).
   b   Anonymity.
   c   Privacy.

2   What is the purpose of a data access statement?

   a   It provides information about how to use a particular dataset.
   b   It provides information about where and how to access data supporting a research publication (correct answer).
   c   It provides information about other publications that have used the data.

3   What does the acronym FAIR stand for, in relation to research data?
   a   Factual, Accurate, Identifiable and Recoverable.
   b   Findable, Accessible, Interoperable and Reusable (correct answer).
   c   Fair, Assessable, Investigable and Replicable.

12

COMPLETION – LET'S WRITE UP AND PASS THE COURSE …

CHAPTER CONTENTS

CHAPTER ACTIVITIES

CHAPTER OBJECTIVES

By the end of this chapter, you will be able to:

- Provide a definition for research findings and discuss how they relate to your research question and design
- Assess whether your findings are interesting and explain how to convey this interest to others
- Discuss when to report research findings and list a variety of methods that can be used to report them
- Summarize the steps required to report findings effectively
- Demonstrate how to act with integrity when reporting findings
- Identify and discuss unethical communication and reporting practice
- List ways in which images are published unethically and consider how this unethical practice can be avoided
- Describe how to improve your chances of success when producing a dissertation or thesis

---

Once you have gathered and analysed your data, you need to work out what to do with all the information. How do you pull out the pertinent points and discard irrelevant information? How do you produce a report that is meaningful and interesting? How do you know that what you produce will be good enough to pass your course?

This chapter will help you to make sense of your data, enabling you to think about what you have found out, how this relates to your research question and how you can present this to others in an interesting and meaningful way. It will also help you to think about the variety of ways in which you can present your findings, when and how you might do this, and how to communicate ethically. Take time to work your way through the activities provided in this chapter: they will assist you through the completion process and provide advice and guidance to help you pass your course successfully.

WHAT HAVE I FOUND OUT?

This seems a straightforward question. However, some students find themselves in difficulty when answering it. They think about all sorts of information that has arisen from their research: they feel overwhelmed, are unsure about how to pull out what is important and do not know how to structure their findings. If this is the case with you, don't panic. Think first about what we mean by research findings. Activity 12.1 will help you to do this.

Activity 12.1: Missing-word puzzle

Complete this missing-word puzzle by filling in the blanks from the list of words provided. This will help you to think about what is meant by research findings and sheds light on how the reporting of findings is related to the type of research you undertake. Answers can be found at the end of the chapter.

Research findings are the results of your research [_____]. They represent the totality of your research outcomes, including your data [_____], interpretation and conclusion. Findings can include, depending on the type of research, theoretical conjecture, empirical evidence, business insight, policy recommendations, objects, equipment, databases, narratives and numerical data.

Research findings answer (or address) the research [_____] and are organized in a way that reflects the research [_____]. For example, quantitative studies might structure findings by statistical tests or answers to the central research question followed by answers to peripheral questions. Qualitative studies might structure findings by themes that have arisen from the data collection phase or as a chronological narrative, for example.

Findings need to be supported by [_____]. This can include quotations, field notes, images, tables, graphs and/or flow charts, depending on the type of research. Data that are not [_____] to the research question should be avoided when findings are reported.

analysis

design

endeavour

evidence

question

relevant

Now that you understand a little more about what research findings are, return to your data analysis and ask yourself again 'What have I found out?'. This is easier to do if you keep your research question in mind, thinking about how your findings help you to answer your research question. If you still struggle with this, seek help from your tutor or supervisor.

ARE MY FINDINGS INTERESTING?

This question covers a number of queries, worries and doubts expressed by students. When students are asked to think about how they might let other people know about their research findings, some ponder whether anyone will be interested. Others are a little concerned that examiners might consider their findings 'boring' or 'of little use'. Some even say that there is no point letting others know about their research: after all, they are only doing it because they have to as part of their undergraduate course. They want to complete their research, pass their course and move on.

Whatever your view, it is important that you take time to think about how your findings are interesting. By doing so you will be able to convey that interest (and your enthusiasm) to others. In terms of examiners, they might have a number of criteria they look for when marking your work, but they also want to see that you display enthusiasm for your work and that you are able to spot and relay interesting findings. Figure 12.1 lists a number of ways in which research findings are interesting. Digest the information provided, then undertake Activity 12.2.

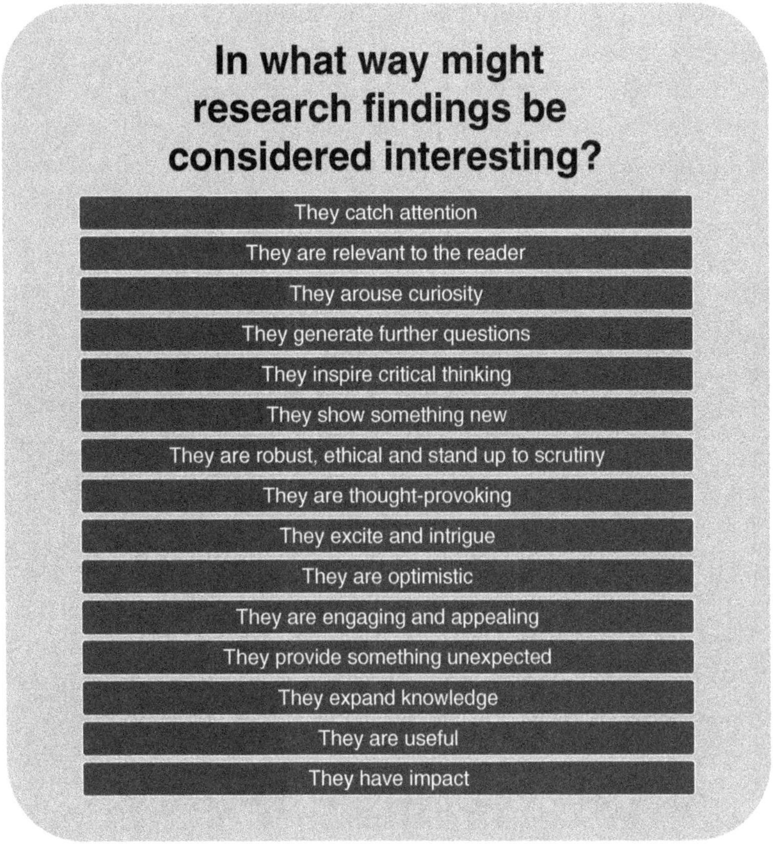

In what way might research findings be considered interesting?

- They catch attention
- They are relevant to the reader
- They arouse curiosity
- They generate further questions
- They inspire critical thinking
- They show something new
- They are robust, ethical and stand up to scrutiny
- They are thought-provoking
- They excite and intrigue
- They are optimistic
- They are engaging and appealing
- They provide something unexpected
- They expand knowledge
- They are useful
- They have impact

Figure 12.1 Assessing whether research findings are interesting

Activity 12.2: Application

Consider the items listed in Figure 12.1 and think about how each relates to your own research findings. Some might relate, whereas others might not. However, going through this process will help you to think in more detail about the interest, impact and relevance of your findings.

WHEN DO I REPORT MY FINDINGS?

I had to present a seminar part-way through my research. It was daunting but actually it really helped because I got feedback on my findings from other students and the tutor. It really made me think and make some changes. **Shonti, economics undergraduate student**

I got bogged down in my themes. Too many that I couldn't make sense of. So, I decided to write a report about them mid-way through the analysis. I shared the report with my supervisors and asked for comments. It made me focus on what was important and helped me to make sure the themes were relevant to my question. **Andrew, sociology postgraduate student**

I discussed some of my findings with my tutor in our meetings and I found it really helpful. But I didn't write a report about them. I didn't have time for that. **Frieda, film studies undergraduate student**

My findings weren't clear until I'd finished my analysis so the first anyone knew of them was when I'd written my long report. **Megan, human geography undergraduate student**

I developed my hypothesis which I tested. Then I made my observation, did my analysis and wrote up my results. It was quite straightforward and my department had quite specific advice about the structure I should follow when I wrote my report. **Kai, chemistry undergraduate student**

I wanted to share my preliminary results with participants. They looked through what I'd done and made comments about whether I was making the correct interpretations. I did this three times before I wrote my dissertation and it was really helpful. **Ilse, anthropology undergraduate student**

Figure 12.2   When to report research findings: practical examples

The time at which you decide to report your findings is closely related to the question of why you report your research findings. Some students, for example, decide to report interim findings. This might be because they wish to share their data with other experts to gain further insight; they might be required to present a seminar or conference paper on their interim findings; or funding bodies or stake-holders require an interim report, for example. Other students concentrate on completing their research and producing their dissertation to meet course deadlines. In this case, findings are reported only when the dissertation is produced. Some postgraduate students choose to produce their thesis and then write a journal paper that presents their research findings to a wider audience.

Consider the practical examples provided in Figure 12.2 and then work through Activity 12.3, which gives further insight into when to report your research findings.

Activity 12.3: Practical examples

Read through the examples in Figure 12.2. Think about whether any of them have resonance with your own research and the time at which you might report your findings. Jot down, or voice record, your thoughts for future reference.

HOW DO I REPORT MY FINDINGS?

The most common way for undergraduate students to report their findings is in an undergraduate dissertation (or long report) and for postgraduate students in their postgraduate thesis (this might also be called a dissertation in some countries). However, as we have seen in the question above (When do I report my findings?) there are other types of report, such as interim written reports and verbal reports to tutors and supervisors.

When you produce a report of your findings, whether this be a dissertation, the-sis, interim report or journal paper, there are some issues that you should bear in mind. They are summarized in Figure 12.3. Take time to digest them as they will help you to produce a better report of your findings.

WHAT DIFFERENT WAYS ARE THERE OF REPORTING MY FINDINGS?

In this chapter we have touched on some of the common ways that students use to report their research findings. Activity 12.4 provides a recap on what they might be, while introducing you to a wide variety of other methods that we have not yet discussed.

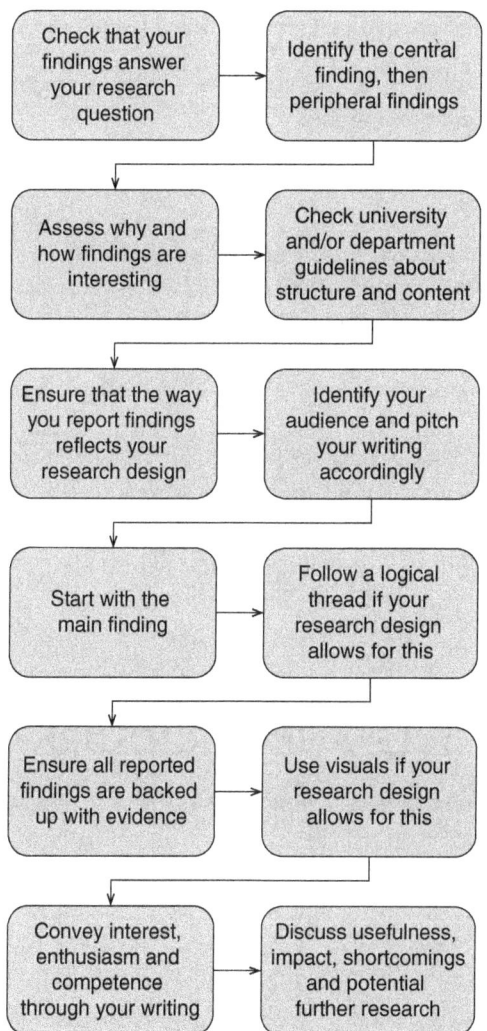

Figure 12.3 Reporting findings successfully

Activity 12.4: Brainstorm

Take a few minutes to brainstorm a list of the different ways that researchers can report their findings. Try to list as many items as possible, as soon as they come into your mind, and write them down (or make a voice note) without analysis or judgement. Once you have spent a few minutes brainstorming, go to the end of the chapter for some examples given by other students. This list provides useful ideas for reporting your own findings.

THINK INTEGRITY 12.1

It is important to build trust and confidence in your research findings. This involves openness and transparency:

- Paying attention to correct referencing and citation, including digital tools and software
- Ensuring all data, codes and analyses are made available
- Providing detailed descriptions of all methods and analyses
- Using language appropriate to the audience (e.g. for examiners or the lay person)
- Providing enough information so that your research can be reproduced and replicated
- Using public access depositories and publishing in open access journals
- Explaining when and why findings cannot be shared (e.g. confidentiality or consent has not been given for sharing data)

DO I HAVE TO FOLLOW A PARTICULAR STYLE AND STRUCTURE?

Most universities require you to follow a particular style and structure when you produce your dissertation or thesis. Consult your university or department website or VLE and/or speak to your tutor or supervisor. It is important that you follow all guidelines and produce your findings in the correct format as you might be penalized if you do not. However, most universities do offer flexibility. If you have undertaken a new and innovative piece of research, perhaps using unusual or inventive methods, there should be scope for you to produce a report in a way that suits your research design. You might have to spend a little time justifying why you are doing this, so seek guidance from your tutor or supervisor prior to producing your report.

Activity 12.5: Action

Now that you understand a little more about how to report your research findings, visit your university website/VLE to assess its guidelines about structure and content. Do this now, while it is fresh in your mind. Write down, or make a voice note of, pertinent points to reference later, when you write up your findings.

HOW DO I COMMUNICATE AND REPORT ETHICALLY?

This question can be addressed through practical examples that illustrate the mistakes researchers make and the potential harmful or negative consequences of their action.

Activity 12.6: Spot the mistakes

Read through each of the scenarios and spot the mistakes that researchers have made in terms of unethical communication and/or reporting. Describe each mistake and then produce a short description of how you think the mistake could be rectified. Go to the end of the chapter to find the answers and some suggestions for solutions.

Scenario 1

A researcher has just completed a project on productivity in a UK factory. Her findings indicate that certain attitudes and behaviours among employees lead to less productivity on the assembly line. She reports these findings to managers who are able to identify the employees. Those who have been working in the factory for less than two years are dismissed (with the correct notice given). Those who have been working in the factory for more than two years are given a written warning, telling them that productivity must improve if they are to remain in their jobs. How has this researcher communicated and/or reported unethically?

Scenario 2

A student is halfway through his research. Twenty-eight people are participating in the study and they are known to each other. Two of these people want to know about the results so far. They want to see what other people have said and check whether everybody participating in the study is saying the same things. The student posts his interim results on his Facebook group, which is a private group that was set up for everyone participating in his study. Some of the participants read the posts and decide to withdraw from the study. How has this researcher communicated and/or reported unethically?

259

THINK ETHICS 12.1

Publication bias is a tendency for researchers to share, disseminate and publish findings with statistically significant positive outcomes and supress or ignore findings with negative or null results. The term can also refer to journal publishers and editors, who are more likely to publish research with positive outcomes. The outcome is that published studies are not representative of completed studies and the published research base is skewed. This can lead to policy and decisions being made, or further research being conducted, on incomplete data. Reasons for publication bias might include the need to publish widely to enhance academic careers; a belief that other researchers, stakeholders and members of the public are interested only in positive outcomes; concern that mistakes have been made if findings contradict, or differ from, other research; and conflicts of interest.

HOW DO I PUBLISH IMAGES ETHICALLY?

Again, let's turn this question on its head and think about how images are published unethically. Figure 12.4 provides some examples of how images are published unethically and Activity 12.7 encourages you to relate these points to your own research.

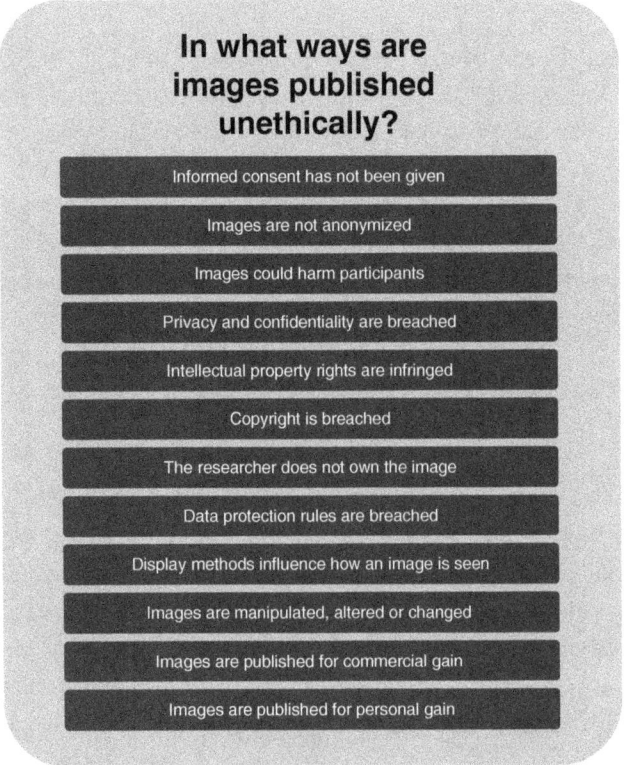

In what ways are images published unethically?

- Informed consent has not been given
- Images are not anonymized
- Images could harm participants
- Privacy and confidentiality are breached
- Intellectual property rights are infringed
- Copyright is breached
- The researcher does not own the image
- Data protection rules are breached
- Display methods influence how an image is seen
- Images are manipulated, altered or changed
- Images are published for commercial gain
- Images are published for personal gain

Figure 12.4 Publishing images unethically

Activity 12.7: Application

Digest the information provided in Figure 12.4. Think about how each item in the list might relate to your own research (if you intend to publish images) and consider the action you need to take to avoid the unethical practice listed.

WHAT DO I NEED TO KNOW ABOUT USING OTHER PEOPLE'S WORK IN MY REPORT?

In Figure 12.5 we see that some of the ways in which images are published unethically involve breach of copyright, infringing intellectual property rights and publishing images that are not owned by the researcher. These issues all involve using the work of others. It is important to note that using the work of others not only relates to images, but to text, designs, software, hardware, creations, objects, scientific equipment, maps, literary works, materials and music, for example. Activity 12.8 encourages you to delve deeper.

Activity 12.8: Action

Data ownership and intellectual property were discussed in Chapter 4. Now that you are thinking more about using other people's work in your research, return to Chapter 4 to refresh your memory. Do it now, while the information is relevant and significant.

TIP 12.1

If there is any doubt about ownership, always check before you communicate. And remember, communication doesn't only involve academic writing, it can also involve sending other people's work in emails or reproducing it on social media, for example.

CAN I MAKE MY RESEARCH AVAILABLE TO EVERYONE?

As researchers we have a duty to make our research available to others. This benefits individuals, society, communities, the environment and/or the economy. However, we must adhere to all relevant ethical and legal obligations when we do this (see Figure 12.4). Go to Chapter 4 for information about legal and regulatory issues about sharing data, and to Chapter 11 for information about the ethical implications of data sharing and for advice about how to share data safely. If, after having re-read this information, you decide that you would like to make your research available to everyone, speak to your tutor first. Explain why you wish to make your research available and discuss how you intend to do so. Your tutor can offer advice and highlight potential problems.

Figure 12.5 'Communicating ethically' image

WHAT CAN I DO TO IMPROVE MY CHANCES OF SUCCESS?

This question tends to be asked by undergraduate students who are in the process of producing their dissertation. They want a bullet point list of how to improve their chances of getting good marks to pass their course successfully. Before the bullet point list is provided, take a little time to work through Activity 12.9.

Activity 12.9: Develop your own checklist

Produce a checklist of action you can take to improve your chances of success. Then go to the end of the chapter to find some suggestions. This list provides a useful checklist that you can refer to when you produce your undergraduate thesis.

Now that you understand more about completing your research, we can move on to the next topic. Before we do, let's test your understanding of what you have learnt so far, with a short quiz.

Activity 12.10: Multiple-choice quiz

Read each question and choose the correct answer. The topics in all three of these questions have been covered in this chapter, so if you can't answer any of the questions, return to some of the activities to refresh your memory. Answers can be found at the end of the chapter.

1   What do research findings address?

    a   Your course learning outcomes.
    b   Your research question.
    c   Your methodology.

2   What is required to support research findings?

    a   Evidence.
    b   Opinions.
    c   Arguments.

3   What is the name given to a tendency for researchers to share, disseminate and publish findings with statistically significant positive outcomes and suppress or ignore findings with negative or null results?

    a   Researcher bias.
    b   Publication bias.
    c   Positive results bias.

ACTIVITY ANSWERS: CHAPTER 12
Activity 12.1: Missing-word puzzle

Research findings are the results of your research *endeavour*. They represent the totality of your research outcomes, including your data *analysis*, interpretation and conclusion. Findings can include, depending on the type of research, theoretical conjecture, empirical evidence, business insight, policy recommendations, objects, equipment, databases, narratives and numerical data.

Research findings answer (or address) the research *question* and are organized in a way that reflects the research *design*. For example, quantitative studies might structure findings by statistical tests or answers to the central research question followed by answers to peripheral questions. Qualitative studies might structure findings by themes that have arisen from the data collection phase or as a chronological narrative, for example.

Findings need to be supported by *evidence*. This can include quotations, field notes, images, tables, graphs and/or flow charts, depending on the type of research. Data that are not *relevant* to the research question should be avoided when findings are reported.

Activity 12.4: Brainstorm

This list gives examples of ways to report findings that were provided by other students when this activity has been undertaken in class. It is a useful resource to reference when you report your own research findings (the list has been arranged alphabetically). Some items will not be relevant to your research; nevertheless, they might encourage you to think creatively:

- Blogs
- Dance
- Dissertations
- Dynamic dashboards
- E-posters/digital posters
- Image slideshows
- Images
- Infographics
- Interactive flowcharts
- Interim reports
- Journal papers
- Long reports
- Magazines
- Mime
- Motion graphics

- Newspapers
- Objects
- Paper posters
- Plays
- Podcasts
- Radio
- Seminar papers
- Stories
- Theses
- TV
- Videos
- Vlogs
- Web and mobile apps

Activity 12.6: Spot the mistakes

Scenario 1

The researcher should not have communicated her research to managers in a way that individuals could be identified. Communication of her findings to managers led to individuals being harmed (in this case dismissal, written warnings and threats to their jobs).

The researcher should have ensured that no individual could be identified from her work. Anonymization would have helped her to do this (see Chapter 11). She should also have considered how communicating her findings might cause harm to others. Although this problem came to light only after she had communicated her findings, the researcher should have carried out a risk assessment in the design stage of her research to ascertain whether participants could be harmed. If she had found that they could, the research should not have gone ahead as it stood (see Chapter 4 for information about carrying out a risk assessment).

There might be issues of funding to consider in this scenario: if the owners of the factory had commissioned the research, for example, the researcher should have considered the owners' motivation and justification for the research and thought about how findings could be misused or abused (in this case to get rid of employees who were deemed unproductive).

Scenario 2

This student should not have posted interim results on a group for all members of the study to see, when it had been requested by only two participants. As all participants are known to each other, and they are all part of the Facebook group, it is easy for any comments to be attributed to individuals. Some of the participants might not want others to know what they had said. This is probably a correct assumption as some decided to leave the study as a result of the communication.

The student should have referred back to what he had told participants at the start of his study in terms of how he intended to communicate results and the consent he'd received to communicate results in the way that he had stated. Some participants might have consented, whereas others might not. It appears that some participants were unhappy about this communication and left the study as a result. While students need to weigh the pros of communication (e.g. openness and transparency) against the cons (e.g. participants being unhappy or breach of confidentiality), the reasons for participants asking for results should also be considered. The student should have explored why the participants wanted to know what others had said and considered how this knowledge might have influenced his study (e.g. affecting what people say later in the study). He should have put together a logical argument as to why he was unable to communicate the results in the way that the two participants had asked, and that he would communicate results at the end of the study, paying close attention to issues of confidentiality.

Activity 12.9: Develop your own checklist

Examples of action you can take to improve your chances of success include the following (you might find that some of them are not relevant to your research or level of study):

- Recognize and avoid academic malpractice (e.g. plagiarism, copyright infringement, cheating, theft of materials, taking credit for someone else's work, using essay mills, falsifying or fabricating results, and/or manipulating data; see Chapter 10).
- Understand what is meant by copyright and ensure that you do not redistribute, reproduce, duplicate or communicate the work of others without permission (see Chapter 4).
- Recognize and address bias in your work (e.g. personal bias, researcher bias and bias in the way you choose to include and omit information; see Chapter 10).
- Refer to, and follow, all university guidelines about producing your dissertation or thesis.
- Understand why and how your work is assessed (see Chapter 7).
- Ensure your writing is clear and concise, and that it displays technical detail and subject knowledge.
- Avoid informalities, generalizations, conversational language and opinions (unless they fit with your methodology).
- Ensure findings are highlighted and well signposted for examiners.

- Check for spelling mistakes, grammatical errors and typing mistakes: ensure your work is presented to the highest standard possible.
- Ensure that your final report demonstrates your ability to carry out independent research and is presented in a coherent document.

Activity 12.10: Multiple-choice quiz

1   What do research findings address?

    a   Your course learning outcomes.

    b   Your research question (correct answer).

    c   Your methodology.

2   What is required to support research findings?

    a   Evidence (correct answer).

    b   Opinions.

    c   Arguments.

3   What is the name given to a tendency for researchers to share, disseminate and publish findings with statistically significant positive outcomes and suppress or ignore findings with negative or null results?

    a   Researcher bias.

    b   Publication bias (correct answer).

    c   Positive results bias.

13

RECAP – LET'S CHECK ON WHAT WE KNOW …

CHAPTER CONTENTS

CHAPTER ACTIVITIES

<hr>

CHAPTER OBJECTIVES

By the end of this chapter, you will be able to:

- Assess your current knowledge and understanding of research methods
- Decide what else you need to know
- List sources of further information
- Produce a plan of action that will help you to complete your research successfully
- List the transferable skills gained from undertaking research and assess how they might be useful for life beyond your research

<hr>

Congratulations – you've reached the last chapter in this book. I hope that you are now feeling more confident and knowledgeable about your research. Embarking on your research project is an exciting time. Yes, it can be daunting, but it can also be fulfilling, intriguing, stimulating and challenging. You are able to pursue your interests, learn something new and pass your course. Your research might provide new insight, inform decision-making, develop something innovative or lead to changes in policy. You are also able to develop skills that will be useful for your future career.

We all have the ability to carry out research: it is not a skill with which we are born. Take time to assess and develop your skills, build your understanding and learn from your experiences. This last chapter encourages you to take a moment to think about what you now know, decide what else you need to know, assess where you can find this information and work out how to move on so that you can produce a good piece of research that will enable you to pass your course successfully.

TEST YOUR KNOWLEDGE

Work your way through Activity 13.1: it will help you to assess how much you know about research methods.

Activity 13.1: Crossword

Read the clues and enter your answer into the relevant section of the crossword (see Figure 13.1). The puzzle covers a wide variety of research areas, subjects and topics, some of which have not been mentioned in this book. However, work your way through the puzzle as you would any other crossword, answering the questions you find easiest first. This will help you to fill in the blanks, even if you are unsure of a specific word. Answers can be found at the end of this chapter.

Figure 13.1 Test your knowledge crossword

Across

1 The science of collecting and classifying numerical data (10)
3 A simple and broad statement of research intent (3)
5 An observational note when undertaking fieldwork (4)
8 In accordance with fact or reality (4)
9 Written copy of the spoken word (10)
10 The study of the nature of human knowledge and how it is acquired (12)

13 Used to record everyday behaviour over time (5)

14 An opinion-gathering tool, ballot or election (4)

15 The average of a set of numbers (4)

16 Value assigned to variables, words or concepts (4)

19 This type of ratio quantifies the strength of association between two events or properties (4)

21 A Boolean search operator that eliminates items that contain the specified term (3)

23 A prejudiced perspective (4)

24 The demonstrable contribution that research makes to society and the economy (6)

27 One of Freud's representations of the three structures of the mind (3)

29 The middle value within a dataset (6)

30 The quality of being factually or logically sound (8)

32 A fixed standard amount or a single person, group, object or number (4)

33 The study and systematic recording of human cultures and human societies (11)

36 Abstract representations of real-world events, systems, behaviour or processes to explain or make predictions (6)

37 A group of people, objects or items that is representative of the larger population (6)

38 With this hypothesis there is no relationship between the two measured phenomena (4)

Down

1 They are used to collect data about thoughts, opinions, attitudes, behaviour and feelings (7)

2 The study of society, human social behaviour and social interaction (9)

4 Relating to more than one branch of knowledge (17)

6 A scientific trial, test or investigation (10)

7 This type of question cannot be answered with a simple yes or no (4)

11 Researchers should act with this to adhere to ethical principles and professional standards (9)

12 The guideline system or framework for a research project (11)

16 This squared test determines whether there is an association between categorical variables (3)

18 A face-to-face or online recorded conversation (9)

20 Word written in brackets to indicate the text was quoted verbatim (3)

22 This type of research is theory-orientated (11)

25 A judgement, decision or result based on reason and argument (10)

26 The number that appears the most often in a set of numbers (4)

28 One of Freud's representations of the three structures of the mind (2)
29 Tools and techniques used to collect and analyse data (7)
31 Supply a research project or kit out a lab (5)
34 A person, item or object within a network (4)
35 A Boolean search operator that finds all the search terms (3)

BUILD A PERSONAL CHECKLIST

After having read this book and completed the crossword in Activity 13.1, you should be feeling more confident about embarking on your research project. Now is the time to look, more specifically, at the action you need to take to begin, work through and complete your project. Activity 13.2 will help you to do this. If you have already begun your project, use this activity to check that you are on the right track and to make sure that you have not missed out something important.

Activity 13.2: Develop your own checklist

Produce a checklist of all the actions you need to take to begin and/or proceed with your research project. Your checklist can be produced in a way that suits you: a numbered list, a bulleted list, a flow diagram or a road map, for example. Once you have done this, go to the end of the chapter for some actions suggested by other students when they were asked to undertake this activity.

DELVE DEEPER

This book cannot cover everything there is to know about research methods: no book can, as there is so much information to convey. However, perhaps this book has built your enthusiasm and encouraged you to want to know more about certain issues, topics or methods. If that is this case, the following list will help you to delve deeper into the areas that are of interest. Topics have been arranged alphabetically for ease of navigation.

Action research

Lenette, C. (2022) *Participatory Action Research: Ethics and Decolonization*. New York: Oxford University Press.

McNiff, J. (2017) *Action Research: All You Need to Know*. London: Sage.

Reason, P. and Bradbury, H. (eds) (2013) *The SAGE Handbook of Action Research: Participative Inquiry and Practice*, 2nd edition. London: Sage.

Bias

Banaji, M and Greenwald, A. (2016) *Blindspot: Hidden Biases of Good People*, reprint edition. New York: Bantam Books.

Hammersley, M. (2000) *Taking Sides in Social Research: Essays on Partisanship and Bias*. London: Routledge.

Noble, S.U. (2018) *Algorithms of Oppression: How Search Engines Reinforce Racism*. New York: New York University Press.

The Catalogue of Bias: https://catalogofbias.org

Children and young people

Alderson, P. and Morrow, V. (2020) *The Ethics of Research with Children and Young People: A Practical Handbook*, 2nd edition. London: Sage.

Graham, H., Powell, M.A. and Taylor, N. (2015) Ethical research involving children: Putting the evidence into practice. *Family Matters, 96*, 23–28. https://aifs.gov.au/research/family-matters/no-96/ethical-research-involving-children

Greig, A., Taylor, J. and Mackay, T. (2013) *Doing Research with Children: A Practical Guide*, 3rd edition. London: Sage.

Groundwater-Smith, S., Dockett, S. and Bottrell, D. (2015) *Participatory Research with Children and Young People*. London: Sage.

Data analysis (qualitative)

Bazeley, P. (2020) *Qualitative Data Analysis: Practical Strategies*, 2nd edition. London: Sage.

Friese, S. (2019) *Qualitative Data Analysis with ATLAS.ti*, 3rd edition. London: Sage.

Jackson, K. and Bazeley, P. (2019) *Qualitative Data Analysis with NVivo*, 3rd edition. London: Sage.

Machin, D. and Mayr, A. (2012) *How to Do Critical Discourse Analysis: A Multimodal Introduction*. London: Sage.

Miles, M., Huberman, M. and Saldaña, J. (2019) *Qualitative Data Analysis: A Methods Sourcebook*, 4th edition. Thousand Oaks, CA: Sage.

The ReStore Depository, Loughborough University, on choosing qualitative data analysis software. www.restore.ac.uk/lboro/research/software/caqdas_primer.php

Data analysis (quantitative)

Blann, A. (2018) *Data Handling and Analysis*, 2nd edition. Oxford: Oxford University Press.

Dawson, J.F. (2017) *Analysing Quantitative Survey Data for Business and Management Students*. London: Sage.

Kent, R. (2015) *Analysing Quantitative Data: Variable-Based and Case-Based Approaches to Non-Experimental Datasets*. London: Sage.

Pallant, J. (2016) *SPSS Survival Manual: A Step-by-Step Guide to Data Analysis Using IBM SPSS*, 6th edition. Maidenhead: Open University Press.

Treiman, D. (2009) *Quantitative Data Analysis: Doing Social Research to Test Ideas*. San Francisco, CA: John Wiley and Sons.

Data analysis (mixed approaches)

Bazeley, P. (2018) *Integrating Analyses in Mixed Methods Research*. London: Sage.

Bergin, T. (2018) *An Introduction to Data Analysis: Quantitative, Qualitative and Mixed Methods*. London: Sage.

Vogt, W., Vogt, E., Gardner, D. and Haeffele, L. (2014) *Selecting the Right Analyses for Your Data: Quantitative, Qualitative, and Mixed Methods*. New York: Guilford Press.

Digital methods

Dawson, C. (2020) *A–Z of Digital Research Methods*. Abingdon: Routledge.

Dunford, M. and Jenkins, T. (eds) (2019) *Digital Storytelling: Form and Content*. London: Palgrave Macmillan.

Foster, I., Ghani, R., Jarmin, R., Kreuter, F. and Lane (eds) (2017) *Big Data and Social Science: A Practical Guide to Methods and Tools*. Boco Raton, FL: CRC Press.

Paulus, T., Lester, J. and Dempster, P. (2014) *Digital Tools for Qualitative Research*. London: Sage.

Plesner, U. and Phillips, L. (eds) (2018) *Researching Virtual Worlds*. Abingdon: Routledge.

Veltri, G. (2020) *Digital Social Research*. Cambridge: Polity Press.

Ethics

Comstock, G. (2013) *Research Ethics: A Philosophical Guide to the Responsible Conduct of Research*. New York: Cambridge University Press.

Israel, M. (2015) *Research Ethics and Integrity for Social Scientists*, 2nd edition. London: Sage.

Ransome, P. (2013) *Ethics and Values in Social Research*. Basingstoke: Palgrave Macmillan.

Richterich, A. (2018) *The Big Data Agenda: Data Ethics and Critical Data Studies*. London: University of Westminster Press.

Social Research Association (SRA) (2021) *Research Ethics Guidance*. https://the-sra.org.uk/SRA/Ethics/Research-ethics-guidance/SRA/Ethics/Research-Ethics-Guidance

Wiles, R. (2013) *What Are Qualitative Research Ethics?* London: Bloomsbury Academic.

Ethnography

Fetterman, D. (2010) *Ethnography: Step-by-Step*, 3rd edition. Thousand Oaks, CA: Sage.

Hammersley, M. and Atkinson, P. (2019) *Ethnography: Principles in Practice*, 4th edition. Abingdon: Routledge.

Hine, C. (2015) *Ethnography for the Internet*. London: Bloomsbury Academic.

Lecompte, M. and Schensul, J. (2013) *Analysis and Interpretation of Ethnographic Data: A Mixed Methods Approach*. Plymouth: AltaMira Press.

Experiments

Duflo, E. and Banerjee, A. (eds) (2017) *Handbook of Field Experiments*, volumes 1 and 2. Amsterdam: North-Holland.

Field, A. and Hole, G. (2003) *How to Design and Report Experiments*. London: Sage.

Harris, P., Easterbrook, M. and Horst, J. (2021) *Designing and Reporting Experiments in Psychology*, 4th edition. Maidenhead: Open University Press.

Interviews

Brinkmann, S. and Kvale, S. (2018) *Doing Interviews*, 2nd edition. London: Sage.

Fujii, L.A. (2018) *Interviewing in Social Science Research*. New York: Routledge.

Seidman, I. (2019) *Interviewing as Qualitative Research: A Guide for Researchers in Education and the Social Sciences*, 5th edition. New York: Teachers College Press.

Questionnaires and surveys

Blair, J., Czaja, R.F. and Blair, E. (2014) *Designing Surveys: A Guide to Decisions and Procedures*, 3rd edition. Thousand Oaks, CA: Sage.

Ekinci, Y. (2015) *Designing Research Questionnaires for Business and Management Students*. London: Sage.

Fink, A. (2015) *How to Conduct Surveys: A Step-by-Step Guide*, 6th edition. Thousand Oaks, CA: Sage.

Gillham, B. (2007) *Developing a Questionnaire*, 2nd edition. London: Continuum.

Nardi, P. (2018) *Doing Survey Research*, 4th edition. New York: Routledge.

Sampling

Daniel, J. (2012) *Sampling Essentials: Practical Guidelines for Making Sampling Choices*. Thousand Oaks, CA: Sage.

Emmel, N. (2013) *Sampling and Choosing Cases in Qualitative Research: A Realist Approach*. London: Sage.

Lohr, S. (2022) *Sampling: Design and Analysis*, 3rd edition. Boca Raton, FL: CRC Press.

Thompson, S. (2012) *Sampling*, 3rd edition. Hoboken, NJ: John Wiley & Sons.

Valliant, R., Dever, J. and Kreuter, F. (2013) *Practical Tools for Designing and Weighting Survey Samples*. New York: Springer.

Sensitive methods/researching people who are vulnerable

Dickson-Swift, V., James, E. and Liamputtong, P. (2008) *Undertaking Sensitive Research in the Health and Social Sciences: Managing Boundaries, Emotions and Risks*. Cambridge: Cambridge University Press.

Liamputtong, P. (2007) *Researching the Vulnerable: A Guide to Sensitive Research Methods*. London: Sage.

Von Benzon, N. and Van Blerk, L. (eds.) (2018) *Geographical Research with 'Vulnerable Groups': Re-examining Methodological and Ethical Process*. Abingdon: Routledge.

Statistics

Dancey, C. and Reidy, J. (2020) *Statistics without Maths for Psychology*, 8th edition. Harlow: Pearson.

Graham, A. (2013) *Statistics: A Complete Introduction*, reprint edition. London: Hodder and Stoughton.

Hand, D. (2008) *Statistics: A Very Short Introduction*. Oxford: Oxford University Press.

Rowntree, D. (2018) *Statistics without Tears: An Introduction for Non-Mathematicians*, 2nd edition. London: Penguin.

Statcheck, for checking for errors in statistical reporting in papers. https://michelenuijten.shinyapps.io/statcheck-web

Visual methods

Gubrium, A. and Harper, K. (2013) *Participatory Visual and Digital Methods*. Walnut Creek, CA: Left Coast Press.

Gubrium, A., Harper, K. and Otañez, M. (eds) (2016) *Participatory Visual and Digital Research in Action*. Abingdon: Routledge.

Margolis, E. and Pauwels, L. (eds) (2011) *The SAGE Handbook of Visual Research Methods*. London: Sage.

WHAT NEXT?

The action plan you developed in Activity 13.2 will help you to think about what you now need to do to move forward with your research. But what happens once you have completed your course? What next? This is a question I am often asked by students who are nearing the end of their research and finishing their three or four years of study. It is useful to think about this question in terms of your research as it enables you to understand more about the useful skills you are developing that are transferable to life beyond your research. Activity 13.3 will help you to consider what these skills might be.

Activity 13.3: Brainstorm

Take a few minutes to brainstorm a list of the skills you are developing, or you think you might develop, as you begin, work your way through and complete your research project. Try to list as many skills as possible, as soon as they come into your mind, and write them down (or make a voice note) without analysis or judgement. Once you have spent a few minutes brainstorming, go to the end of the chapter for some examples given by other students.

You might be asking 'What do I do now? 'How do I make use of my research skills?' 'Has this all been worthwhile?' Put some order to your questions by keeping a reflective diary. It will help you to record and analyse your feelings, reactions, insights and experiences.

Figure 13.2 Questions about what next image

A reflective diary is a useful way to record, and reflect upon, your experiences and the skills to be gained when completing your research project. Use the list provided at the end of the chapter to stimulate the reflection process. Your diary will help you to consider whether you have developed particular skills, record how they have been developed and enable you to list evidence for the development of each skill. This record will be useful for life beyond your research (see Figure 13.2).

We started this book with a story: it seems fitting, therefore, to conclude with a story. This really happened...

Activity 13.4: Story

Anna decided to research behaviour in schools in two locations, one rural, the other urban. Her own school experiences had not been positive: she had received several detentions and a couple of suspensions for unruly behaviour. She had been told by her teachers that she wouldn't pass her exams and would find it difficult to get work. She didn't like or enjoy school and couldn't wait to leave.

Despite this, she scraped through her exams and went on to study at her local further education college. Anna was not ready to enter the world of employment and felt that continuing study would be a good way to delay entering paid employment. After completing her college course, she managed to get enough qualifications to get into university through the clearing system in the UK. This system enabled her to find a university that could offer her an available place, despite her low grades.

For the first two years Anna didn't study too hard. She enjoyed the social life, the sports and the entertainment. Studies came last. However, in the third year she undertook her dissertation. The topic was of great interest to her, given her own experiences at school. She interviewed some children who were experiencing similar issues and others who had much worse problems. This helped to put her own experiences into perspective. Although it surprised her, she found that she enjoyed carrying out the interviews, visiting schools and speaking to teachers.

Anna also enjoyed working independently, planning and organizing her work, finding relevant sources, analysing her data and writing her report. She learnt how to listen, working hard to ensure that she did not pre-judge or pre-empt what young people were saying, especially given her own experiences.

Her tutor had known Anna since the start of her degree. He was amazed at how well she'd done in her project. Previously, she had only just scraped through each assessed piece of work and she had failed one of her modules in the first year, which she had to re-sit. He arranged a tutorial to discuss her dissertation and her research experiences. He congratulated her and asked whether research might be something she might wish to pursue once she had completed her degree.

Anna knew it was something she wanted to pursue. For the first time in her life, she was interested in continuing with her studies. She applied to study a Master's degree. She was accepted on the course. All of a sudden, she enjoyed learning. She sought out information of her own volition. She went to seminars and workshops without being told. She planned, designed and executed an excellent piece of research which saw her pass her course with distinction. Then she went on to complete a PhD, before moving into academia, where she remains to this day, researching to her heart's content!

TO CONCLUDE ...

We have now come to the end of this book. I hope you've found it useful, interesting, entertaining and different from the traditional, text-based research methods books. My aim is to guide, inform and inspire: I hope you feel confident and motivated enough to get started, or continue with, your research. Remember, research can be fun: you will learn a lot and develop as a person along the way, as did Anna in our story. I wish you every success with your research project and with your life beyond.

Activity 13.5: Multiple-choice quiz

Let's finish with one final multiple-choice quiz. This quiz is different: there are no right or wrong answers. Instead, it encourages you to reflect on your confidence levels when conducting your research, writing your report and passing your course. Go to the end of the chapter for feedback on your responses.

1   How confident do you feel about moving forward with your research?

   a   Very confident.
   b   Somewhat confident.
   c   Not at all confident.

2   How confident do you feel about writing your research report, dissertation or thesis?

   a   Very confident.
   b   Somewhat confident.
   c   Not at all confident.

3   How confident do you feel about producing a piece of work that will enable you to pass your course?

   a   Very confident.
   b   Somewhat confident.
   c   Not at all confident.

ACTIVITY ANSWERS: CHAPTER 13
Activity 13.1: Crossword

This is the solution to the crossword (see Figure 13.3). If you have struggled to find answers to some of the clues, take a little time to find out more about the word, what it means and how it is used in research. This will help you to learn something new from the crossword and serves to reinforce your learning.

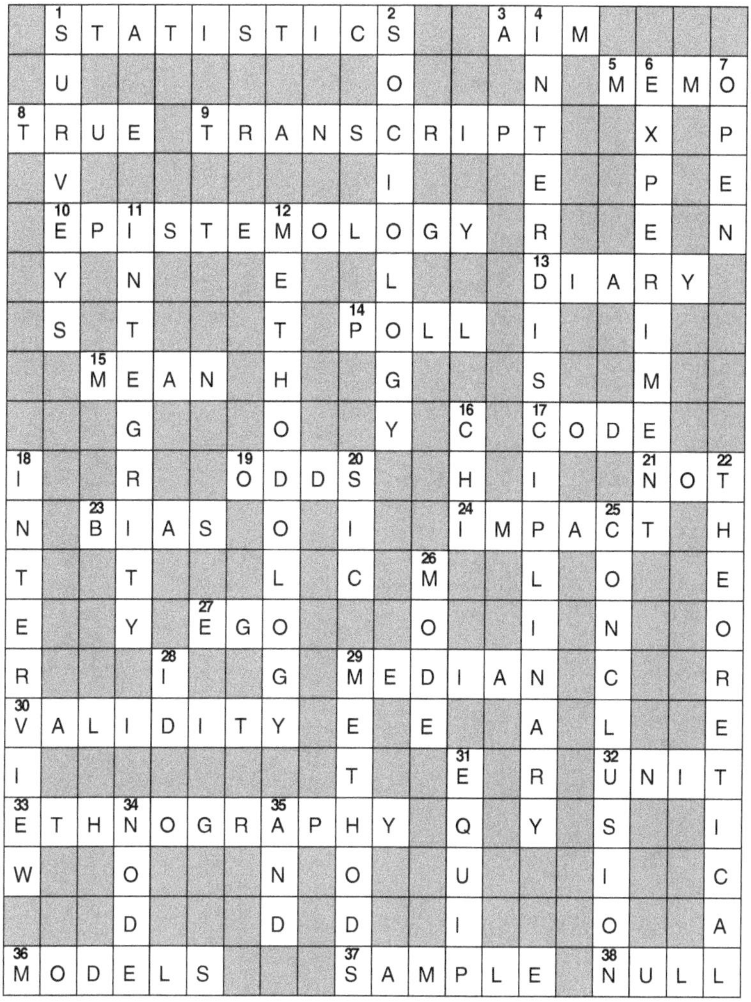

Figure 13.3 Test your knowledge crossword answers

Activity 13.2: Develop your own checklist

The following are examples of checklists provided by other students when they have been asked to undertake this activity. Each checklist is unique to a specific student and their project, and some cover parts of a project whereas others cover the whole project. There are some points mentioned that are relevant to most or all students: they provide useful examples to follow when you produce your own checklist.

Student 1

1 Are interviews the best way forward for my research? I need to:

   a   Speak to my tutor

   b   Look at alternative methods

    c   Read some books

    d   Look at previous dissertations that have used interviews to find out why they were used, whether they worked and whether anything might have been better

2   If I use interviews, how am I going to record them? I need to:

    a   Assess the different types of technology

    b   Consider the pros and cons

    c   Speak to others who know about this: perhaps my tutor, IT members of staff or maybe other students who've already started using the tech

3   Do I know enough about analysing qualitative data? I need to:

    a   Assess the different software available

    b   Speak to IT staff at the help desk

    c   Look at what other students and researchers use and see what they say about them

    d   Practise using some different software packages to see how easy they are and whether they will be suitable for my research

    e   Read up on qualitative data analysis techniques

Student 2

Here is my flowchart, which provides a visual representation of what I need to do next (see Figure 13.4)

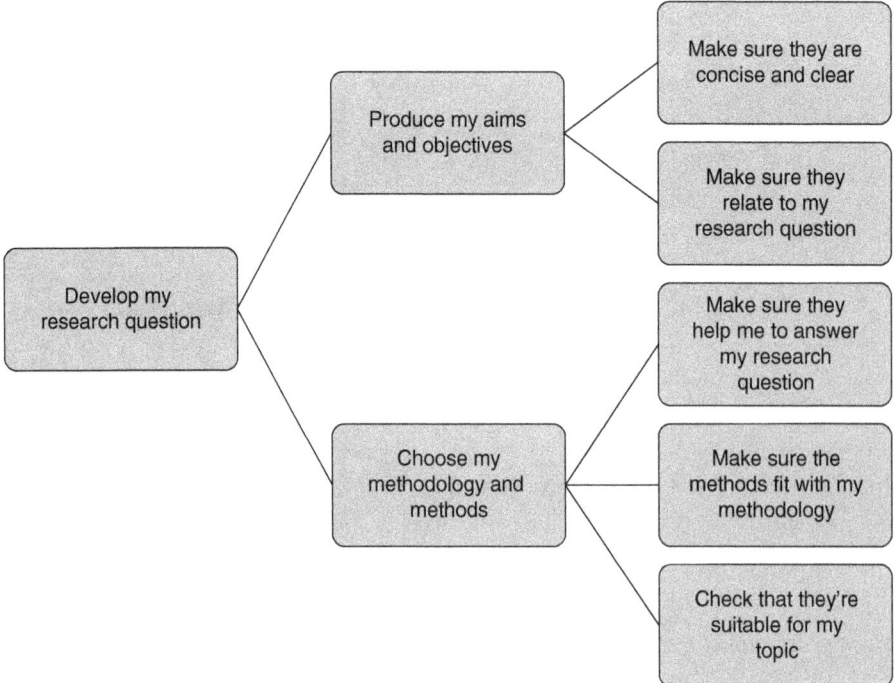

Figure 13.4 Student 2 flowchart

Student 3

- Stop procrastinating and get on with it!
- Talk through my ideas with [names of two other students on the course]
- Check I'm okay to go with [name of tutor]
- Read some more. Especially about observation methods. Try to be specific and not be put off by difficult reading
- Start to think about the people I'm going to study. What's in it for them? Why should they do it? Then think about how to get their consent, what I need to produce for them
- Check all this regulations stuff. Have a word with [name of tutor]. Probably should do that first actually
- Probably ought to look at some other dissertations:

    o   my university repository
    o   Networked Digital Library of Theses and Dissertations: http://search.ndltd.org
    o   Open Access Theses and Dissertations: https://oatd.org

- Then get on with it. Time's moving on
- Take time to work out how it's going as I move on. Realize things can change and be ready for this
- Speak to [name of tutor] if I have any problems as I carry on.

Activity 13.3: Brainstorm

This list provides examples of skills that might be developed during a research project mentioned by other students when we have undertaken this activity. It provides a useful resource for those of you who intend to look for jobs or apply for further study once you have finished your studies (you can find additional transferable skills, along with evidence for their development, in Activity 6.1). The list has been arranged alphabetically and some items have been shortened or amalgamated for brevity and clarity:

- Citing, referencing and producing a bibliography
- Critiquing and questioning
- Data protection and privacy awareness
- Editing and proof-reading skills
- Ethical awareness
- Evaluating sources
- Finding and using datasets effectively
- Finding and using primary and secondary sources effectively
- Groupwork skills

- Hypothesizing and theorizing
- Interpreting graphs, charts and visual representations
- Interview skills
- IT skills
- Learning independently
- Listening skills
- Numerical, mathematical and statistical skills
- Meeting deadlines
- Observation skills
- Online collaboration skills
- Organization skills
- Overcoming problems/acquiring problem-solving skills
- Paraphrasing, quoting and summarizing
- Producing an effective argument
- Project management
- Reading skills
- Reasoning inductively and/or deductively
- Recognizing and addressing bias
- Recognizing the differences between statistics, facts, arguments and opinions
- Skills of analysis, synthesis and evaluation
- Taking notes/using note-taking apps
- Teamwork skills
- Time management
- Using digital methods
- Working with integrity and to high professional standards
- Written and oral communication skills
- Written, oral and visual presentation skills

Activity 13.5: Multiple-choice quiz

Question 1 Feedback

If you have answered 'a' that is great news! Progress conscientiously, taking care to work with integrity and meet all ethical requirements.

If you have answered 'b' you might find it useful to clarify some issues with your tutor or talk through any concerns with peers who are also conducting research. Follow up relevant resources listed in this book so that you can become more confident about moving forward. Your confidence will increase as you build your understanding and expand your knowledge.

If you have answered 'c' to this question, don't worry. Seek advice from your tutor and from peers who are also conducting research. Return to relevant sections in this book as they provide advice and guidance that will help build your understanding. Follow up some of the resources listed in this book and ask your tutor for advice about other resources that are specific to your research. You will become more confident as you learn more. Remember, you are not alone and there is a lot of support and guidance available at your university. Look into workshops or support groups: ask your tutor for recommendations. Think about methods to build resilience (this is the ability to protect yourself, physically and psychologically, so that you can cope with life's ups and downs). This could include celebrating your progress, goal-setting, reflection and feeling part of a learning community where you can seek, and offer, support.

Question 2 Feedback

If you have answered 'a' that is great news! Make sure that you adhere to university requirements about structure, content and format. Keep your writing clear and concise; display subject knowledge and technical detail; avoid generalizations; highlight and signpost findings; edit and proofread, checking for spelling mistakes and grammatical errors.

If you have answered 'b' you might find it useful to discuss any concerns with your tutor or supervisor. Use your university repository or library to find other reports, dissertations or theses in your discipline or subject, or ask your tutor to recommend those that provide good examples for you to follow. Begin your writing as soon as you can; give a draft to your tutor or supervisor and ask for comments. Listen to feedback and act on it as this will help to improve your writing and increase your confidence.

If you have answered 'c', don't worry. There is a lot of support, encouragement and guidance available for students who are struggling to produce their report. Speak to your tutor or supervisor: ask them about support groups, writing circles, workshops or short courses. Re-read relevant sections in this book and follow up some of the resources listed. Create a space for writing: ensure you are not disturbed and distracted. Get into a routine, brainstorm ideas and read around your subject. Sometimes it is hard to start at the beginning. If this is the case, try writing a middle section or even the end section. Return to the first section when you feel more confident. Also, if you struggle with writing your report, try writing something else, perhaps a blog, story or poem. The action of writing may help you to become more confident with your report writing. Or, if you prefer, use a voice recorder to make sense of your thoughts and to help put some order to them.

Question 3 Feedback

If you have answered 'a' that is great news! It might be prudent to check with your tutor, or return to your university requirements, just to make sure that you have got it right.

If you have answered 'b' note that most people have some doubts about their ability to produce a good piece of work at the level required to pass their course. Doubts can be a good thing: they make us work harder and encourage us to produce a better piece of work. Continue with your writing, seeking advice from your tutor or supervisor as you go. They will offer advice about whether your work is at the right standard and provide suggestions about how it can be improved. Listen to their advice and act on it.

If you have answered 'c', don't worry. Speak to your tutor or supervisor to discuss your concerns. They will be able to offer advice and reassure you. Build a network with your peers to offer support and encouragement to each other. Remember that you are part of a learning community in which you can all work together to achieve positive outcomes. Working together in this way will help to build your confidence and enable you to produce a successful piece of work that meets all requirements. Remember also to build your resilience and look after your well-being as you complete your research: useful tips are available on the Mind website: www.mind.org.uk/information-support/tips-for-everyday-living/wellbeing [accessed 15 February 2024].

INDEX